STYLE
Ten Lessons in Clarity and Grace

SIXTH EDITION

Joseph M. Williams
The University of Chicago

LONGMAN

An imprint of Addison Wesley Longman, Inc.

New York • Reading, Massachusetts • Menlo Park, California • Harlow, England
Don Mills, Ontario • Sydney • Mexico City • Madrid • Amsterdam

To my mother and father

. . . English style, familiar but not coarse,
elegant, but not ostentatious. . . .

Samuel Johnson

Publishing Partner: Anne Smith
Sponsoring Development Manager: Arlene Bessenoff
Development Editor: Meg Botteon
Marketing Manager: Renee Ortbals
Supplements Editor: Donna Campion
Full Service Production Manager: Joseph Vella
Project Coordination and Text Design: York Production Services
Electronic Page Makeup: York Production Services
Cover Designer/Manager: Nancy Danahy
Senior Print Buyer: Hugh Crawford
Printer and Binder: R.R. Donnelley & Sons Company
Cover Printer: The Lehigh Press, Inc.

For permission to use copyrighted material, grateful acknowledgment is made to the copyright holders on p. 303, which is hereby made part of this copyright page.

Library of Congress Cataloging-in-Publication Data

Williams, Joseph M.
    Style: ten lessons in clarity and grace/Joseph M. Williams.—
6th ed.
      p.   cm.
    Includes bibliographical references and index.
    ISBN 0-321-02408-7
    1. English language—Rhetoric. 2. English language—
Technical English. 3. English language—Business English.
4. English language—Style. 5. Technical writing. 6. Business
writing. I. Title.
PE1421.W545 1999
808'.042—dc21   98–20555
                                          CIP

Copyright © 2000 by Addison-Wesley Educational Publishers, Inc.

Please visit our website at http://www.awlonline.com

ISBN 0-321-02408-7

345678910—DOC—02010099

CONTENTS

Preface   *v*

PART I   *Style as Choice*   *1*

LESSON ONE   Understanding Style   3

LESSON TWO   Correctness   14

PART II   *Clarity*   *39*

LESSON THREE   Clarity 1: Actions   41

LESSON FOUR   Clarity 2: Characters   68

LESSON FIVE   Cohesion and Coherence   97

LESSON SIX   Emphasis   118

PART III   *Grace*   *137*

LESSON SEVEN   Concision   139

LESSON EIGHT   Shape   165

LESSON NINE   Elegance   191

PART IV   *Ethics*   *217*

LESSON TEN   The Ethics of Prose   219

Appendix: Punctuation   *251*
Glossary   *273*
Suggested Answers   *287*
Acknowledgments   *303*
Index   *305*

PREFACE

Most people won't realize that writing is a craft.
You have to take your apprenticeship in it like anything else.
KATHERINE ANNE PORTER

WHAT'S NEW IN THIS EDITION

The most obvious difference from the fifth edition of *Style* is that I have moved the lesson on "Point of View" to the end and retitled it "The Ethics of Style," and I've added to it some thoughts that have been flitting through my mind for the last few years about some issues larger than clarity and grace. When we write for others, we engage in a social act with ethical consequences. When we read, we engage in a social act that also has an ethical dimension. I think the issue is worth a few pages. I hope it won't be seen as self-indulgent, though I understand those who might think so.

I've made some less obvious but substantial changes: I've again tried to make Lessons 3 and 4 on agents and actions less dense and more patient. There are new examples scattered throughout. And I've tinkered with probably half the sentences. I used to think that if I wrote this book often enough, I would eventually get it right. I was wrong.

WHAT'S THE SAME

This edition still aims at answering the same three questions I asked in earlier ones:

- What is it about a sentence that influences how readers judge its clarity?
- How can we diagnose our own prose to anticipate their judgments?
- How can we revise it so that readers will think better of it?

The standard advice about drafting is well intentioned, but largely useless, because it consists mostly of truisms like "Make a plan" and "Think of your audience," or trivia like "Don't begin a sentence with *and* or end it with *up*," advice that most of us ignore in the act of wrestling our ideas out onto the page. As I first drafted this paragraph, I wasn't thinking about you; I was struggling to get my own ideas straight; I had no plan for it, much less for the next one; and the first time I drafted this sentence, I stopped to edit it several times before I finished it.

What I did know was that I would go back to that paragraph again and again, and that it was likely to be only then—as I revised—that I could think about you, the reader, and figure out the plan that fit my draft. I also knew that as I did so, there were a few principles that I could rely on. This book is about them.

PRINCIPLES AND PREDICTIONS RATHER THAN PRESCRIPTIONS

Those principles may seem to some readers prescriptive. That is not how I intend them. What I offer are not rules, but ways to help you predict how your readers will read your prose, and then help you decide whether and how to revise it, but only if you *choose* to. You can write in any way you like; it's a free country. But it's useful to know how readers are likely to react to your choices.

You may find that after reading all this you will write more slowly. That's inevitable. Whenever we reflect on what we do as we do it, we become self-conscious, sometimes to the point of paralysis. It passes. You can avoid some of the paralysis, even the slowdown, if you remember that the principles offered here have little to do with how you write, but with how you *re*write. If there is a first principle of drafting, it is to forget these principles of diagnosis and revision.

In fact, to get the most out of this book, you should try writing *against* the principles offered here to see what happens. Try writing in the bureaucratic style, just to get the feel of it. Try creating a passage in a style elegant beyond your needs, to see whether you can pull it off. Try writing the longest sentence you can, just to see how far you can stretch it before it collapses. Do not let habits of style box you in, even good ones, especially good ones.

SOME DEMANDS ON YOUR TIME AND ATTENTION

To learn how to revise efficiently, though, you have to know a few things:

- I will use a few grammatical terms you may have forgotten: SUBJECT, VERB, NOUN, ACTIVE, PASSIVE, CLAUSE, PREPOSITION, and COORDINATION. All key terms are capitalized the first time they appear in a lesson and defined in the Glossary.
- You will have to learn new meanings for two familiar words: TOPIC and STRESS.
- You will have to learn six terms that you probably do not know at all. Two are important: NOMINALIZATION and METADISCOURSE; four are useful: RUNNING MODIFIER, RESUMPTIVE MODIFIER, SUMMATIVE MODIFIER, and FREE MODIFIER.

But just knowing these words won't help you write better. Only when you understand how to use nouns and verbs will you understand why some prose seems clear and other prose does not. And that will help you rewrite unclear prose more quickly.

Some students think that since they see so much unclear writing in print, it must be less important than good ideas. The truth is that even good ideas need all the help they can get, especially for readers who have neither the time nor the patience to dig them out of muddy prose. Indeed, whenever professionals are asked what they wish they had studied more diligently, first or second on their list is always communication, especially writing. In any field, the person who can deliver a clear and readable document quickly has an invaluable skill.

If you are reading this book on your own, go slowly. It is not an amiable essay that you can read in a sitting or two. Take the lessons a few pages at a time, up to the exercises. Do the exercises, edit someone else's writing, then edit some of your own that you wrote at least a few weeks ago. You will be surprised at how much less you admire it. Then look hard at what you've written today, first for elements addressed by the current lesson, then for other points, and then if you have time, for the rest.

So many have offered support, suggestions, and criticisms over the last twenty years, that I cannot thank you all. But once again I begin with those English 194 students (now in their forties!) who put up with faintly dittoed pages (that tells you how many years ago this book was born) and with a teacher who at times was as puzzled as they. I remain grateful to you all.

In more recent years, I have learned much from those undergraduate, graduate, and professional students, and post-docs who have gone through the Little Red Schoolhouse writing program here at the University of Chicago (a.k.a. Advanced Academic and Professional Writing). I am equally grateful to the graduate students who have taught these principles and offered important feedback. Students and teachers alike have encouraged us that this way of thinking about writing and teaching pays off, particularly to those who teach it.

I have intellectual debts to those who broke ground in psycholinguistics, text linguistics, and functional sentence perspective. Those who keep up with such matters will recognize the distant influence of Charles Filmore, Jan Firbas, Nils Enkvist, Michael Halliday, Noam Chomsky, Thomas Bever, Vic Yngve, and others. More recently, the work of Eleanore Rosch has provided a rich explanation for why verbs should be actions and characters should be subjects. Her work in prototype semantics is a powerful theoretical account for the kind of style urged here. The Teachers Manual that comes with this book sketches those theoretical foundations.

I am indebted to colleagues who have taken time to read the work of another. For reading earlier versions of this book, I must thank in particular Randy Berlin, Ken Bruffee, Douglas Butturff, Donald Byker, Bruce Campbell, Elaine Chaika, Avon Crismore, Constance Gefvert, Maxine Hairston, George Hoffman, Ted Lowe, Susan Miller, Neil Nakadate, Mike Pownall, Peter Priest, Margaret Shaklee, Nancy Sommers, Mary Taylor, and Stephen Witte. I am grateful for the feedback from the class taught by Stan Henning at the University of Wisconsin–Madison, and for the error in usage caught by Linda Ziff at Johns Hopkins University. I am grateful to John Ruszkiewicz, Bill Vande Kopple, and Margaret Batschelet. I am indebted to Christina Devlin for the Wesley quotation in Lesson Seven and to James Vanden Bosch for the Montaigne quotation in the Glossary. I gratefully acknowledge the assistance of Frederick C. Mish, editorial director, G. & C. Merriam Company, in locating the best examples of three citations in Lesson Two, and Charles Bazerman, whose work on Crick and Watson led me to the first paragraph of their DNA paper.

And for this edition in particular, I am in debt to another group of especially thoughtful and careful reviewers: Theresa Ammirati, Connecticut College; Yvonne Atkinson, University of California, Riverside; Cheryl Brooke, Cleveland State University; Jeanne Gunner, Santa Clara University; Rebecca Moore Howard, Texas Christian University; Richard Jenseth, St. Lawrence University; Elizabeth Bourque Johnson, University of Minnesota; Patricia Murray, California State University, Northridge; John W. Taylor, South Dakota State University; Joseph F. Wappel, University of Maryland; Alison Warriner, California State University, Hayward; Kevin S. Wilson, Boise State University. I am particularly indebted to an exchange with Keith Rhodes, Northwest Missouri State University, about Lesson 10. He made me think as hard as I should have about some claims that, as I think of them now, I am lucky to have escaped committing to print.

The editors of Addison Wesley Longman have saved me from more than a few gaffes. I remain in the debt of the editor who first urged me to write this book, Harriett Prentiss, and my current editors, Anne Smith and Meg Botteon, who have more than restored my faith in the competence of that profession. I think they are now friends as well as colleagues. They have both demonstrated more patience with me than I deserve.

I would also like to thank Stephanie Magean, who edited the manuscript. I have been fortunate to have good copy editors, but her careful reading reflected not just for a scrupulous job of editing, but a deeply intelligent one. And finally, my thanks to my careful assistant, Charles Chandler, who helped proof the galleys and assemble the index.

For several years, I have had the good fortune to work with two people who have been both good colleagues and good friends and whose careful thinking has helped me think better about many matters, both professional and personal: Don Freeman and Greg Colomb. Don's careful readings have saved me from more than a few howlers; I am indebted to him for the quote from William Blake in Lesson Eight. Greg has put up with more than most friends would. It has been a pleasure and a privilege to work and hang out with him and Sandra for almost twenty years now.

And again, those who have contributed more to the quality of my life than I have let them know. Once six, they now are nine: Chris, Oliver, Megan and Phil, Dave and Patty, and Joe and Christine. And at beginning and end still, Joan, whose patience, good judgment, and love seem inexhaustible.

J. M. W.
April 1999

PART I

Style as Choice

Have something to say, and say it as clearly as you can.
That is the only secret of style.

MATTHEW ARNOLD

LESSON ONE

Understanding Style

Style is the physiognomy of the mind.
ARTHUR SCHOPENHAUER

*To me, style is just the outside of content,
and content the inside of style, like the outside
and inside of the human body—both go together,
they can't be separated.*
JEAN-LUC GODARD

The great enemy of clear language is insincerity.
GEORGE ORWELL

*In matters of grave importance, style,
not sincerity, is the vital thing.*
OSCAR WILDE

PRINCIPLES AND AIMS

This book builds on two principles: It's good to write clearly, and anyone can. That first principle is self-evident, especially to those who have to deal with prose like this:

> Better evaluation of responses to treatment modalities depends on the standardization of an index allowing accurate descriptions of learning disorder behaviors.

But that second principle may seem optimistic to those who hide their ideas not only from their readers, but sometimes even from themselves. Hard as they struggle, they can't get close to this:

> We could better evaluate how those with learning disorders respond to treatment if we could standardize an index that accurately describes how they behave.

We could say that such writers have a problem with their style, but they have no style, if by style we mean how we choose to arrange words to their best effect: Those writers do not choose how they write, any more than they choose whether to put *the* before *dog* rather than after.

But choice is at the heart of clear writing, because to meet the needs of different readers, we have to choose between this word and a more exact one, between this order of words and some other that better helps a reader get from the beginning of a sentence to its end without feeling, as one of my teachers said of my writing forty years ago, that she was slogging through a field of wet mud.

Writing can fail for reasons more serious than its style, of course. We bewilder readers when we cannot organize new and complex ideas in a way that seems to them coherent. We cannot hope to gain their assent if we ignore their predictable questions and objections. As important as those issues are, this book addresses a different matter: Once we've assembled our ideas, formulated our claims, supported them with good reasons, and organized our text coherently, we still have to express our ideas clearly. Before readers can accept our claims, they have to understand them.

That's my aim: to explain how you can overcome a problem that has afflicted generations of writers—a style that, instead of revealing ideas, hides them. When we read that kind of writing in government regulations, we call it bureaucratese; when we find it in contracts and judicial pronouncements, legalese; in scholarly articles and books that inflate small ideas into gassy abstractions, academese. Intended or not, it feels like a style of pretension and intimidation. When it is the product of carelessness or indifference, it expresses contempt for its intended readers. When written deliberately, it is an exclusionary language that a democratic society cannot tolerate as its standard of ethical civic discourse. Unfortunately, that style has become so common that it seems to have established itself as an institutional standard, beguiling many inexperienced writers into imitating it. The problem has a long history.

A SHORT HISTORY OF UNCLEAR WRITING

The Past

It was not until the late sixteenth century that writers of English finally decided that their language was eloquent enough to replace Latin and French in intellectually respectable discourse, but their first impulse toward elegance was a style complex beyond the needs of their readers:

> If use and custom, having the help of so long time and continuance wherein to [re]fine our tongue, of so great learning and experience which furnish matter for the [re]fining, of so good wits and judgments which can tell how to refine, have griped at nothing in all that time, with all that cunning, by all those wits which they will not let go but hold for most certain in the right of our writing, that then our tongue has no certainty to trust to, but write all at random.
>
> —Richard Mulcaster, *The First Part of the Elementary,* 1582

Within a century, this inflated style had spread to scientific prose. As one critic complained,

> Of all the studies of men, nothing may sooner be obtained than this vicious abundance of phrase, this trick of metaphors, this volubility of tongue which makes so great a noise in the world.
>
> —Thomas Sprat, *History of the Royal Society,* 1667

When the New World was settled, American writers had a chance to establish a new prose style, not viciously voluble, but lean and direct. In 1776, Thomas Paine published *Common Sense,* a pamphlet whose plain language helped rouse American colonists to a revolution.

> In the following pages I offer nothing more than simple facts, plain arguments, and common sense; and have no other preliminaries to settle with the reader, than that he will divest himself of prejudice.

It was a good start. His straightforward language helped spark a revolution in our form of government. But not, sad to say, in the style of our prose.

By the early nineteenth century, James Fenimore Cooper was complaining that "the common faults of American language were an ambition of effect, a want of simplicity, and a turgid abuse of terms":

> The love of turgid expressions is gaining ground, and ought to be corrected. One of the most certain evidences of a man of high breeding, is his simplicity of speech: a simplicity that is equally removed from vulgarity and exaggeration. . . . He does not say, in speaking of a dance, that "the attire of the ladies was exceedingly elegant and peculiarly becoming at the late assembly," but that "the women were well dressed at the last ball"; nor is he apt to remark, "that the Rev. Mr. G— gave us an elegant and searching discourse the past sabbath," but that "the parson preached a good sermon last sunday."
>
> The utterance of a gentleman ought to be deliberate and clear, without being measured. . . . Simplicity should be the firm aim, after one is removed from vulgarity, and let the finer shades of accomplishment be acquired as they can be attained. In no case, however, can one who aims at turgid language, exaggerated sentiments, or pedantic utterances, lay claim to be either a man or a woman of the world.
>
> —James Fenimore Cooper, *The American Democrat*, 1838

Unfortunately, in condemning that style, Cooper adopted it. He criticizes *the attire of the ladies was exceedingly elegant,* but in his next sentence he echoes it: *The utterance of a gentleman ought to be deliberate.* Had he followed his own advice, he might chosen to write this:

> We should discourage writers who love turgid language. A well-bred person speaks simply, in a way that is neither vulgar nor exaggerated. We should not measure our words, but speak them clearly and deliberately. After we rid our language of vulgarity, we should aim at simplicity, and then as we can, acquire the finer shades of accomplishment. No one can claim to be a man or woman of the world who exaggerates sentiments or deliberately speaks in language that is turgid or pedantic.

About fifty years later, Mark Twain wrote what we now like to think is classic American prose—easy, clear, concise, direct, emphatic:

> There have been daring people in the world who claimed that Cooper could write English, but they are all dead now—all dead but Lounsbury [an academic who praised Cooper's style]. I don't remember that Lounsbury makes the claim in so many words, still he makes it, for he says that *Deerslayer* is a "pure work of art." Pure, in that connection, means faultless—faultless in all details—and language is a detail. If Mr. Lounsbury had only compared Cooper's English with the English which he writes himself—but it is plain that he didn't; and so it is likely that he imagines until this day that Cooper's [style] is as clean and compact as his own. Now I feel sure, deep down in my heart, that Cooper wrote about the poorest English that exists in our language, and that the English of *Deerslayer* is the very worst tha[t] even Cooper ever wrote.

Everyone admires Twain's easy directness; few have chosen to emulate it.

The Present

In the best-known essay on English style, "Politics and the English Language," George Orwell anatomized the inflated language of twentieth-century politicians, bureaucrats, and other chronic dodgers of responsibility:

> The keynote [of a pretentious style] is the elimination of simple verbs. Instead of being a single word, such as *break, stop, spoil, mend, kill,* a verb becomes a phrase, made up of a noun or adjective tacked on to some general-purposes verb such as *prove, serve, form, play, render.* In addition, the passive voice is wherever possible used in preference to the active, and noun constructions are used instead of gerunds (*by examination* of instead of *by examining*). The range of verbs is further cut down by means of the *-ize* and *de-* formations, and the banal statements are given an appearance of profundity by means of the *not un-* formation.

But just as Cooper did, in abusing that style Orwell modeled it. Had he avoided PASSIVES and NOUN constructions (capitalized words are defined in the Glossary), he could have chosen to write more directly:

Those who write pretentiously eliminate simple verbs. Instead of using one word, such as *break, stop, spoil, mend, kill,* they turn a verb into a noun or adjective and then tack it on to a general-purpose verb such as *prove, serve, form, play, render.* Wherever possible, they use the passive voice instead of the active and noun constructions instead of gerunds (*by examination* instead of *by examining*). They cut down the range of verbs with *-ize* and *de-,* and try to make banal statements profound by the *not un-* formation.

If in attacking this style Orwell could not avoid imitating it (I don't think he was being ironic), we ought not be surprised that today's academic and professional writers fare worse. On the language of the social sciences:

A turgid and polysyllabic prose does seem to prevail in the social sciences. . . . Such a lack of ready intelligibility, I believe, usually has little or nothing to do with the complexity of thought. It has to do almost entirely with certain confusions of the academic writer about his own status.

—C. Wright Mills, *The Sociological Imagination*

On the language of medicine:

It now appears that obligatory obfuscation is a firm tradition within the medical profession. . . . [Medical writing] is a highly skilled, calculated attempt to confuse the reader. . . . A doctor feels he might get passed over for an assistant professorship because he wrote his papers too clearly—because he made his ideas seem too simple.

—Michael Crichton, *New England Journal of Medicine*

On the language of law:

In law journals, in speeches, in classrooms and in courtrooms, lawyers and judges are beginning to worry about how often they have been misunderstood, and they are discovering that sometimes they cannot even understand each other.

—Tom Goldstein, *New York Times*

On the language of scholarship (from a review of a book about teaching apes to communicate):

There are times when the more the authors explain, the less we understand. Apes certainly seem capable of using language to communicate. Whether scientists are remains doubtful.

—Douglas Chadwick, *New York Times*

Some postmodern critics now even think clarity is ideologically suspicious:

> [T]hose . . . who make the call for clear writing synonymous with an attack on critical educators have missed the role that the "language of clarity" plays in a dominant culture that cleverly and powerfully uses "clear" and "simplistic" language to systematically undermine and prevent the conditions from arising for a public culture to engage in rudimentary forms of complex and critical thinking.
>
> Stanley Aronowitz, Postmodern Education

(I'll revisit claims like this in Lesson 10.)

Students often confront this kind of turgidity in their textbooks. Here is a sentence from one that is clearer than many, but more difficult than it had to be:

> Recognition of the fact that systems [of grammar] differ from one language to another can serve as the basis for serious consideration of the problems confronting translators of the great works of world literature originally written in a language other than English.

More concisely:

> When we recognize that languages have different grammars, we can consider the problems of those who translate great works of literature into English.

Generations of students have struggled with prose they could not understand, often blaming themselves, thinking they were not smart enough to grasp ideas seemingly so complex. Some may have been right about that, but more should have blamed the tangled writing they were trying to understand.

Some students, sad to say, give up; sadder still, many who learn to read that style imitate it and then go on to write their own books in the same way, confounding more students, some of whom master that same tangled style and go on to write yet more books. . . . And thus the style of one generation insinuates itself into that of the next, sustaining a 400-year-old tradition of wretched prose.

Some Private Causes of Unclear Writing

The most common reason we write unclearly, however, is that we don't know we do, much less how to revise prose into something better. When we read our own writing, we all think it clearly expresses what we mean, because when we read it, we are only reminding ourselves of what we had in mind when we wrote it. But beyond that chronic inability to read our prose as others will, there are other private causes of unclear writing.

Hiding Behind Language

Michael Crichton mentioned the most common one: Some writers choose complicated language not only to plump up their ideas, but to mask their absence, hoping that complexity will impress those who confuse difficulty with substance. When we don't know what we're talking about and don't want anyone else to know that we don't, we typically throw up a screen of big words in long, complicated sentences.

Others choose intimidating language to protect what they have from those who want a piece of it—the power and privilege that go with the ruling class. We control information by locking it up, but we can also conceal it behind a style so complex that it can be understood only by those trained to endure and interpret it.

Bad Memories

Others write graceless prose because they are gripped by the memory of someone who taught them that writing was good only when it was free of errors that only a teacher of grammar could explain. Too many of us now approach a blank page not as a space for fresh thinking, but as a minefield to be traversed gingerly. We inch our way from word to word, concerned less with our readers' understanding than with our own survival, and in the process create sentences as awkward as they are error-free.

Temporary Aphasia

Finally, many of us write unclearly not because we choose to, but because we are seized by a kind of literary aphasia, a dismaying experience that renders us unable to write as well as we thought we once could, or in some severe cases, unable to write at all. This typically happens when we are learning to think and write in a new academic or professional field, when we start to write about matters we do not entirely understand for readers who do. The afflicted include not just undergraduates taking their first course in economics or psychology, but graduate students, business people, doctors, lawyers, professors—anyone writing about a new topic, aimed at readers who are unfamiliar to them and therefore intimidating.

As we struggle to master complex ideas, many of us, probably most of us, have to pass through this period of stylistic confusion. If you find yourself in that situation, your floundering should dismay you less if you know you are sharing an experience endured by generations of other writers. You will discover that you can write more clearly once you more clearly understand what you are writing about.

In all of this, of course, there is a great irony: When you write about a subject that confuses you, you are likely to write in ways that confuse others. But when you struggle through prose that confuses you not just because of its unavoidably difficult content, but also because of its gratuitously difficult style, you can too easily assume that such stylistic complexity must signal the complexity of deep thought, and so you try to imitate it in your own prose, compounding your own already confused style. Thus your inability to write clearly conspires with an impulse to write complexly, a conspiracy of influences resulting in prose that thoroughly confuses your readers.

The aim of this book is to help you cut through that confusion by showing you how to make better choices.

ON WRITING AND REWRITING

As I emphasized in the Preface, this book is not, in fact, about writing. It is about *re*writing. You can use the principles presented here to help you plan what to write and to revise what you have written, but they help no one caught up in the moment of writing to write clearly. In fact, if you think about these principles as you draft, you may never draft anything. Experienced writers know that they have to get something down on paper (or up on the screen) as fast as they can, just to have a draft that they can revise into a better one, and if they are lucky, to discover in the process something new.

When you revise your early confusion into something clearer you better understand your own ideas. And when you understand your ideas better, you express them more clearly, and when you express them more clearly, you understand them even better . . . and so it goes: You write to help yourself think better, then think to help yourself write better, until you run out of energy, interest, or time. For a fortunate few, that moment comes weeks, months, even years after they begin. (Over the last eighteen years, this book has been through several dozen drafts, and there are parts I still can't get right.) For most of us, though, the deadline is closer to tomorrow morning. And so we have to settle for prose that is less than perfect, but as readable as possible given the complexity of its subject and the time available for revising it. Perfection is an admirable goal, but it is the enemy of done.

You should therefore treat what you read here not as a set of rules to apply to every sentence you write, but as principles to apply quickly to your early drafts. To that end, I'll suggest ways to identify quickly those passages most likely to need revising and then ways to revise them just as quickly.

As important as clarity is, though, some occasions call for more:

> Now the trumpet summons us again—not as a call to bear arms, though arms we need; not as a call to battle, though embattled we are; but a call to bear the burden of a long twilight struggle, year in and year out, "rejoicing in hope, patient in tribulation," a struggle against the common enemies of man: tyranny, poverty, disease and war itself.
>
> —John F. Kennedy, Inaugural Address, January 20, 1961

Few of us write presidential addresses. But in even our most modest prose, we may want more than just readability, especially when we have something to say that calls for special dignity. Or even just to take a bit of pleasure in the craft of writing, regardless of whether anyone will notice, like a cabinetmaker who makes even the back of a drawer look right. Those who take that kind of pleasure in crafting their sentences will find some suggestions in Lesson 9. And in Lesson 10, I address some of the ethical issues involved in style: Writing is a social act, and all social acts imply motives that might or might not be in the best interests of readers.

About sixty years ago, H. L. Mencken wrote this:

> With precious few exceptions, all the books on style in English are by writers quite unable to write. The subject, indeed, seems to exercise a special and dreadful fascination over school ma'ams, bucolic college professors, and other such pseudoliterates. . . . Their central aim, of course, is to reduce the whole thing to a series of simple rules—the

overmastering passion of their melancholy order, at all times and everywhere.

That melancholy judgment has hovered over every sentence I've written, because Mencken was right: No one can teach good writing by rule, especially to those who cannot feel or think or see. But I know that many who do see clearly, feel deeply, and think carefully cannot share their feelings and thoughts and visions. I also know that the more clearly we write, the more clearly we see and feel and think. Rigid rules help no one, but there are some principles that do.

Here they are.

LESSON TWO

Correctness

*No grammatical rules have sufficient authority to control the firm
and established usage of language. Established custom, in speaking
and writing, is the standard to which we must at last resort for
determining every controverted point in language and style.*
HUGH BLAIR

*It is not the business of grammar, as some critics seem
preposterously to imagine, to give law to the fashions which regulate
our speech. On the contrary, from its conformity to these, and from
that alone, it derives all its authority and value.*
GEORGE CAMPBELL

*English usage is sometimes more than mere taste, judgment, and
education—sometimes it's sheer luck, like getting across the street.*
E. B. WHITE

*God does not much mind bad grammar, but He does not take any
particular pleasure in it.*
ERASMUS

Any fool can make a rule and every fool will mind it.
HENRY DAVID THOREAU

Choice Versus Obedience
Clarity and Choice

To a competent writer, nothing is more important than choice, the ability to choose not just what to write but how. In some matters, of course, we have no choice—whether to put *the* before or after a NOUN, as in *the street* versus *street the*. But for other matters, choice should always be at the front of a writer's mind. For example, which of these sentences would we choose to write if we wanted readers to think we wrote clearly and directly?

1. There was a lack of evidence on their part in support of their claim.
2. Their claim suffered because of their lack of evidence in its support.
3. They could not support their claim because they lacked evidence.

All three are grammatically "correct," but most of us would choose (3), because of the three, it feels most direct.

Correctness and Obedience

Unlike matters of style, though, correctness seems not to offer choice, but to demand obedience. When the *American Heritage Dictionary* says that *irregardless* is "nonstandard . . . never acceptable" (except, they say, for humor), our freedom to choose between *irregardless* and *regardless* seems at best academic. In this matter, we choose not between better and worse, but between right and utterly, irredeemably, unequivocally, existentially Wrong.

That seems to simplify things: "Correctness" requires neither good taste nor sound judgment, much less informed choice, but only a reliable memory. If we can remember that *irregardless* is always Wrong, it ought no more rise to even the lowest level of choice than does *street the*. Some teachers and editors think that we should do the same with dozens of other "rules" like these:

- Don't begin a sentence with *and* or *but*.
- Don't use double negatives.
- Don't split INFINITIVES.
- Don't end a sentence with a PREPOSITION.

Unfortunately, it's not that simple. Some "rules" allegedly governing correct usage are less important than many think (indeed, some are not important at all), and that if you obsess on every point of usage, you will hinder yourself from writing quickly and easily. In fact, that's why I am addressing this matter of correctness now, before I turn to matters of clarity, not because clarity runs second to "good" grammar. Quite the contrary: I want to put this matter of correctness where it belongs—behind us, before we tackle more difficult and important issues.

Three Kinds of Rules

We have to distinguish three kinds of rules that allegedly govern good usage:

- Classroom folklore, invented by eighteenth-century grammarians out of whole cloth and still taught by those who repeat what textbooks tell them, even though such "rules" are widely ignored by respected writers and by their careful readers.
- Other rules are imperatives whose violations mark us as at least careless, if not illiterate. These rules are observed by even the less-than-best writers.
- And then there are points of usage that we may choose to observe or not, depending on how we want our readers to respond.

Before we look at these points in detail, though, we should take a moment to think about how rules like these originated. Once we understand their history, we can see them not as Rules Handed Down From Above but as the social conventions they really are.

REASONS FOR RULES

Opinion is split on the social role of Standard English. To some, it is just one more device invented by the ruling class to control the rest: A standard grammar helps them keep the underclasses under by stigmatizing their speech and blocking their social ambitions. To others, Standard English is the refined product of a sifting and winnowing conducted by generations of grammarians, the best of all possible Englishes, codified in rules observed by the best writers, or, at least according to some grammarians, should be.

Both views are correct, partly. For centuries, most of those who govern our affairs have used grammatical "errors" to identify those who are unwilling or unable to acquire the habits of diligence, self-discipline, and obedience—values that the gatekeepers of our institutions look for in those whom they screen for admission. But the conservatives are also right: Many features of Standard English did originate in apparent efficiencies of expression. For example, we don't really need the complex set of verb endings required a thousand years ago, so now we omit present tense endings in all but one context (and in fact, we don't even need it there):

	1ST PERSON	2ND PERSON	3RD PERSON
Singular	I know +_.	You know +_.	She know + **S**.
Plural	We know +_.	You know +_.	They know +_.

Correctness as Historical Accident

But if the radical critics are right to claim that Standard English has been used to discriminate, they are wrong to claim that it is *devised* to achieve socially vicious ends. Linguistic standards originate in historical accidents of geography and economic power. When a country has different regional dialects, that of the wealthiest region is likely to become most prestigious and the basis for that nation's standard form of writing. Thus if a thousand years ago, Scotland had by some geographical accident been closer to the Continent than was London, and its capital, Edinburgh, had been a great port and the center of Britain's economic, political, and literary life, we might be writing and speaking less like Shakespeare and more like the Scottish poet Robert Burns:

A ye wha are sae guid yourself	(All you who are so good yourselves
Sae pious and sae holy,	So pious and so holy,
Ye've nought to do but mark and tell	You've nothing to do but talk about
Your neebours' fauts and folly!	Your neighbors' faults and folly!)

But the conservative critics are also wrong when they claim that Standard English is superior to other forms because it has been refined by the logic and taste of countless educated speakers and their grammarian overseers. True, many features of Standard English seem to reflect an evolution toward efficiency. But most of those features are shared by all speakers, whatever their dialect. Every speaker of Modern English, for example, enjoys (or should) the demise of the distinction that made adjectives and nouns grammatically masculine, feminine, or neuter, as they still are in Spanish and German.

Correctness as Unpredictability

If the features that define Standard English are not the product of historical inevitability, neither do they reflect any intrinsic logic, if by logical we mean systematic and therefore predictable. In fact, many features of Standard English are less "logical" than their corresponding features in nonstandard English:

- The person who says *I **knowed*** makes the same "mistake" as the first person who said *I **climbed** the tree* instead of the earlier "correct" *I **clum** the tree*. Both speakers regularize an inconsistent pattern, an act that in other contexts is taken as a sign of intelligence.
- Those who say *hisself* and *theirselves* regularize an inconsistency among the reflexive pronouns: If we have **myself, our**selves, **yourself, your**selves, **herself,** and **its[s]elf,** all possessive pronouns, we should predict the possessives **hisself** and **their**selves.
- The person who says, *I'm here, ain't I?* uses a wholly logical (and once widely acceptable) contraction of *am + not.* It is precisely parallel to *He's here, isn't he?*

   I am here, am I not? → amn't I? → ain't I?
   He is here, is he not? → isn't he?

   What is illogical is the "correct" form—*I'm here, **aren't** I?*—because that *aren't I* is equivalent to an "ungrammatical" *I are not.*

   We could cite a dozen other examples where, strictly applied, principles of logic and history should approve a form we now condemn, because that nonstandard form reflects a logical mind regularizing gratuitous irregularity. In fact, it is in their *ir*regularity that the features of Standard English prove most useful to those who would use it to discriminate: To speak and write Standard

English, we must either be born into it or spend lots of time learning its idiosyncrasies. Those determined to discriminate use any social difference available, of course. But since our language seems to reflect our quality of mind more directly than does our ZIP code, it is easy for those inclined to look down on others to imagine that their grammatical "errors" signal mental or moral deficiency.

> *Here's the point:*   We must reject the notion that Standard English makes its speakers intellectually or morally superior. That belief is not just factually wrong: In a democracy, it is destructive. Yet even if logic predicts *hisself* and *knowed* and both history and logic attest to a once-respectable *ain't*, so much greater is the power of social convention that we must still exclude those words when we write for serious purposes, which is just about all the time.

THREE KINDS OF CORRECTNESS

These confused attitudes about correctness have been encouraged by generations of grammarians who, in their zeal to codify and certify "good" English, have confused themselves (and many others) about three kinds of errors:

1. Some rules define the fundamental structure of English—ARTICLES precede nouns: *the book,* not *book the;* SUBJECTS usually precede verbs: *I see you,* not *See I you.* These rules are violated by native speakers of English only when they are tired or rushed, and they recognize and correct those violations the moment they see them.

2. A few rules reliably distinguish standard speech from non-standard: *you were* versus *you was, I don't know anything* versus *I don't know nothing.* The only writers who *consciously* choose to follow these rules are those striving to join the educated class. Schooled writers think about such rules only when they notice someone else violating them.

3. Finally, some grammarians have invented rules they think everyone *should* observe. Most date from the last half of the eighteenth century:

   Don't split infinitives, as in *to **quietly** leave.*

   Don't use *than* after *different*, as in *This is different **than** that.* Use *from.*

   Don't use *between* with three or more, as in ***between** the three of us.*

A few date from this century:

   Don't use *hopefully* for *I hope,* as in ***Hopefully**, it won't rain.*

   Don't use *which* for *that* in a RESTRICTIVE CLAUSE, as in *a car **which** I sold.*

The fact is, none of these rules reflects the consensus usage among our best writers.

By confounding these three quite different kinds of errors, grammarians have misled countless teachers and their students into believing that splitting an infinitive is an error as egregious as a double negative, and that both are almost on a par with scrambled syntax.

We will concentrate on the third kind of rule—the trivia of usage, because only they vex educated writers. They are the rules that we remember from high school and whose "violation" newspaper columnists endlessly rehearse as reason to fear for the future of Western Civilization. But since grammarians have been accusing the best writers of violating these rules for the last 200 years, we have to conclude that for 200 years the best writers have been ignoring both the rules and grammarians. Which is lucky for grammarians, because if writers did obey all their rules, grammarians would have to keep inventing new ones, or find another line of work.

Some educated and careful writers honor every rule, but most choose to observe fewer, and their educated and careful readers notice fewer still. A few know all the rules, but also that they need observe only certain ones, and that other rules they can observe or ignore, as they choose.

Observing Rules Thoughtfully

But what do you do if you want to be thought of as someone who writes not only well but "correctly"?

The Worst (i.e., Safest) Case Policy

You could choose the worst-case policy: Follow all the rules all the time because somewhere, sometime, someone might criticize you for something—for beginning a sentence with *and* or ending it with *up*. And so you scrutinize every sentence for "errors" until you learn to obey the rules without thought.

But if you obey all the rules all the time, you surrender a measure of choice. Worse, you may find yourself so obsessed with rules that you tie yourself—and your writing—into knots. And sooner or later, you will try to impose those rules—real or not—on others. After all, what good is learning a rule if all you can do is obey it?

A More Thoughtful (i.e., Riskier) Approach

The alternative to blind obedience is selective observance. But then you have to decide which rules to observe, which to ignore, and which to observe or ignore as you choose. And then if you do decide to ignore some alleged rule, how do you deal with those whose passion (and memory) for "good" grammar seem to endow them with the ability to see in your split infinitive a sign of moral laxity?

If you want to avoid being labeled "permissive," or worse "without standards," but if you also decline to submit mindlessly to whatever "rule" someone can dredge up from memories of an English class, you have to know more about the rules than do the rule-mongers. For example, some teachers and editors like to abuse those who begin a sentence with *and* or *but*. For matters of this kind, it is useful to consult the guide used by the most conservative writers: the second edition of H. W. Fowler's *A Dictionary of Modern English Usage* (first edition, Oxford University Press, 1926; second edition, 1965; third edition, 1997). (The second edition is the choice of critics on the grammatical right because they have judged the third too permissive.) The second edition was edited by Sir Ernest Gowers, who to Fowler's original entry on *and* in the first edition, added this:

> That it is a solecism to begin a sentence with *and* is a faintly lingering superstition. (p. 29)

And to the original entry for *but,* he added "see *and.*"

Now to be sure, even the best writers commit occasional errors. We all have used a singular verb distant from a plural subject (or vice versa), and when told about it, we gratefully fix it. But we must define the standard for what is or is not an error by the consensus of usage of writers whom we consider competent and by the unself-conscious judgment of their most competent readers.

> *Here's the point:*   If writers and readers we judge competent do not think that sentences beginning with *and* are a problem, then it is not those writers who should change their usage but grammarians who should change their rules. If vast numbers of otherwise careful writers choose to "violate" some alleged rule of usage and the vast majority of their otherwise careful readers don't notice, then regardless of what any editor or grammarian says, the usage in question cannot be a grammatical error.

DISTINGUISHING TWO KINDS OF RULES

We can sort just about all the rules that some grammarians think define "good usage" into two groups: Folklore and Options.

1. *Folklore.* When you violate "rules" like these, few careful readers notice, much less care. So these are not rules at all, but folklore you can ignore, unless you are writing for someone with the power to demand whatever kind of writing that person idiosyncratically prefers.
2. *Options.* When you ignore these rules, few readers notice. But paradoxically, some readers notice when you observe them, because when you do, you signal special formality. So you can observe these rules or not, depending on how you want to impress different groups of readers.

Folklore

These rules include those whose observance and violation careful readers and writers largely ignore. I decided what to include in this category based on reading a good deal of prose that was carefully written and intended to be read just as carefully. The quotations that illustrate "violations" of these nonrules are from writers who are of substantial intellectual and scholarly stature or who, on matters of usage, are reliable archconservatives (or both). Some of these "rules" may be unfamiliar, but even if you have not yet had one inflicted on you, chances are that eventually you will. (A check mark indicates those sentences that are acceptable Standard English.)

1. "Don't begin sentences with *and* or *but*." This passage ignores the "rule" twice:

✓　　**But,** it will be asked, is tact not an individual gift, therefore highly variable in its choices? **And** if that is so, what guidance can a manual offer, other than that of its author's prejudices—mere impressionism?

> —Wilson Follett, *Modern American Usage: A Guide*,
> edited and completed by Jacques Barzun et al.

The vast majority of highly regarded writers begin sentences with *and* or *but,* some more than two or three times a page.

　　Some insecure writers now even think they should not begin a sentence with *because.* They would criticize this:

✓　　**Because** we have access to so much historical fact, today we know a good deal about changes within the humanities which were not apparent to those of any age much before our own and which the individual scholar must constantly reflect on.

> —Walter Ong, S.J., "The Expanding Humanities
> and the Individual Scholar,"
> *Publication of the Modern Language Association*

Though it is gaining currency, this proscription about *because* appears in no handbook ever published (so far as I know). It must stem from advice intended to avoid sentence FRAGMENTS like this one:

> The application was rejected. **Because** the deadline had passed.

The introductory *because* is correct when attached to a MAIN CLAUSE:

✓　　**Because** the deadline had passed, the application was rejected.

A recent variation on this theme is the suspicion that neither should a sentence begin with a preposition:

✓   **In** the morning, everyone left.

This bit of folklore probably results from overgeneralizing the "rule" about not *ending* a sentence with a preposition combined with uncertainty about how to begin one. Neither "rule" has any substance. Ignore them both.

2. "Use the RELATIVE PRONOUN *that*—not *which*—for restrictive clauses." Allegedly, not this:

✓   Next is a typical situation **which** a practiced writer corrects "for style" virtually by reflex action.

> —Jacques Barzun, *Simple and Direct.* (p. 69).

Yet just a few sentences earlier, Barzun himself had just asserted that rule:

> Us[e] *that* with defining clauses except when stylistic reasons interpose.

(No reasons interposed.) A rule can have no force when a writer as eminent and accomplished as Barzun asserts it on one page and on the next unselfconsciously violates it, and that *which* is never caught, not by his editors, not by his proofreaders, apparently not even by Barzun himself.

This "rule" is relatively new. It first appeared in 1906 in Henry and Francis Fowler's *The King's English* (Oxford University Press; reprinted as an Oxford University Press paperback, 1973). The Fowlers thought that the random variation between *that* and *which* in restrictive clauses was messy, so they simply asserted that henceforth writers should (with some exceptions) limit *which* to nonrestrictive clauses.

A nonrestrictive clause, you may recall, describes a noun that you can identify unambiguously without the help of that clause. In this function, *which* enjoys the support of historical and contemporary usage:

✓   ABCO Inc. ended its bankruptcy, **which** it had filed in 1997.

A company can have only one bankruptcy at a time, so we unambiguously identify that bankruptcy as the only one in question. The clause is called *nonrestrictive*, because in the mind of the reader, that clause beginning with *which* cannot "restrict" the meaning of the noun phrase *a bankruptcy* any more precisely than it already is. We must therefore put a comma before the modifying clause and begin that clause with *which*.

But, according to the Fowlers, we should use only *that* to introduce a restrictive clause, a clause that the reader needs in order to identify the *particular* noun it modifies:

✓   ABCO Inc. finally developed a product **that** [*not* **which**] made millions.

Since ABCO has probably developed many products, the reader would not know which one the writer refers to with *a product,* so the writer singles out that one product by the identifying clause, *that made millions.* In this case, we do *not* put a comma before the modifying clause, and, at least according to some grammarians, we should begin the clause not with *which* but with *that.*

In truth, this "rule" did not then and does not now enjoy the support of either historical or contemporary usage.

Francis died in 1918, but Henry continued the family tradition with *A Dictionary of Modern English Usage.* In that landmark reference work, he devoted more than a page to discussing the finer points of choosing between *which* and *that,* and then added this:

> Some there are who follow this principle now; but it would be idle to pretend that it is the practice either of most or of the best writers. (p. 635)

That wistful observation must have been judged still relevant to our own usage, because it was retained in the second edition and again in the third. (For another example of this usage, see the passage by Walter Ong on p. 23.)

Having said all that, I confess I follow Fowler's advice, not because I think that a restrictive *which* is wrong, but because *that* is less noisy. I do choose a *which* when it is within a few words of a *that* because I don't like the sound of the two of them close together:

We all have **that** one principle **that** we will not compromise.

✓   We all have **that** one principle **which** we will not compromise.

3. "Use *fewer* with nouns you count, *less* with nouns you can't." Allegedly not this:

✓   I can remember no **less** than five occasions when the correspondence columns of *The Times* rocked with volleys of letters . . .

—Noel Gilroy Annan, Lord Annan,
"The Life of the Mind in British Universities Today,"
American Council of Learned Societies Newsletter

No one uses *fewer* with uncountable mass nouns (*fewer sand*) but educated writers often use *less* with countable plural nouns (*less resources*).

A few other words are commonly used in ways proscribed by many conservative critics. Some critics think that we should use *since* to refer only to a point in time, but most careful writers use *since* with a meaning close to *because* but with an added sense of "What follows *since* is information I assume you already know":

✓   **Since** asbestos causes lung disease, it is considered a dangerous substance.

Careful writers use *while* in a similar way: They do not restrict it to its temporal sense (*We'll wait **while** you eat*), but use it as well with a meaning close to "What I state in this clause I assume you know, but what I assert in the next qualifies it":

✓   **While** we agree on the problem, we disagree about its solution.

On the other hand, you might observe the advice to avoid *as* to signal cause and effect, because it does so weakly:

As the expenses are minor, we need not discuss them.

Use *since* instead.

On the most formal of public occasions, when you are under the closest scrutiny, you might choose to observe each of these rules. In ordinary contexts, though, they are ignored by most careful writers, which is to say that they are not rules at all, but rather a guide to self-consciously formal usage. If you adopt the worst-case approach and observe them all, all the time—well, private virtues are their own reward.

OPTIONS THAT SIGNAL DELIBERATE CARE

These next bits of advice complement the Real Rules: Most readers will not notice when you violate them, but when you observe

them, a few careful readers will note your grammatical fastidious-
ness, especially if you are young.

1. "Do not split infinitives." Purists would condemn Dwight Mac-
   Donald, a linguistic archconservative, for this sentence:

   ✓   One wonders why Dr. Gove and his editors did not think
         of labeling *knowed* as substandard right where it occurs,
         and one suspects that they wanted **to *slightly* conceal**
         the fact or at any rate to put off its exposure as long as
         decently possible.

                         —"The String Untuned," *The New Yorker*

   They would require

         One suspects that they wanted **to conceal** the fact *slightly* . . .

   Infinitives are now so commonly split by the best writers
   that if you avoid splitting one, you invite careful readers to
   think you are trying to be especially correct, whether you
   are or not.

2. "Use *shall* as the first person simple future, *will* for second and
   third person simple future; use *will* to mean strong intention
   in the first person, *shall* for second and third person." Purists
   would condemn F. L. Lucas, a highly regarded writer on matters of style, for this, preferring *shall*.

   ✓   I **will** end with two remarks by two wise old women of
         the civilized eighteenth century.

                         —"What Is Style?" *Holiday*

   They would be right, but only if readers had reason to expect
   formal usage. When they have no reason to expect a *shall*, they
   may be close to astonished to find one.

3. "Use *whom* as the OBJECT of a verb or preposition." Purists
   would condemn William Zinsser for this use of *who:*

   ✓   Soon after you confront this matter of preserving your
         identity, another question will occur to you: "**Who** am I
         writing for?"

                         —*On Writing Well*

   They would insist on

         . . . another question will occur to you: "For **whom** am I writing?"

Most readers take *whom* to be a small but distinct flag of self-conscious correctness, as it in fact is. So when a writer uses it incorrectly, that choice is probably a sign of insecurity.

An actual rule: If you want to use *who* or *whom*, decide whether it is the subject or the object *of its own clause*. Use *who* if it is a subject, *whom* if an object. Not this:

The committee must decide **whom** should be promoted.

In that sentence, *whom* is the subject of the verb *should be promoted,* so that *whom* should be *who.*

Those who self-consciously use *whom* probably do so from from the same impulse that motivates them to use *I* in *between you and I* instead of the preferred *me.* Though the *I* there has been common in conversation since at least the middle of the eighteenth century, it still rankles a good many purists.

4. "Do not end a sentence with a preposition." Purists would condemn Sir Ernest Gowers for this:

✓   The peculiarities of legal English are often used as a stick to beat the official **with.**

—The Complete Plain Words

and insist on this revision:

. . . a stick **with which** to beat the official.

The first is correct; the second more formal. (Again, see the Walter Ong example on p. 23.) And when you choose to move both the preposition and its *whom* back to the left, you make that sentence even more formal. Compare:

✓   The man I spoke **with** was the man I had written **to.**

✓   The man **with whom** I spoke was the man **to whom** I had written.

We should note, however, that a final preposition can seem to make a sentence end weakly. George Orwell may have chosen to end this next sentence with the preposition *from* to make a sly point about English grammar, but I suspect it just ended up there (and note the *which* five words from the end):

[The defense of the English language] has nothing to do with archaism, with the salvaging of obsolete words and turns of speech, or with the setting up of a "standard English" **which** must never be departed **from.**

—George Orwell, "Politics and the English Language"

This would have been less awkward and more emphatically concise:

> We do not defend the English language just to preserve archaisms or to create a "standard English" whose rules we must always obey.

5. "Contrary-to-fact statements require the subjunctive." Purists would correct this, written by H. W. Fowler himself:

✓ Another suffix that is not a living one, but is sometimes treated as if it **was,** is *-al.*

> —*A Dictionary of Modern English Usage*

They would insist on this:

✓ Another suffix that is not a living one, but is sometimes treated as if it **were,** is *-al.*

To express subjunctives, we usually use just a simple past tense:

✓ If we **knew** what to do, we **would** do it.

The problem is with *be:* Strictly construed, the subjunctive demands *were,* but it is giving way to *was:*

✓ If this **were** 1941, a loaf of bread would cost 20 cents.
✓ If this **was** 1941, a loaf of bread would cost 20 cents.

As the subjunctive fades into the sunset of linguistic history, it casts over a sentence a faintly archaic and therefore formal glow. When readers expect formal English, it is wise to choose it, but the emphasis is on *choice.*

6. "Use the singular with *none* and *any.*" Historically *none* and *any* were singular and so took singular verbs, but today most writers use them as plurals. Therefore, if you use them as singular, some readers are likely to notice. The second is a bit more formal than the first:

✓ **None** of the reasons **are** sufficient to end the project.
✓ **None** of the reasons **is** sufficient to end the project.

SOME WORDS THAT ATTRACT SPECIAL ATTENTION

The preceding points of style are matters of grammar and word order. Observe them, and very careful readers will think you are a bit formal, or at least self-consciously correct. There is also a small group of words whose careful use not only will make you seem formal, but may distinguish you in the eyes of your most exacting readers as one of the few who has learned how to use them.

For example, fewer writers today distinguish *flaunt* from *flout*. So if you actually use either word correctly, the few readers who think the difference is worth preserving will take note that at least you still know that *flaunt* means to display oneself or something in a deliberately conspicuous way and that *flout* means to ignore a rule or standard scornfully: Thus if you chose to flout the rule about *flaunt* and *flout* in a particularly public and scornful way, you would not flout your flaunting it, but flaunt your flouting it.

Here are some others:

aggravate, meaning "to make worse." It does not mean simply to "annoy" or "irritate." You can aggravate an injury but not a person.

anticipate, meaning "to plan ahead in order to prepare for a contingency." It does not mean just "expect." You can anticipate a question if you prepare its answer before you think it will be asked; otherwise you only expect it.

anxious, meaning "uneasy and worried." It does not mean "eager." If you fear bad news, you might await it anxiously, but if it is good news, you would await it eagerly.

blackmail, meaning "to extort by threatening to reveal damaging information." It does not mean simply "coerce." One country cannot blackmail another with nuclear weapons; it threatens or coerces.

cohort, meaning "a group of people who attend on someone." It does not mean a single accompanying person. If Prince Charles marries his friend she will become his *consort;* all of his hangers-on are his *cohort.*

continuous, meaning "without interruption." It is not synonymous with *continual,* which means an activity extending over a period of time possibly with interruptions. If you continually interrupt, the person you interrupt will never say a word because your interruption will go on and on. If you continuously interrupt, you let that person start sentences from time to time, but not finish them.

disinterested, meaning "neutral." It does not mean "not interested." A judge should be disinterested in the outcome of a case, but not uninterested.

enormity, meaning something "monstrously evil." It does not mean just "huge." In private, a sneeze might be enormous, but at a state funeral, it would be an enormity.

fortuitous, meaning "by chance." It does not mean "fortunate." You are fortunate when you fortuitously pick the right number in the lottery.

fulsome, meaning "sickeningly excessive." It does not mean just "a lot." All of us enjoy praise, except when it becomes fulsome.

notorious, meaning "well known for bad behavior." It does not mean simply "famous." Frank Sinatra was notorious for treating people badly, but famous as a great singer.

comprise, meaning "to include all parts in a single unit." It does not mean on the one hand, to constitute a whole out of its parts nor on the other, the looser meaning of a whole merely "including" a few parts from among many.

This word *comprise*, in fact, is a bit complex. When parts make up a whole, they *constitute* it. Thus these words *constitute* this sentence. On the other hand, the whole *comprises* all of its parts. Thus this whole sentence *comprises* all of its words. The ACTIVE form of each verb is almost synonymous with the other's PASSIVE:

ACTIVE		PASSIVE
Words **constitute** a sentence.	=	Words **are comprised by** a sentence.
A sentence **comprises** its words.	=	A sentence **is constituted by** its words.

And then, of course, there are the words *consist* and *compose*.

A whole **consists of** its parts.	=	A whole is **composed out of** its parts.

Now in fact, relatively few readers care about these distinctions anymore, but they are often just those readers whose approval is not without meaning, especially when we respect their judgment in larger matters. It takes only a few minutes to learn how to use these words in ways that testify to your precision, so it may be worth your time to do so, especially if you also think that these distinctions are worth preserving.

On the other hand, you win no distinction for correctly distinguishing *imply* and *infer, principal* and *principle, accept* and *except, affect* and *effect, proceed* and *precede, discrete* and *discreet*. That's just what we expect of schooled writers. Most educated readers also notice when a plural Latinate noun is incorrectly used as a singular, so you might want to keep them straight too:

Singular	datum	criterion	medium	stratum	phenomenon
Plural	data	criteria	media	strata	phenomena

HOBGOBLINS

For some reason, a few items of usage have become the object of particularly zealous abuse. There's no explaining why, but they have become the flags around which those most dedicated to linguistic goodness have agreed to rally. None of these so-called "errors" interferes with clarity or concision. But because they arouse such animus, you should both know their special status and understand that judgments about them are capricious, unfounded in logic, history, or linguistic efficiency.

1. "Never use *like* for *as* or *as if*." Not this:

   These operations failed **like** the earlier ones did.

   But this:

   ✓ These operations failed **as** the earlier ones did.

   Like evolved into a SUBORDINATING CONJUNCTION in the eighteenth century when some writers began to drop *as* from the phrase *like as*, leaving just *like* to serve as the conjunction. This dropping of an element is called *elision*, and is a common linguistic change. We might note that the editor of the second edition of Fowler deleted *like* for *as* from the original list of Illiteracies and moved it into the category of Sturdy Indefensibles.

2. "Use *hopefully* only when the subject of the sentence in fact feels hopeful." Not this:

   Hopefully, the matter will be resolved soon.

   But this:

   ✓ We **hopefully** ~~requested [that is, we were hopeful when we requested]~~ that the matter be resolved soon.

   This "rule" is so entrenched in the thinking of some that it is impossible to convince them by mere reason and evidence that it has no basis in logic or grammar. In fact, at the beginning of a sentence, as every native speaker knows, *hopefully* self-evidently means 'I am hopeful':

   ✓ Hopefully, it will not rain tomorrow.

   It parallels other introductory words such as *candidly, frankly, sadly,* and *happily:*

   ✓ Candidly, we may fail. (That is, I am candid when I say we may fail.)

   ✓ Seriously, we must leave. (That is, I am serious when I say we must leave.)

But no one condemns the analogous use of *candidly* or *seriously* to describe the speaker's attitude.

3. "Never use *finalize* to mean 'finish' or 'complete.'" But *finalize* does not mean just 'finish.' It means 'to clean up the last few details,' a sense captured by no other word. Some think *finalize* smacks of the bureaucratic mind, an understandable objection. But we ought not believe the word *finalize* is bad because its ending *-ize* is ugly. If we did, we would have to reject *nationalize, synthesize, rationalize,* along with hundreds of other common words.

4. "Never never use *irregardless* for *regardless*." The word blends *irrespective* and *regardless,* but that doesn't legitimize it (or should we say, "make it legitimate"?).

5. "Never use *impact* as a verb, as in *The survey* **impacted** *our strategy.* Use it only as a noun, as in *The survey had an* **impact** *on our strategy. Impact* has been a verb since the seventeenth century, but on some people, historical evidence has none.

6. "Do not modify absolute words such as *perfect, unique, final,* or *complete* with *very, more, quite,* and so on," a rule that would have ruled out this familiar sentence:

✓   We the People of the United States, in order to form a **more perfect** union . . .

A SPECIAL PROBLEM: PRONOUNS AND SEXISM

We expect literate writers to make verbs agree with subjects:

✓   Our reasons **are** based on solid evidence.

We also expect pronouns to agree with antecedents. Not this:

Early **efforts** to oppose the hydrogen bomb failed because **it** was not coordinated with political communities. **No one** wanted to expose **themselves** to anti-Communist hysteria unless **they** had the support of others.

But this:

✓   Early **efforts** to oppose the hydrogen bomb failed because **they** were not coordinated with political communities. **No one** wanted to expose **himself** to anti-Communist hysteria unless **he** had the support of others.

We must use a singular pronoun to refer to a singular referent:

✓   His early **effort** to oppose the hydrogen bomb failed because **it** was ...

But there are two problems. First, do we use a singular or plural pronoun to refer to a noun that is singular in grammar but plural in meaning: When we refer to a *group, committee, staff, administration,* and so on, do we use *it* or *they?* Some writers use a singular pronoun when the group acts as a single entity:

✓   The **committee has** met but has not yet made **its** decision.

But they use a plural pronoun when members of the group act individually:

✓   The **faculty have** received the memo, but not all of **them** have read it.

These days the plural is sometimes used in both senses.

Second, what personal pronoun should we use to refer to the indefinite pronouns *someone, everyone, no one* and to singular nouns that do not indicate gender: *teacher, doctor, person, student?* We casually use *they:*

> **Everyone** realizes why **they** must take responsibility for **their** own actions.
>
> When **a person** is on drugs, it is hard to help **them.**

But more formal usage requires a singular pronoun:

✓   **Everyone** realizes why **he** must take responsibility for **his** own actions.

✓   When **a person** is on drugs, it is hard to help **her.**

But observe the formal rule, and you risk the thorny problem of sexist language.

GENDER AND LANGUAGE

Common sense demands that we write in ways that do not gratuitously offend readers. And we give up nothing when we substitute *police officer* for *policeman* and *synthetic* for *man-made,* and we stop reinforcing stereotypes. (Those who ask whether we should also substitute *person-in-the-moon* for *man-in-the-moon* are being merely tendentious.)

But if we reject *he* as a generic pronoun because it is sexist and *they* because careful readers consider it ungrammatical, we are left with either a clumsily intrusive *he or she*, a substantially worse *he/she*, or the worst, *s/he*.

> If **a writer** does not consider the ethnic background of **his or her** readers, **s/he** may respond in ways **the writer** would not expect to words that to **him or her** are innocent of ethnic bias.

So we rewrite. We can begin by substituting plurals for singulars:

✓   When **writers** do not consider the ethnicity of **their** readers . . .

But to the careful ear, plurals seem less precise than singulars. When appropriate, we can substitute a second person *you* or a first person *we* (though some readers object to the royal *we*):

✓   If **we** do not consider the ethnic background of **our** readers, they may respond in ways **we** would not expect to words that to **us** are innocent of ethnic bias.

We can also drop people altogether, but that leads to fuzzy abstraction, a problem this book aims at eliminating:

> Failure to consider ethnic background may lead to an unexpected response to words considered innocent of ethnic bias.

Finally, we can alternately use *he* and *she*, as I have. But that is not a perfect solution either, because to some readers, *she* is as intrusive as *he/she*. A reviewer in the *New York Times* wondered what to make of an author whom the reviewer charged with attempting to

> right history's wrongs to women by referring to random examples as "she," as in "Ask a particle physicist what happens when a quark is knocked out of a proton, and she will tell you . . . ," which strikes this reader as oddly patronizing to women.

We might wonder how that "she" struck women who happened to be particle physicists.

For years to come, we will have a problem with the singular generic pronoun, and to some readers, any solution will seem awkward. I suspect that eventually we will accept the plural *they* as an entirely correct singular:

✓   **No one** should turn in **their** writing unedited.

There is precedent: Our second person singular pronoun was once *thou*. But in the fifteenth century, English speakers began to replace it with *you*, originally strictly plural. The same thing will probably happen with *they*. In fact, the change has already been approved by at least one highly respected style guide, *The Chicago Manual of Style*. Some claim, predictably, that such compromises mean that we are surrendering all aspiration to precision. Until the issue is decided, though, that point of dispute gives us a choice, and that's not entirely a bad thing, because choices define character.

PRECISION

We must think about this matter of precision precisely: We must write correctly. But if in defining correctness we ignore the difference between truth and folklore, we risk overlooking what is important—the choices that make prose wordy and confusing or clear and precise. We are not being precise when we merely get straight all the *which*es and *that*s, mend every split infinitive, eradicate every *finalize* and *hopefully*. Many who obsess on such details are oblivious to the more serious matter of imprecise thought and expression, and it is that kind of substantive imprecision that will allow obtuse prose to become the national standard, prose like this next passage that actually made it into print. Its grammar is as impeccable as its style is impenetrable:

> Too precise a specification of information processing requirements incurs the risk of overestimation resulting in unused capacity or inefficient use of costly resources or of underestimation leading to ineffectiveness or other inefficiencies. Too little precision in specifying needed information processing capacity gives no guidance with respect to the means for the procurement of the needed resources.

That means,

✓ When you specify too precisely the resources you need to process information, you may overestimate. If you do, you risk having more capacity than you need or using costly resources inefficiently. But if you do not specify what you need precisely enough, you may fail to guide others in how to procure those resources.

How we revise the one into the other is the object of the next several lessons.

SUMMING UP

The finer points of correct English are unpredictable, so I can offer no principles to help you remember them all, much less decide whether any particular point is Real, Folklore, or Optional. Indeed, if correctness did yield to principle, it would cease being a social issue, because most "errors" of usage occur when someone levels out the idiosyncrasies of Standard English for principled, if unintended, reasons. But, of course, it is the very idiosyncrasy of each rule that makes it so useful. Its unpredictability guarantees that it will be mastered only by those born into the right social world or by those willing to learn such rules as the price of admission.

Actually, I think that those of us who choose to observe all the rules all the time do so not because we think we are protecting the integrity of the language or the quality of our culture, but because we want to assert a style of our own. Some of us are self-consciously straightforward and plain speaking; others take pleasure in a bit of elegance, in a touch of fastidiously self-conscious "class." The *shalls* and *whoms,* the aggressively unsplit infinitives, the subjunctive verbs: these are the private choices that let some of us display a careful sense of linguistic decorum and social conservatism. It is an impulse that we ought not scorn, but only so long as it is informed and thoughtful, only so long as it is not used as a pretext for invidious discrimination, and only so long as those who choose to follow all the rules all the time include in their concern the more important matters to which we now turn—the choices that define not what is correct, but what is clear and graceful.

PART II

Clarity

Everything that can be thought at all can be thought clearly.
Everything that can be said can be said clearly.

LUDWIG WITTGENSTEIN

LESSON THREE

Clarity 1: Actions

Whatever is translatable in other and simpler words of the same language, without loss of sense or dignity, is bad.
SAMUEL TAYLOR COLERIDGE

It takes less time to learn to write nobly than to learn to write lightly and straightforwardly.
FRIEDRICH NIETZSCHE

I am unlikely to trust a sentence that comes easily.
WILLIAM GASS

Words and deeds are quite different modes of the divine energy. Words are also actions, and actions are a kind of words.
RALPH WALDO EMERSON

Suit the action to the word, the word to the action.
WILLIAM SHAKESPEARE, *HAMLET*, 3.2

Action is eloquence.
WILLIAM SHAKESPEARE, *CORIOLANUS*, 3.2

MAKING JUDGMENTS

We have words enough to praise writing we like: *clear, direct, concise, flowing,* and more than enough to abuse writing (and writers) we don't: *unclear, indirect, wordy, confusing, abstract, awkward, turgid, disjointed, complex, obscure.* We could use those words to distinguish these two sentences:

> 1a. The cause of our educational system's failure at teaching basic skills to children is not understanding the influence of their cultural background on learning.

> 1b. Our educational system has failed to teach children basic skills because we do not understand how their cultural background influences the way they learn.

Most of us would call (1a) complex and abstract, (1b) clearer and more direct. But though we point to (1a) and call *it* unclear, we aren't referring to anything that is unclear *in that sentence.* We in fact describe how that sentence makes us feel as we read it. If we say that (1a) is "less clear" than (1b), we really say that we have a harder time understanding it. If we say that (1a) is "wordy," we really say that we feel we have to read too many words to get what it says. In other words, if we say we have a hard time understanding (1a) because it is unclear, we say only that we have a hard time understanding it, because we have a hard time understanding it.

How our readers judge our writing is crucial, of course, but we have to understand not just how they feel, but what it is *on the page* that makes them feel as they do. For that, we need a vocabulary that is less impressionistic than words like *dense* and *turgid.* We need a vocabulary that helps us pinpoint what it is *about* (1a) that makes us want to say that it seems unclear. More important, we need ways to help us both identify sentences like (1a) that need revising, and then help us revise them.

We can find those ways in the way we tell a good story.

TELLING STORIES ABOUT CHARACTERS AND ACTIONS

✓ Every story needs CHARACTERS and ACTIONS. This one has a problem:

> 2a. Once upon a time, there was Little Red Riding Hood, Grandma, the Woodsman, and the Wolf. The end.

Interesting characters maybe, but no action. Here's some action:

> 2b. Once upon a time, as a walk through the woods was taking place, a jump out from behind a tree occurred, causing fright.

Lots of action, but no characters. Here's a version with both:

> 2c. Once upon a time, as a walk through the woods was taking place on the part of Little Red Riding Hood, the Wolf's jump out from behind a tree occurred, causing fright in Little Red Riding Hood.

Something is still wrong. That story has both characters and actions, but we don't like the way they are expressed. What we expect—indeed what we *want*—is this (I will again check the sentences I think are clearer and more direct):

> ✓ 2d. Once upon a time, Little Red Riding Hood was walking through the woods, when the Wolf jumped out from behind a tree and frightened her.

Why does that sentence (2d) seem to tell its story clearly while (2c) does not, and why do (2a) and (2b) tell no story at all?

We respond to those sentences differently because each one tells the story in a different way. In the sentences we don't much care for, the writer has mismatched the elements of the story—characters and actions—with the grammatical elements of the sentences, with their SUBJECTS and VERBS. In brief, the simple difference is this:

- In (2c), the sentence we like less, the characters are *not* subjects of verbs, and their actions are *not* verbs.
- But in (2d), the sentence we like more, the characters *are* subjects of verbs and their actions *are* verbs.

Characters as Subjects

For example, look at the underlined subjects in (2c) below. The subjects (underlined) and the main characters (italicized) do *not* come together:

> 2c. Once upon a time, as <u>a walk through the woods</u>_{subject} was taking place on the part of *Little Red Riding Hood*_{main character}, <u>*the Wolf's*</u>_{main character} <u>jump out from behind a tree</u>_{subject} occurred causing fright in *Little Red Riding Hood*_{main character}.

In (2c), the subjects are not characters but rather actions represented as abstractions (verbs are capitalized):

a **walk** through the woods WAS TAKING place

Wolf's **jump** out from behind a tree OCCURRED.

Contrast those abstract subjects in (2c) with the concrete subjects in (2d). The subjects (underlined) and the main characters (italicized) *do* come together:

✓   2d. Once upon a time, <u>*Little Red Riding Hood*</u>_{subject / main character} was walking through the woods, when the <u>*Wolf*</u>_{subject / main character} jumped out from behind a tree and frightened her.

✓ Actions as Verbs

Now compare how the actions and verbs differ in (2c) and (2d). In (2c), the actions and verbs do *not* come together either: The actions are expressed as abstract NOUNS and the verbs express little action at all (the actions are boldfaced; the verbs are capitalized):

2c. Once upon a time, as a **walk**_{action / noun} through the woods WAS TAKING_{empty verb} place on the part of Little Red Riding Hood, the Wolf's **jump**_{action / noun} out from behind a tree OCCURRED_{empty verb}, causing **fright**_{action / noun} in Little Red Riding Hood.

Now in (2d), contrast how the actions and verbs do work together:

✓   2d. Once upon a time, Little Red Riding Hood WAS WALKING_{verb / action} through the woods, when the Wolf JUMPED_{verb / action} out from behind a tree and FRIGHTENED_{verb / action} her.

> *Here's the point:*   In the version of Little Red Riding Hood that seems indirect and confusing, we do not see the main characters in the subjects, nor do we see in the verbs the actions that those characters are connected with: Thus the structure of the story does *not* match the structure of the sentence.
>
> On the other hand, in the version we thought was clearer and more direct, we do see the main characters in the subjects and we do see the main actions in the verbs: In that version, the structure of the story *does* match the structure of the sentence.
>
> So here are the first two principles of good story telling:
>
> • Express main characters as subjects.
>
> • Express their actions as verbs.

Fairy Tales and Academic Writing

You may think that writing in college or on the job is distant ✓ from writing fairy tales. But behind even the most scholarly or professional abstraction, all sentences have a story to tell, like this one:

> 3a. The Federalists' argument that the destabilization of government was the result of popular democracy was based on their belief in the tendency of factions to further their self-interest at the expense of the common good.

Is it fair to say that we struggle to get through that sentence? We can make it clearer (which is to say we understand it better) if we revise that sentence to make its subjects name its characters and its verbs name their actions:

> ✓ 3b. The Federalists argued that popular democracy destabilized government, because they believed that factions tended to further their self-interest at the expense of the common good.

When we compare these two versions about the Federalists and factions with the two versions of Little Red Riding Hood, we can see the same pattern of differences. In (3a), the subjects (underlined) and characters (italicized) do not come together

> 3a. _The Federalists'_$_\text{character}$ argument that the destabilization of _government_$_\text{character}$ was the result of _popular democracy_$_\text{subject}$ was based on _their_$_\text{character}$ belief in the tendency of _factions_$_\text{character}$ to further _their_$_\text{character}$ self-interest at the expense of the common good.

Nor do the actions (boldfaced) come together with verbs (capitalized):

> 3a. The Federalists' **argument**$_\text{action}$ that the **destabilization**$_\text{action}$ of government WAS$_\text{verb}$ the result of popular democracy WAS BASED$_\text{verb}$ on their **belief**$_\text{action}$ in the **tendency**$_\text{action}$ of factions to FURTHER$_\text{verb}$ their self-interest at the expense of the common good.

We can see that lack of fit in (3a) more clearly if we break out its subjects and verbs. Notice that its subjects are quite long and abstract and that the two verbs express no specific meaning:

SUBJECTS	VERBS
The Federalists' argument that the destabilization of government	was
The Federalists argument that the destabilization of government was the result of popular democracy	was based

But in (3b), characters coincide with subjects, and actions coincide with verbs:

3b. *The Federalists*_{subject/character} **ARGUED**_{action/verb} that *popular democracy*_{subject/character} **DESTABILIZED**_{action/verb} *government*_{character} because *they*_{subject/character} **BELIEVED**_{action/verb} that *factions*_{subject/character} **TENDED** to **FURTHER**_{action/verb} *their*_{character} self-interest at the expense of the common good.

Again, we can see this more clearly if we break out the subjects and verbs:

SUBJECT / CHARACTER	VERB / ACTION
Federalists	argued
popular democracy	destabilized
they	believed
factions	tended to further

▬▬▬▬▬▬▬▬▬▬▬▬▬▬▬▬▬▬▬▬

Exercise 3.1

You can see how writers move characters and actions around inside sentences if you start with a sentence that seems clear, then revise it into one that is not.

✓   4a. Although the governor knew that the cities needed more money for schools, she vetoed a bigger education budget to encourage the cities to increase their local taxes.

That sentence seems clear because we know who the main characters are and what they are doing: The characters are the governor and the cities (a legislature is implied). The governor is the source or agent of three actions, all of which are verbs:

1. The governor **knew** [something],
2. [yet] she **vetoed** a bigger education budget,

3. [because] she **wanted** to **encourage** the cities to [do something].

The cities are involved in two actions, both of which are verbs:

4. The cities **need** money,
5. [so] they [should] **increase** their local taxes.

In that reasonably clear sentence, each of those characters plays the same role: They are subjects of verbs. And each of their five actions—*knew, vetoed, encourage, need, increase*—is the same part of speech: They are verbs.

Stop now and write a different version of that story, but instead of using those five verbs to express actions, use their corresponding noun forms. Two of those nouns differ from their corresponding verbs:

to know	→	knowledge
to encourage	→	encouragement

The other three nouns are identical to their corresponding verbs:

to need	→	the need
to veto	→	the veto
to increase	→	the increase

Here is one new version. Yours may differ (we underline subjects, italicize characters, boldface actions, and capitalize verbs):

4b. Despite *her* **knowledge** of the **need** by *cities* for more money, <u>*her* **veto** of a bigger education budget</u> AIMED at GIVING **encouragement** to *cities* for an **increase** in local taxes.

Compare how the characters in this revision do not come together with subjects and how the actions do not come together with verbs. Here's the original again:

✓   4a. Although <u>*the governor*</u> KNEW that <u>*the cities*</u> NEEDED more money for schools, <u>*she*</u> VETOED a bigger education budget to ENCOURAGE <u>*the cities*</u> to INCREASE their local taxes.

At some level, both sentences tell the same story. But when we compare their clarity, they differ as much as the two versions of Little

Red Riding Hood and the Federalists. What *causes* them to differ so much? It again has to do with the way the writer brought together characters and subjects and brought together actions and verbs.

In the rest of this lesson, we look closely at actions and verbs. In the next lesson, we focus on characters and subjects.

VERBS AND ACTIONS

As we use the word here, *action* covers all literal or figurative movement, mental processes, relationships, and conditions. Your sentences will seem clearer if you express those actions in verbs. Look at how sentences (5a) and (5b) express the actions.

> 5a. Our lack of data prevented evaluation of state action in targeting funds to areas in need of assistance.

> ✓   5b. Because we lacked data, we could not evaluate whether the state had targeted funds to areas that needed assistance.

In (5a), actions (boldfaced) are not verbs (capitalized), but nouns:

> 5a. Our **lack**$_{noun\,/\,action}$ of data PREVENTED$_{verb}$ **evaluation**$_{noun\,/\,action}$ of state **action**$_{noun\,/\,action}$ in **targeting**$_{noun\,/\,action}$ funds to areas in **need**$_{noun\,/\,action}$ of **assistance**$_{noun\,/\,action}$.

In (5b), on the other hand, the actions are almost all verbs:

> 5b. Because we LACKED$_{verb\,/\,action}$ data, we COULD NOT EVALUATE$_{verb\,/\,action}$ whether the state HAD TARGETED$_{verb\,/\,action}$ funds to areas that NEEDED$_{verb\,/\,action}$ **assistance**$_{noun\,/\,action}$.

If your readers think that you have written in ways that seem complex, impersonal, or abstract, you have almost certainly used too many abstract nouns, particularly nouns derived from verbs ✓ and ADJECTIVES, nouns ending in *-tion, -ment, -ence,* and so on, *particularly if you begin your sentences with them.*

Such nouns have a technical name: NOMINALIZATIONS. The word illustrates its own meaning: When we nominalize the verb *nominalize,* we create the nominalization *nominalization.*

VERB	→ NOMINALIZATION	ADJECTIVE	→ NOMINALIZATION
discover	→ discovery	careless	→ carelessness
resist	→ resistance	different	→ difference
react	→ reaction	proficient	→ proficiency

We can also nominalize a verb by adding *-ing* (making it a GERUND):

She flies → her flying   We sang → our singing

Some nominalizations are identical to their corresponding verb:

hope→hope   result→result   repair→repair   charge→charge

We REQUEST$_{verb}$ that when you RETURN$_{verb}$, you REVIEW$_{verb}$ the data.

Our **request**$_{noun}$ IS that on your **return**$_{noun}$ you DO a **review**$_{noun}$ of the data.

Had I relied on nominalizations to tell this story about nominalizations, I would have written this:

> The frequent use of nominalizations instead of verbs results in the frustration of reader expectations. Their expectation is of characters as subjects and their actions as verbs. Increased reader frustration results from dropping characters from sentences altogether. That feeling no doubt occurred in your reading of this:
>
> > Once upon a time, as a walk through the woods was taking place, a jump out from behind a tree caused surprise.
>
> Dropping Little Red Riding Hood and the Wolf from the story became a possibility subsequent to the nominalization of the verb *walk* into the nominalization *walking*, the verb *jump* into the nominalization *jump*, and the verb *surprise* into the nominalization *surprise*. And had I done that, you would have stopped reading long ago.

No feature of style more typically characterizes abstract, indirect, difficult academic and professional writing than lots of nominalizations.

ACTIONS IN ADJECTIVES

You can also hide an action in adjectives. Such adjectives usually ✓ appear after a form of *be:*

> The results ARE **indicative** that the data ARE **representative** of the population.
>
> The results INDICATE that the data REPRESENT the population.

Some examples:

applicable → apply deserving of → deserve dubious → doubt
fearful of → fear hopeful → hope indicative→ indicate

reflective → reflect   representative → represent
suggestive → suggest

Exercise 3.2

Analyze the subject/character and verb/action patterns in this pair of sentences in the same way we analyzed the other pairs of sentences:

> There is opposition among voters to nuclear power plants near population centers because of a widespread belief in their threat to human health.

> Many voters oppose nuclear power plants near population centers because they believe that such plants threaten human health.

REFORMULATING SOME FAMILIAR DEFINITIONS

Most of what you've read here modifies what many of us learned about subjects and verbs. In grade school, most of us learned that the order of Subject–Verb–Object was relatively predictable, and so were their meanings: subjects *are* characters (or "doers"), verbs *are* actions, objects *are* "receivers." That's true in a sentence like this:

subject   verb   object
We discussed the problem.
doer   action   receiver

But it's not true for this almost synonymous sentence:

subject   verb complement modifier object
The problem was the topic of our discussion.
receiver   doer   action

It's better to forget the idea that subjects, verbs, and objects *must* be anything at all. Instead, you need a sense of a sentence that gives you the freedom to move characters and actions where you choose.

But you can't make that choice independently of your readers. Though you can move characters and actions around, your readers prefer that you keep most of your characters in subjects and actions in verbs. *And in what you read, so do you.* If that's so, then the Writer's Golden Rule applies:

Write to others as you would have others write to you.

If you prefer to *read* sentences that start with subjects as charac- ters and that move quickly to verbs as actions, then that's a lesson in how to *write* them.

Exercise 3.3

Here are several verbs, adjectives, and nominalizations. If you are feeling uncertain about their differences, spend a few minutes turning the verbs and adjectives into nominalizations and nominalizations into adjectives and verbs. Recall that some verbs and nominalizations have the same form:

Poverty predictably CAUSES social problems.
Poverty IS a predictable **cause** of social problems.

analysis	believe	attempt	conclusion	emphasize	evaluate
suggest	approach	comparison	define	discuss	explanation
expression	failure	acquisition	appeal	appearance	description
decrease	improve	increase	accuracy	careful	clear
intelligence	important	precise	relevant	decide	explicit

Exercise 3.4

Now make up a few sentences using in each of them some of the verbs and adjectives in Exercise 3.3. Then rewrite those sentences you just created by using the corresponding nominalizations to express the same idea. In some cases, you change an adjective to an adverb. For example, picking *suggest, discuss,* and *careful,* you first write:

I SUGGEST that we DISCUSS the issue CAREFULLY.

Then rewrite that sentence into its nominalized form:

My **suggestion** is that our **discussion** of the issue be done with **care.**

It may seem odd to ask you to make a clear sentence unclear. But only when you see how a sentence can be less clear than it could be will you understand why it seemed clear in the first place.

Exercise 3.5

Exchange with other students some of the nominalized sentences that you made up to see whether you can revise theirs and they can revise yours back to the originals.

Exercise 3.6

Now do the reverse. Make up some sentences using some of the nominalizations you created in Exercise 3.3; then try to express the same idea using corresponding verbs, adjectives, and adverbs. If you can, exchange papers again and try to revise each other's sentences into their original forms. This is much harder.

Exercise 3.7

Revise any paragraph in Lesson 1 (or in any text that you think is clearly written) by substituting nominalizations for the important verbs. For example, we could rewrite the preceding sentence like this:

> Do a revision of any paragraph in Lesson 1 (or any text whose writing is, in your thinking, characterized by clarity) by substituting nominalizations for verbs of importance.

Then exchange your paragraph with someone to see if you can return each other's revision to the original.

Exercise 3.8

Revise that nominalized passage on p. 49.

FROM DIAGNOSIS TO ANALYSIS TO REVISION

You can use these two principles about characters as subjects and actions as verbs to explain why your readers might judge a passage to be clear or unclear. But more important, you can also use these principles to help you know when you should revise it. (Again, note the emphasis on *revise*. Only after you have thoroughly assimilated these principles as habits of revision will they work their way into your habits of drafting.)

Here's a tip that might save you some time: Try to recall where in the process of drafting you found yourself struggling because you were a bit confused or not confident about your ideas. When you revise, go to that passage first, because the kinds of problems we've looked at here predictably show up when you aren't quite certain of what you're writing about. Revising is a three step process:

1. **Diagnosis:** If you want to predict whether a reader might think your prose is hard to read, do this:

    a. Ignoring short (four or five word) introductory phrases, underline the first seven or eight words in each sentence.
    b. Look for three characteristics:

        • Sentences that begin not with characters, but with abstract nouns.

        • Sentences that take you more than six or seven words to get to a verb.

        • Verbs that are less specific than the actions buried in the nouns around them.

2. **Analysis:** If you find such sentences, do this:

    a. Find or invent your cast of characters. For the moment, that will be flesh-and-blood characters. In the next chapter, we'll complicate this notion of character a bit.
    b. Find nominalizations that name the actions those characters perform.

3. **Revision:** Once you locate the characters and their actions, do this:

    a. Change the nominalizations into verbs and adjectives.
    b. Make the characters the subjects of those new verbs.
    c. Rewrite the sentence with conjunctions like *because, if, when, although, why, how, whether, that.*

Some Common Patterns

You can easily spot a few common patterns of nominalizations.

✓ 1. A nominalization follows a verb with little specific meaning.
   In these cases, the subject is probably already a character:

   The *agency* CONDUCTED an **investigation** into the matter.

   a. Change the nominalization to a verb: *investigation* → *investigate*
   b. Replace the empty verb with the new verb: *conducted* → *investigate*

   ✓ The *agency* INVESTIGATED the matter.

✓ 2. A nominalization follows *there is* or *there are:*

   There IS no **need** for *our* further **study** of this problem.

   a. Change the nominalization to a verb: *need* → *need, study* → *study*
   b. Find a new subject: *our* → *we*

   ✓ *We* NEED not STUDY this problem further.

✓ 3. The nominalization is the subject of an empty verb: ?

   The **intention** of *the committee* IS to audit the records.

   a. Change the nominalization to a verb: *intention* → *intend*
   b. Find a character to be its subject:

   The committee INTENDS to audit the records.

✓ 4. Two or three nominalizations in a row are joined by prepositions:

   There WAS first a **review** of the **evolution** of the dorsal fin.

   a. Turn the first nominalization into a verb: *review* → *review.*
   b. Either leave the second nominalization as it is or turn it into a verb in a CLAUSE beginning with *how* or *why: evolution of the dorsal fin* → *how the dorsal fin evolved.*

   First, *she* REVIEWED the **evolution** of the *dorsal fin.*

   ✓ First, *she* REVIEWED how *the dorsal* fin EVOLVED.

✓ 5. Often, one nominalization appears in a subject and a second in the COMPLEMENT of a verb or phrase like *be, seems, has the result of,* etc.:

   Their **increase** in revenues WAS a result of their **expansion** of outlets.

You have to revise sentences like those more extensively:

   a. Identify the nominalizations in the two halves:

Subject:	*Their* **increase** in revenues
Connecting verb or phrase:	WAS a result of
Complement:	*their* **expansion** of outlets.

   b. Revise nominalizations into verbs:

      increase → increase, expansion → expand.

   c. Find subjects for those verbs:

      they increase, they expand.

   d. Link the new clauses with a word that expresses their logical connection. That connection will typically express some kind of causal relationship:

- To express simple cause: *because, since, when*
- To express conditional cause: *if, provided that, so long as*
- To contradict expected causes: *though, although, unless*

Their **increase** in revenues	→	*They* INCREASED revenues
was the result of	→	**because**
their **expansion** in outlets.	→	*they* EXPANDED outlets.

Exercise 3.9

These pairs contrast in style: One tells its story in a direct, concise way, expressing characters as subjects and actions as verbs; the other is indirect, with actions in nominalizations and characters anywhere but as their subjects. Identify which is which. You might try this: Circle nominalizations, and highlight verbs. If you are good at grammar, underline subjects, as well. Then put a "c" through characters.

  1a. Some have argued that carbon dioxide in the atmosphere will almost certainly elevate global temperature.

  1b. There has been speculation by educators as to the positive effect of a good family environment on educational achievement.

  2a. Smoking during pregnancy may lead to fetal injury.

  2b. When we write concisely, readers understand more easily.

3a. AIDS researchers have identified the AIDS virus but have failed to develop a vaccine that will immunize those at risk.

3b. Attempts by economists at formulating principles for the definition of full employment have not achieved full success.

4a. Complaints by editorial writers about voter apathy do not often provide suggestions about dispelling it.

4b. Although many critics have claimed that when children watch television they tend to become less able readers, no one has yet demonstrated that to be true.

5a. The loss of market share to Japan by domestic auto makers resulted in the loss of employment of hundreds of thousands of workers and a decline in domestic auto production.

5b. If educators could discover how to use computer-assisted instruction, our schools could teach more complex subjects and students could learn faster.

6a. We need to know which areas of our national forests are being logged most extensively so that we can save virgin stands at greatest risk.

6b. There is a need for an analysis of the intensity of library use to provide a reliable base for the projection of needed new resources.

7a. Professional athletes often fail to realize that they are unprepared for life after stardom because their teams protect them from the problems that the rest of us adjust to every day.

7b. Many colleges have come to the realization that continued increases in tuition are no longer possible because of strong resistance from parents to the high cost of higher education.

8a. In this article, we examine how buyers influence advertising and how advertising agencies respond to those influences when they create a strategy that appeals to consumers.

8b. This study is a review of responses to rhetorical patterns and of judgments of textual well-formedness by readers with prior knowledge of a subject before reading.

Exercise 3.10

Go back to Exercise 3.9 and change the clear sentence in each pair into a nominalized sentence. You can use the paired nominal version as a pattern for your revision. For example, if the nominalized sentence in the pair begins with *There,* begin your revised sentence with *There:*

Sentence to revise: 1a. Some have ARGUED that carbon dioxide in the atmosphere will almost certainly ELEVATE global temperature.

Model: 1b. There has been **speculation** by educators as to the positive effect of a good family environment on educational **achievement.**

Your revision: 1c. There have been **arguments** by some as to . . . .

Exercise 3.11

Revise the original nominalized sentences in 3.9 into corresponding verbal sentences. You can use the paired verbal version as a pattern. For example, if the verbal sentence in the pair begins with a *when,* begin your revised sentence with *when:*

Sentence to revise: 2a. **Smoking** during pregnancy may lead to fetal **injury.**

Model: 2b. When we WRITE concisely, readers UNDERSTAND more easily.

Your revision: 2a. When pregnant women SMOKE . . .

Exercise 3.12

Revise these next sentences so that the nominalizations are verbs and characters are the subjects of those verbs. In (1) through (5), characters are italicized and nominalizations are boldfaced.

1. *Lincoln's* **hope** was for the peaceful **preservation** of the Union, but the *South's* **attack** on Fort Sumter made it an **inevitability.**
2. **Attempts** were made on the part of the *President's aides* to assert *his* **immunity** from a *Congressional* subpoena.
3. There were **predictions** by *his supporters* that the *nominee* would receive quick committee **approval.**
4. The *author's* **analysis** of our data omits any **citation** of *sources* that would provide **support** for *his* **criticism** of our **argument.**

5. The *health industry's* **ability** to exert cost **controls** could lead to the *public's* **decision** that *congressional* **action** is not needed.

In sentences 6 through 10, the agents are italicized; you find the actions.

6. A *papal* appeal was made to the *industrialized nations of the world* for assistance to those in *Africa* facing the threat of starvation.
7. Attempts at explanations for increases in *voter* participation in this year's elections were offered by *several candidates.*
8. The agreement by the *participants* on the program was based on the assumption that there was a promise of *federal* funds.
9. There was no independent *business-sector* study of the cause of the sudden increase in the trade surplus.
10. Agreement as to the need for revisions in the terms of the treaty was reached by *the two sides.*

In 11 through 15, only the nominalizations are boldfaced; you find or invent the characters.

11. There was **uncertainty** in the White House about Serbian **intentions** in regard to **withdrawal** from Albania's borders.
12. Thorough **preparation** of the specimen sections is the **responsibility** of laboratory personnel.
13. Any **contradictions** among data in any result requires an **explanation** of the reasons for the **inconsistencies.**
14. The board's **rejection** of our proposal was a **disappointment** but not a **surprise** because of our **expectation** that a **decision** had already been made in regard to a **delay** of any new initiatives.
15. Their **performance** of the music was marked by great **enthusiasm** but lacked historical **accuracy.**

SOME HAPPY CONSEQUENCES

We began with these two principles:

✓ • Express central characters as the subjects of verbs.
✓ • Express the actions those characters are involved in as verbs.

When you draft or revise sentences to reflect those principles, you make other useful changes:

1. You may have been told to write more concretely. Your sentences will seem more concrete if you name characters in subjects and actions in verbs. Compare:

   There WAS an affirmative **decision** for program **expansion.**

   ✓ *The Director* DECIDED to EXPAND the program.

2. You may have been told to order your ideas logically. When you string nominalizations through prepositional phrases, you can distort the logical sequence of your story. This next sequence of actions distorts their chronology. (The numbers refer to the sequence in which the actions actually occur.) Compare:

   Decisions[4] in regard to **administration**[5] of medication despite **inability**[2] of an *irrational patient* **appearing**[1] in Trauma Centers to PROVIDE legal **consent**[3] REST with *the attending physician* alone.

   When we revise those actions into their chronological order, we get something more coherent:

   ✓ When *a patient* APPEARS[1] in a Trauma Center and BEHAVES[2] so irrationally that *he* cannot legally CONSENT[3] to treatment, only *the attending physician* can DECIDE[4] whether to ADMINISTER[5] medication.

3. You may have been told to make logical relationships clearer. When you nominalize verbs, you often have to use diffuse connectors like prepositions and phrases such as *as a result of* and *in regard to*. But when you use verbs, you must link the new clauses with more precise SUBORDINATING CONJUNCTIONS like *because, although,* and *if:*

   Our more effective **presentation** of *our* **needs** RESULTED in *our* **success** in **acquiring** federal funds, despite more intensive **lobbying** efforts by *others.*

   ✓ Although *others* LOBBIED more intensively, *we* ACQUIRED federal funds because we PRESENTED our **needs** more effectively.

4. You may have been told not to use too many prepositional phrases. It's not clear what counts as "too many," but when you use nominalizations, you usually have to add prepositional phrases to keep the characters in the sentence. You can eliminate most prepositions by using verbs and conjunctions:

A **revision** of the program WILL RESULT in **increases** in *our* **efficiency** in **servicing** *clients.*

✓   If *we* REVISE the program, *we* CAN SERVE *clients* more EFFICIENTLY.

A COMMON PROBLEM AND ITS SOLUTION

At this point you can probably identify problems in the writing of others but have a harder time recognizing them in your own. That problem is entirely predictable. Just about everyone recognizes this experience: You write something you think is great, but when you get it back from a reader, you are told that your ideas are confusing and your organization is hard to follow. You wonder whether your critic is just being difficult, but you bite your tongue and try to fix what you are certain should have been clear to anyone who can read prose more complex than stories about My Dog Spot.

When that happens to me, I almost always realize—eventually—that my critics were, in fact, right: They were better able than I at recognizing where I had not made myself clear. (That's why I have acknowledged so many names in the Preface; they all found passages in earlier editions and in the draft for this one that needed revision. I was wholly oblivious to those problems.)

How can we be right about other people's writing, and so often so wrong about our own? The answer lies in this paradox: We can judge the writing of others more accurately than we can our own because we usually know less about their subject than they do.

This explains why you are your own worst editor: No one knows more about what you've written than you do. In fact, as you reread your own writing, you usually don't read it; you just remind yourself of what you intended to mean when you wrote it. But since your readers know less than you do, they are likely to respond in ways that you cannot predict. This also explains why two readers can disagree about the clarity of the same passage: Someone who understands its content is more likely to think the passage is more clearly written than someone who knows less. Both are right.

Since you can never read as your readers will, you have to look at your writing in ways that sidestep your too quick and easy understanding of it, and to do that, you need a way to diagnose your prose that is just as quick:

1. The quickest and most reliable way to revise is not to read, hoping that you will somehow "sense" what's not clear, but to underline the first seven or eight words of every sentence. If ✓ in those first seven or eight words you don't see a character as subject and a verb as an action, you have a candidate for revision:

   Our analysis of the results of the experiment did not provide an explanation of its failure, because our data collection lacked the precision needed.

2. A method more demanding but more reliable is to look at the subject of *every* verb in *every* clause.

   Our analysis of the results of the experiment did not provide an explanation of its failure, because our data collection lacked the precision needed.

3. The most demanding method is to look for *any* nominalization that you can turn into a verb. ✓

   Our **analysis** of the results of the experiment did not provide an **explanation** of its **failure,** because our data **collection** lacked the **precision** needed.

Now revise: turn as many actions as you can into verbs (and conditions into adjectives and adverbs) and then find subjects for them:

✓   When we ANALYZED the results of the experiment, we could not EXPLAIN why it FAILED, because we did not COLLECT data PRECISELY.

USEFUL NOMINALIZATIONS

I have so relentlessly urged you to revise nominalizations, that I may now seem to contradict myself when I say that, in fact, you cannot write well without them (the next lesson will expand on this idea). The trick is to know which nominalizations to keep and which to turn into verbs. Keep these:

1. The nominalization in the subject refers to a previous sentence: ✓

✓   **These arguments** all depend on a single unproven claim.

✓   **This decision** can lead to positive outcomes.

   Those nominalizations link one sentence to another into a cohesive flow.

2. A succinct nominalization replaces an awkward *The fact that:*

   The fact that she ACKNOWLEDGED the problem impressed me.

   ✓ Her **acknowledgment** of the problem impressed me.

   But then, why not

   ✓ She IMPRESSED me when she ACKNOWLEDGED the problem.

3. A nominalization names what would be the object of the verb:

   I accepted what she REQUESTED.

   ✓ I accepted her **request.**

   This kind of nominalization feels more concrete than an abstract one. However, contrast *request* above with this next sense of *request,* one that is more of an action:

   Her **request** for **assistance** CAME after the deadline.

   ✓ She REQUESTED **assistance** after the deadline.

4. A nominalization at the end of the first sentence of a paragraph introduces a topic you intend to develop in the following sentences:

   ✓ There is no need, then, for **argument** about the **existence**, the **inevitability**, and the **desirability** of **change** [in language]. There is need, however, for **argument** about the **existence** of such a thing as good English and correct English. Let us not hesitate to assert that "The pencil was laying on the table" and "He don't know nothing" are at present incorrect no matter how many know-nothings say them.

   —Theodore M. Bernstein, *The Careful Writer*

   Of course, Bernstein might have revised those first two sentences into this:

   ✓ While we need not DEBATE whether language CHANGES in ways that are inevitable and desirable, we can ARGUE that some English is correct and good.

5. A nominalization refers to a concept so familiar that the concept itself is almost a character (more about this in the next chapter).

   ✓ Few problems have so divided us as **abortion** on **demand.**

   ✓ The Equal Rights **Amendment** was an issue in past **elections.**

   ✓ **Taxation** without **representation** was not central to the American **Revolution.**

These nominalizations name concepts familiar to all of us: *abortion on demand, amendment, election, taxation, representation, revolution*. We almost always compress familiar concepts into nouns so that we don't have to spell them out repeatedly in subjects and verbs: *freedom, death, love, life*. Without such abstract words, we would find it at least difficult to write about subjects that have preoccupied writers for millennia. You have to develop an eye for the nominalization that expresses one of these common ideas and the nominalization that hides a significant action:

> There is a **demand** for a **repeal** of the **inheritance** tax.
>
> ✓ We **DEMAND** that the government **REPEAL** the **inheritance** tax.

Exercise 3.13

Revise these sentences. At the end of each is a hint. For example,

> Congress's **reduction** of the deficit resulted in the **decline** of interest rates. [because]
>
> ✓ Interest rates **DECLINED** because Congress **REDUCED** the deficit.

1. The use of models of good prose in teaching prose style does not invariably result in improvements of clarity and directness in the writing of students. [Although teachers have used . . .]

2. Precision in plotting the location of fragments of a vase or other object enhances the possibility of its accurate reconstruction. [When you precisely . . .]

3. Any departures by the staff from the established procedures may cause delays and even termination of the experiment. [If the staff . . .]

4. A student's lack of socialization into a field may lead to writing problems because of her insufficient knowledge about the construction of arguments by professionals in that field. [When . . . , ... , because . . . .]

5. The successful implementation of a new curriculum depends on the cooperation of faculty with students in setting achievable goals within a reasonable time. [In order to . . . , ...]

6. Our evaluation of the outcomes of the programs placed emphasis on objective measures despite our recognition of

the low level of rater agreement. [When . . . , . . . , even though . . . .]

Exercise 3.14

On any page in the Preface or Lesson 1, find five nominalizations and decide whether they should be changed or left as they are.

Exercise 3.15

Look through your old papers for the kinds of problems we have considered here. Revise them, then bring the originals to class to exchange with other students who will have done the same thing. Revise each other's prose; then compare your revisions of your own writing with someone else's revision of your writing. Whose do you like better?

Exercise 3.16

Find some professional writing and revise specific verbs into nouns. Exchange your revisions with someone else, revise each other's passages, then compare your revision with the original.

CLARITY, NOT SIMPLEMINDEDNESS

To the degree that you can match actions to verbs and characters to subjects, your readers will think that you write clearly. But you also have to avoid a prose style that makes you sound as if you are unable to go beyond Dick-and-Jane prose. This was written by a student aspiring to academic sophistication:

> After Czar Alexander II's emancipation of Russian serfs in 1861, many freed peasants chose to live on communes for purposes of co-operation in agricultural production as well as for social stability. Despite some communes' attempts at economic and social equalization through the strategy of imposing low economic status on the peasants, which resulted in their reduction to near poverty, a centuries-

long history of social distinctions even among serfs prevented social equalization.

In his struggle to follow these principles, he revised that paragraph into sentences that could have been written by a 12-year old:

> In 1861, Czar Alexander II emancipated the Russian serfs. Many of them chose to live on agricultural communes. There they thought they could cooperate with one another in agricultural production. They could also create a stable social structure. The leaders of some of these communes tried to equalize the peasants economically and socially. As one strategy, they tried to impose on all a low economic status. That reduced them to near poverty. However, the communes failed to equalize them socially. This happened because even serfs had made social distinctions among themselves for centuries.

In Lessons 8 and 9 we look at ways to revise a series of too-short, too-simple sentences into a style that is readable but still complex enough to communicate complex ideas. When that student applied those principles to his primer-style passage, he revised again:

> After the Russian serfs were emancipated by Czar Alexander II in 1861, many chose to live on agricultural communes, hoping they could cooperate in working the land and establish a stable social structure. At first, those who led some of the communes tried to equalize the new peasants socially and economically by imposing on them a low economic status, a strategy that reduced them to near poverty. But the communes failed to equalize them socially because the serfs had for centuries been observing their own social distinctions.

Those sentences are long but clear, because the writer consistently aligned major characters with subjects and actions with verbs. Admittedly, you cannot do this with every subject and every verb. But to the degree that you can, your readers will think that you write clearly.

Summing Up

We can represent these principles systematically and graphically. As we read, we have to integrate two levels of sentence structure.

One level is a predictable and relatively fixed grammatical sequence of subject and verb (the empty box is for everything that follows the verb):

Fixed	Subject	Verb	———

The other level of structure is variable, based on its story, on character, and action. This is a level of meaning whose elements have no fixed order, but can appear in one that our readers expect and prefer:

Variable	Character	Action	———

We can graphically represent the conjunction of these principles:

Fixed	Subject	Verb	———
Variable	Character	Action	———

Readers expect to see characters not just *in* a subject, as in these two:

The *President's* **veto** of the bill_{subject} **INFURIATED** Congress.

The **veto** of the bill by the *President*_{subject} **INFURIATED** Congress.

Instead, readers prefer to see the character *as* the subject, like this:

✓   When *the President*_{subject} **VETOED**_{verb} the bill, *he*_{subject} **INFURIATED** Congress.

They also expect to see verbs express important actions involving those characters. When you fail to meet your readers' expectations, you make them work harder than they should have to. So keep these principles in mind as you revise:

1. When appropriate, express actions and conditions in verbs:

The **intention** of the committee IS improvement of morale.

✓   The committee INTENDS to improve morale.

2. When appropriate, make subjects of verbs the agents of actions.

    <u>A decision by the *Dean* in regard to the funding by *the Department* of the program</u> IS necessary for there to be adequate *staff* preparation.

✓   If <u>*the staff*</u> is to prepare adequately, <u>*the Dean*</u> must decide whether <u>*the Department*</u> will fund the program.

3. Don't revise nominalizations that do the following:

    a. Refer to a previous sentence:

✓   <u>These **arguments**</u> all depend on a single unproven claim.

    b. Replace an awkward "The fact that":

    <u>The fact that she strenuously OBJECTED</u> impressed me.

✓   Her strenuous **objections** impressed me.

    c. Name what would be the object of a verb:

    I do not know <u>what she INTENDS.</u>

✓   I do not know <u>her **intentions.**</u>

    d. After *there is/are,* introduce a topic that you develop in the next few sentences:

✓   <u>There are</u> *three ways to explain our* **successes.** First, we . . .

    e. Refer to a familiar and often repeated concept:

✓   The Equal Rights **Amendment** was an issue in past **elections.**

Delivery of Resources

WON'T REMEMBER ALL THE Rules + if u DO
      Your WRITING will NOT be good

cf these 10 say TO GREAT Books of Adler
   DO Authors follow these guides
   IF NOT -11 IT REAlly us IF we HAVE TROUBLE

LESSON FOUR

Clarity 2: Characters

*I have never had a thought which I could not set down in words,
with ever more distinctiveness than that which I conceived it.*
EDGAR ALLAN POE

There is no artifice as good and desirable as simplicity.
ST. FRANCIS DE SALES

Affected simplicity is refined imposture.
LA ROCHEFOUCAULD

When character is lost, all is lost.
ANONYMOUS

THE IMPORTANCE OF CHARACTERS

As we saw in the last lesson, we get close to a style that readers judge to be clear and direct when we consistently express crucial ACTIONS in VERBS. Compare the directness of (1a) with the wordiness of (1b) (subjects are underlined, characters italicized, actions boldfaced, verbs capitalized). In (1a), all the actions are verbs; in (1b), those actions are in NOMINALIZATIONS.

✓   1a. The *CIA* FEARED <u>*the president*</u> would RECOMMEND to Congress that <u>*it*</u> should REDUCE its budget.

    1b. The *CIA* HAD **fears** that <u>*the president*</u> would SEND a **recommendation** to *Congress* that <u>*it*</u> MAKE a **reduction** in *its* budget.

Most of us probably prefer (1a) to (1b) for the reason we focused on in Lesson 3: We like to see actions expressed not as nouns, but as verbs.

But some readers don't sense a big difference between (1a) and (1b). Why should that be? It's because most sentences with characters as subjects will seem reasonably clear, and both (1a) and (1b) have characters as subjects. Even so, most readers prefer (1a) because it is more direct and more concise.

To see the difference subjects make, compare (1b) and (1c). Sentence (1c) has as many nominalizations as (1b), but most readers think it is much less clear than (1b):

    1b. The *CIA* HAD **fears** that *the president* would SEND a **recommendation** to *Congress* that *it* MAKE a **reduction** in *its* budget.

    1c. <u>The **fear** on the part of the *CIA*</u> WAS that <u>a **recommendation** from *the president*</u> WOULD GO to *Congress* for a **reduction** in *its* budget.

Readers find (1c) less clear than (1b) because in (1c) the main characters—the CIA, the president, and Congress—have been changed from subjects of verbs into PREPOSITIONAL OBJECTS:

        of the *CIA*   **from** *the President*   **to** *Congress*

But if we had never read any of these sentences before, even (1c) would be clearer than this next sentence, (1d), which has no characters at all:

    1d. <u>There</u> WERE **fears** that <u>there</u> would BE a **recommendation** for a **reduction** in the budget.

> *Here's the point:* Readers generally prefer to see impor-
> tant characters *as* (not just in) the subjects of your verbs, es-
> pecially when those characters are the AGENTS of the actions
> expressed by the verbs. You risk giving readers problems
> when for no good reason you move characters away from
> subjects, or worse, delete them entirely.

Exercise 4.1

If you're having a hard time making these distinctions, it's probably because you are getting to know these sentences too well.
Compare these:

> 2a. There were proposals put forth by Student Government for a de-
> crease of student activity fees by the University.
>
> 2b. Student Government proposed that the university decrease stu-
> dent activity fees.
>
> 2c. Student Government made a proposal that the University insti-
> tute a decrease in student activity fees.

Which of them seems most direct? Why?

FINDING AND RELOCATING CHARACTERS

To revise dense, abstract sentences, you have to know three
things:

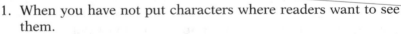

1. When you have not put characters where readers want to see
   them.
2. If so, where you should look for them.
3. What you should do once you find them.

Assume you have drafted a sentence like this:

> In the twentieth century, governmental intervention in fast changing
> technologies has commonly resulted in a distortion of the evolution
> of a market or interference in its dissemination of new products.

Do this:

1. First, look at how each sentence begins. Don't read the whole sentence; just skim the first six or seven words (ignore short introductory phrases like *In the 20th century, For the most part,* and *In London*). Your readers are likely to have a problem if in those first six or seven words they don't see a character as a subject. For example:

   > In the twentieth century, <u>governmental intervention in fast changing technologies</u> has commonly resulted in a distortion of the evolution of a market or interference in *its* dissemination of new products.

   A character is in an adjective *in* the subject, *governmental,* but *government* is not *the* subject.

2. If your sentences begin with abstractions like that, next look for the characters. They may be in POSSESSIVE PRONOUNS attached to a nominalization, in objects of prepositions, particularly *by* and *of,* or even implied in an adjective:

   > In the 20th century, *governmental* intervention in fast changing technologies has commonly resulted in a distortion of the evolution of a *market* or interference in *its* dissemination of new products.

   Decide which character you want to make your central character. In this case, it looks like the government first, the market second.

3. Skim the passage for important actions, particularly those buried in nominalizations, then convert them to verbs, and make the relevant characters their subjects:

   > In the twentieth century, *governmental* **intervention** in fast changing technologies has commonly resulted in *its* **distortion** of the **evolution** of a *market* or **interference** in *its* **dissemination** of new products.

governmental **intervention**	→	The *government* **intervenes**
its **distortion**	→	*it* **distorts**
evolution of a *market*	→	a *market* **evolves**
interference in *its*	→	*government* **interferes** in its
dissemination of new products	→	ability to **disseminate** new products.

4. Finally, the hardest task: Reassemble those propositions into a complete sentence. As you do this, keep in the front of your mind the words *if, although, because, that, when, how,* and *why,* words you can use to stitch a new sentence together:

> In the twentieth century, when *government* has **INTERVENED** in fast changing technologies, *it* has commonly **DISTORTED** how *a market* **EVOLVES** or **INTERFERED** with its ability to **DISSEMINATE** new products.

Be aware that some characters hide out in ADJECTIVES:

> *Medieval theological* **debates** often ADDRESSED issues that to *modern philosophical* thought ARE CONSIDERED trivial.

When you find a character in an adjective, revise in the same way:

✓   *Medieval theologians* often **DEBATED** issues that *philosophers today* CONSIDER trivial.

RECONSTRUCTING MISSING CHARACTERS

Readers have their biggest problem when they see no characters at all:

> A **decision** WAS MADE in favor of **conducting** a **study** of the **disagreements.**

When we write sentences like this in the context of other sentences that do name characters, we may take those characters for granted. But that assumption can be a mistake, because our readers know less than we do, and so they usually need more help than we think they do. That sentence could mean any of these, and more:

> *We* DECIDED that *I* should STUDY why *they* DISAGREED.
>
> ✓   *I* DECIDED that *you* should STUDY why *HE* DISAGREED.

Sometimes we omit characters not by accident but to make a general statement.

> Multivariate strategies ARE of more **use** in **understanding** factors that CONTRIBUTE to psychiatric disorder than strategies based on the **assumption** that the **presence** or **absence** of psychopathology IS **dependent** on a single major gene or on strategies in which a single biological variable is STUDIED.

When we revise, we face the problem of creating characters and then deciding what to call them. Do we use *one* or *we*, or name some generic "doer?"

✓   If *one / we / researchers* ARE to **UNDERSTAND** what causes psychiatric disorder, *one / we / they* should USE multivariate strategies rather than ASSUME that a *single major gene* is **RESPONSIBLE** for psychopathology or ADOPT a strategy in which *one / we / they* STUDY only a single biological variable.

Most readers feel that *one* is stiff, but *we* may seem ambiguous because it can refer just to the writer (the "royal" *we*), to a group that includes the writer and others like her (we researchers) but not the reader, to just reader and writer (you and me), or to people in general. And *they* may seem ambiguous if a sentence has several plural nouns. But when we try to avoid both nominalizations and vague pronouns, we easily slide into PASSIVE verbs (we'll discuss passives in a moment):

To understand <u>what</u> makes patients vulnerable to psychiatric disorders, <u>multivariate strategies</u> **SHOULD BE USED** rather than strategies in which <u>it</u> **IS ASSUMED** that <u>a major gene</u> causes psychopathology or only <u>a single biological variable</u> **IS STUDIED.**

In extreme cases, characters may be so remote from the surface of a sentence that we just have to start over and write a new sentence:

<u>There</u> ARE good reasons that ACCOUNT for the **lack** of evidence.

✓   *I* can **EXPLAIN** why *I* have not **FOUND** any evidence.

I can offer no pat solution to this problem. The only certain principle is that the more distant and abstract you make your characters, the less likely your readers will admire your prose. So the first six or seven word test is an important one: It helps you anticipate when your readers will find your prose impersonal, abstract, and distant.

A MAJOR COMPLICATION: ABSTRACTIONS AS CHARACTERS

So far, we've discussed characters as if they were always flesh-and-blood doers. But now I have to complicate matters by defining character in a more general way, because we can tell stories whose main characters are abstractions, including nominalizations. Here's a story about a character called "freedom of speech."

✓   No right is more fundamental to a free society than *freedom of speech.* *Free speech* served the left in the 1960s when it protested the Vietnam War, and *it* is now used by the right when it claims the federal government is conspiring with the UN to take over the country. *The doctrine of free speech* has been embraced by all sides of all questions to guard against those who would silence their unpopular views. As a distinct legal concept, *it* arose out of . . .

The phrase *free speech* (or its equivalents *freedom of speech* and *it*) does not refer to any flesh-and-blood character. But in that passage, I turned it into a virtual character when I made it the subject in a series of sentences and assigned to it actions such as *served, is used, has been embraced,* and *arose.*

So for our purposes, a character is now whomever or whatever you *think* you can tell a story about, and you can tell a story about whatever you can make the subject of a series of sentences. Though prototypically characters are the flesh-and-blood kind, you can tell stories about abstractions like *free speech, upward mobility, trade pact violations*—anything at all, so long as you make that abstraction the subject of a lot of verbs through a lot of sentences.

But when you do that, you face some potential problems. When you tell stories about abstract concepts as familiar to your readers as *free speech*, they respond to those abstractions as they would to real characters, because to them such phrases refer to concepts with a shape as conceptually well-defined as Little Red Riding Hood. But if your readers are not familiar with those abstractions, they may find it difficult to distinguish them from other abstractions in the same sentence, and when that happens, they may feel your passage collapses into a muddle of nominalizations and prepositional phrases.

For example, if you are unfamiliar with "intention" as a philosophical concept, you may find it difficult to understand a story abut two strange characters called "prospective intention" and "immediate intention," both nominalizations. If you are not familiar with such concepts, you will find this next passage difficult, not only because the two characters are unfamiliar, but because they are embedded in a field of other nominalizations (*intention* is underlined; actions are boldfaced; human characters are italicized):

> The **argument** is this. The cognitive component of **intention** exhibits a high degree of **complexity.** **Intention** is temporally **divisible** into two: prospective **intention** and immediate **intention.** The cognitive **function** of prospective **intention** is the **representation** of a *subject's* similar past **actions,** *his* current situation, and *his* course of future

actions. That is, the cognitive component of <u>prospective **intention**</u> is a **plan**. The cognitive **function** of <u>immediate **intention**</u> is the **monitoring** and **guidance** of ongoing bodily **movement**.

—Myles Brand, *Intending and Acting*

When we revise the surrounding nominalizations into verbs and introduce flesh-and-blood characters, we make the passage clearer to someone unfamiliar with such stories (flesh-and-blood characters are italicized; subjects are underlined; "de-nominalized" verbs and one adjective are in boldface and capitalized):

✓ *I* ARGUE this about **intention**. <u>It</u> has a COMPLEX cognitive component of two temporal kinds: <u>prospective intention</u> and <u>immediate intention.</u> <u>Prospective intention</u> lets *us* REPRESENT how *we* have ACTED in the past, our present situation, and how *we* will ACT in the future. That is, *we* USE the cognitive component of <u>prospective intention</u> to help *us* PLAN. <u>Immediate intention</u> lets *us* MONITOR and GUIDE our bodies as *we* MOVE them.

I have, though, changed the writer's voice into my own, something he might well reject. But have I made him say something he did not mean? Some argue that any change in grammatical form changes meaning. Sometimes that's true, but not always. In this case, the writer could offer an opinion, but the reader can decide whether the writer is right. Writers know what they intend to mean, but only readers know what a passage actually means.

Here's the point: Most readers prefer that subjects of verbs be main characters. When you write about concepts, though, you can treat them almost as if they were real characters by making them the subjects of verbs that feel like actions:

<u>Intention</u> HAS a complex cognitive component.
<u>Prospective intention</u> LETS us represent . . .
<u>Immediate intention</u> LETS us monitor and guide . . .

When your readers are familiar with these abstractions, they have no problem understanding the sentences in which they appear. But when readers are not familiar with them, then you have to avoid using a lot of other nominalizations around them. If you do, your readers may well think your prose is a swamp of abstraction.

An Overview: Two Principles

I know that all this may seem complicated, but in fact you have to learn just four terms to understand two principles that help you understand, analyze, and revise either your own prose or that of others.

1. Two of the terms refer to the two central elements in the grammatical structure of your sentences: *subject* and *verb*. In most sentences, subjects are first, verbs second:

   The scientists$_{\text{subject}}$ + solved$_{\text{verb}}$ + the problem$_{\text{object.}}$

2. Two other terms refer to the two central elements of your story: *character* and *action*. In most stories, the main characters are agents that perform actions directed toward a goal, and those elements usually (but not always) come in that order:

   The scientists$_{\text{agent}}$ → solved$_{\text{action}}$ → the problem$_{\text{goal.}}$

You understand style best when you imagine a reader working to integrate and interpret these two "levels" of organization or structure simultaneously:

1. A fixed level of grammatical structure involving subjects and verbs
2. A variable level of meaning involving characters and actions:

Fixed	Subject	Verb	————
Variable	Character	Action	————

When readers see that you have consistently matched characters to subjects and actions to verbs, they are likely to judge you to be a clear and direct writer. When you depart from that pattern, particularly when you move characters out of the subject position and actions into it, your readers are likely to think your writing more difficult than it has to be.

You can test this principle easily enough. The next time you read a passage that feels like wet wool, just skim the beginning of each sentence in a passage. Odds are you will not see many flesh and blood characters as subjects followed by verbs expressing specific actions. You are more likely to see a lot of sentences beginning with abstract nominalizations.

Exercise 4.2

Before you revise these next sentences, practice diagnosing them. Look at the first six or seven words of every sentence (ignore introductory phrases). Then revise them so that each has a specific character as subject of a specific verb. You may have to invent characters. Use *we, I,* or any other word that seems appropriate.

1. In recent years, the existence of differences in interpretation about the meaning of the discovery of America has led to a reassessment of Columbus's place in Western history.
2. According to most experts, a solution to the UFO problem is impossible without a better understanding about the possibility of extraterrestrial life.
3. Tracing the transitions in a book or a well-written article will provide assistance in efforts at improving coherence in prose.
4. In almost all cases, decisions about forcibly administering medication in an emergency room setting despite the inability of an irrational patient to provide legal consent is an on-scene medical decision.
5. As reported in recent media stories, resistance has been growing against building new mental health facilities in residential areas because of a distrust founded on the belief that the few examples of improper management are typical. There is a need for a modification of these perceptions.
6. With the decline in network television viewing in favor of cable and rental cassettes, awareness is growing at the networks of changes in tastes and viewing habits, resulting in a need to change programming accordingly.
7. Of concern is the increasing cost of protecting museum artifacts. Their mere storage is a contributing factor to deterioration, to say nothing of the effects of their display. The concept of conservation means that higher expenditures are necessary to ensure the availability of skills and equipment to ensure their preservation for future generations.
8. Recent assertions about failures to present information fairly are accurate in regard to journalism in the Middle East today. A comparison of press coverage from different countries reveals many inaccuracies in reporting by politically biased newspapers. The omission of facts and the

slanting of stories show the failure of the press to carry out its mission with objectivity. As a result, lack of knowledge has resulted in a public opinion based more on emotion than on reason.

CHARACTERS AND PASSIVE VERBS

You have probably heard this bit of advice more than any other: "Don't write verbs in the passive. Write in the active voice." That's not bad advice, but it's by no means always reliable. This is what happens when you write in the active voice:

- You typically name the agent of the action in the subject of a sentence.
- You name the goal or receiver of an action in its DIRECT OBJECT:

subject   verb   object
Active: I   lost   the money.
agent   action   goal

When you turn from an active to a passive verb, you reverse that sequence:

                             past participle prepositional
          subject   be +   verb   phrase
Passive: The money   was   lost   [by me].
          goal   action   agent

The passive differs from the active in three ways:

1. The subject expresses the goal of the action.
2. A form of *be* precedes a verb in its PAST PARTICIPLE form.
3. The agent of the action appears after the verb in a *by*-phrase, but it may also be dropped:

The money was lost ~~by me~~.
agent

Like some other terms we've looked at, though, the terms *active* and *passive* can be confusing, because we use them not only to name these two grammatical constructions but also to describe how they *feel*. We often call a sentence passive if it merely feels flat, regardless of whether its verb is in the passive voice. For example, both of these sentences are in the active voice:

The **success** of *the project* DEPENDS on cost **control.**

The project will SUCCEED if *we* can CONTROL costs.

But while that first sentence has no passive verbs in the grammatical sense of the term *passive,* it certainly feels less active than the second, for two reasons.

*   Neither of its actions—*success* and *control*—are verbs; they are both nominalizations.
*   It is missing an important character: *we.*

We have seen how to create this kind of passive, impersonal effect with nominalizations: Once you nominalize the verb, you drain the active life of a sentence, and then on top of that, you can drop the characters associated with the action:

> *We* EXPECTED that *we* would RECRUIT *the staff* quickly.
>
> *Our* **expectation** WAS that *our* **recruitment** of *the staff* would BE quick.
>
> ~~Our~~ The **expectation** WAS for ~~our~~ quick **recruitment** ~~of the staff.~~

If your cast of mind is impersonal and aloof, you will typically combine passives with nominalizations:

Active-verbal:	*We* INVESTIGATED why *the employment office* INTERVIEWED so *few minority applicants.*
Active-nominalized:	*We* CONDUCTED an **investigation** into why *the employment office* DID so few **interviews** of *minority applicants.*
Passive-nominalized:	**An investigation** WAS CONDUCTED into why so few **interviews** WERE DONE.

When writers in the professions combine nominalizations with passives, they create what readers variously call *sociologicalese, educationese, legalese, bureaucratese*—a kind of prose written by those who confuse authority and objectivity with polysyllabic abstraction and remote impersonality.

MORE COMPLICATED ADVICE: CHOOSING BETWEEN ACTIVE AND PASSIVE

Unreflective critics of style relentlessly urge us to avoid the passive, because they think it encourages impersonality and needs an extra word or two (a form of *be* and perhaps the preposition *by*). In general, that's not bad advice, but like so many other clichés, it is often wrong, because the passive is often the better choice.

To choose whether to make the verb active or passive, you have to answer three questions:

1. *Must your readers know who is responsible for the action?*

    Often, you won't say who is responsible for an action, because your readers won't care or because you don't know. For example, you would naturally choose the passive in these sentences:

✓   The president **WAS RUMORED** to have considered resigning.

✓   Those who **ARE FOUND** guilty can **BE FINED.**

✓   Valuable records should always **BE KEPT** in a fireproof safe.

If you do not know who was spreading rumors, you cannot say. And since everyone knows who finds criminals guilty, who fines them, and who should keep records in a safe, no one would wonder. On those grounds, the passive version of this active sentence would be more concise:

Once <u>someone</u> **CIRCULATED** the information, <u>people</u> widely **BELIEVED** it.

✓   Once <u>that information</u> **WAS CIRCULATED,** <u>it</u> **WAS** widely **BELIEVED.**

Sometimes, of course, writers do deliberately avoid assigning responsibility to a character when they don't want readers to know who was responsible for an action with bad consequences, especially when that person is the writer. In this next sentence, we might predict the passive, for reasons having less to do with style, more with avoiding responsibility:

Because the inspection **WAS NOT DONE,** the flaw **WAS LEFT UNCOR-RECTED,** a fact that **WAS KNOWN** months before it **WAS LEAKED** to the press.

Here's the point: Choose the passive when you don't know who did it, your readers don't care who did it, or you don't want them to know who did it.

2. *Would the active or passive verb let you arrange words in an order that helps your readers move smoothly from one sentence to the next?*

    When we read, we depend on the beginning of a sentence to locate us in a context of what we know before we follow the sentence to what is new. Therefore, a sentence can confuse us if it starts not with familiar information, but with information that is new and unexpected. For example, in the second sentence of this next short passage, the subject (double underlined) communicates new and complex information; its object (single underlined) names a concept that would be more familiar to us because it refers to the previous sentence:

> We must **decide** whether to focus on improving education in the sciences alone or to attempt to raise the level of education across the whole curriculum. The weight given to two factors, industrial competitiveness and the value we attach to the liberal arts, $_{\text{new information}}$ WILL INFLUENCE $_{\text{active verb}}$ **this decision** $_{\text{familiar information}}$.

That verb in the second sentence is in the active voice. But we could follow the sentence more easily if it were passive, because we would then read familiar information first and the new and complex information last, the order all readers prefer (I'll devote much of the next lesson to this matter):

> ✓ We must decide whether to focus on improving education in the sciences alone or to attempt to raise the level of education across the whole curriculum. **This decision** $_{\text{familiar information}}$ WILL BE INFLUENCED $_{\text{passive verb}}$ by the weight we give to two factors, industrial competitiveness and the value we attach to the liberal arts $_{\text{new information}}$.

Here's the point: Your readers have a problem with sentences that begin with long, complex subjects expressing information that seems to them new. You can sometimes use a passive verb to shift that long and complex bundle of information to the end of its sentence, especially when it also lets you move to its beginning a chunk of information that is shorter and more familiar. In fact, that's the main reason we have the passive in the language.

3. *Would the active or passive create a consistent and appropriate sequence of subjects representing characters that you want your readers to focus on?*

Look at the subjects in this next paragraph about energy. In the first version, the subjects (underlined) of the verbs (capitalized) seem to have been chosen almost at random:

> It WAS FOUND$_{passive}$ that <u>data about resources allocated to the states</u> WERE NOT OBTAINED$_{passive}$. <u>This action</u> IS NEEDED$_{passive}$ so that <u>it</u> can BE DETERMINED$_{passive}$ how <u>resources</u> can BE REDIRECTED$_{passive}$ when <u>conditions</u> CHANGE$_{active}$. <u>Support</u> must BE PROVIDED$_{passive}$ to the agency so that <u>data on fuel consumption</u> may BE GATHERED$_{passive}$ on a regular basis.

We can revise this to focus on a consistent set of characters, but only if we decide what characters we *want* to focus on, and then *choose* an active or passive verb to help us do that:

✓   <u>We</u> FOUND$_{active}$ that <u>the Department of Energy</u> did not OBTAIN$_{active}$ data about resources that <u>federal offices</u> WERE ALLOCATING$_{active}$ to the states. <u>The agency</u> NEEDS$_{active}$ these data so that <u>it</u> can DETERMINE$_{active}$ how to REDIRECT$_{active}$ resources when <u>conditions</u> CHANGE$_{active}$. <u>The energy secretary</u> must BE PROVIDED$_{passive}$ with support so that *his office* can GATHER$_{active}$ data on fuel consumption on a regular basis.

Note the passive in the last sentence:

✓   The energy secretary **MUST BE PROVIDED** with support . . .

That passive focuses us on the energy secretary appropriately because the energy secretary is one of a consistent set of characters: *Department of Energy, federal offices, the agency, it, the energy secretary, his office.*

When we read a series of sentences with a *consistent* set of subjects, we feel we are reading a coherent story. Imagine this:

> Once upon a time, Little Red Riding Hood was skipping her way to Gramma's house when suddenly the Wolf jumped out from behind a tree. Gramma was home lying in bed wondering when her lunch would arrive, while the Woodsman was chopping down some trees behind her house. The mayor of the village was still in bed, but his brother in the next town had been up for several hours. His wife was visiting her sister. Their mother . . .

That story has characters as the subject of every verb, but it is incoherent because it focuses on no one character.

But if a series of subjects must seem consistent, it should also be appropriate. Almost every story has more than one character, and we can tell a story from almost any character's point of view:

Once upon a time, Little Red Riding Hood was walking to Gramma's house.

Once upon a time, the Wolf was loitering behind a tree in the woods.

Once upon a time, Gramma was wondering where her lunch was.

We always have to decide whose story to tell, and that choice always has consequences on how our readers understand it. The writer of this next passage reports the end of World War II in Europe from the point of view of the Allies. In so doing, she used a series of active verbs:

✓ By early 1945, <u>the Allies</u> HAD essentially DEFEATED_{active} Germany; all that remained was a bloody climax. <u>American, French, British, and Russian forces</u> HAD BREACHED_{active} its borders and WERE BOMBING_{active} it around the clock. But <u>they</u> HAD not yet so DEVASTATED_{active} it as to destroy its ability to resist.

But if she had wanted us to understand history from the point of view of Germany, she could have used passive verbs:

✓ By early 1945, <u>Germany</u> HAD essentially BEEN DEFEATED_{passive}; all that remained was a bloody climax. <u>Its borders</u> HAD BEEN BREACHED_{passive}, and <u>it</u> WAS BEING BOMBED_{passive} around the clock. <u>It</u> HAD not BEEN SO DEVASTATED_{passive}, however, that <u>it</u> could not RESIST.

Here's the point: If in a series of sentences with active or passive verbs, you find yourself shifting randomly from one subject to another, or worse, you have no consistent subjects at all, then decide whom you want to tell a story about, and then rewrite verbs to *either* passive or active to make those subjects more consistent. If you need a passive verb—choose the passive.

Exercise 4.3

In the following, change as many active verbs as you can into passives, and passives into actives. Which sentences improve? Which do not? (In the first five, the active verbs that you could make passive if you choose to are italicized. The verbs that are already passive that you could make active, if you choose to, are boldfaced.)

1. Independence is **gained** by those on welfare when skills are **taught** that the marketplace *values*.
2. In this textbook students are **trained** to perceive rhythm not as a series of individual notes but as a larger movement that *creates* a sense of musical architecture.
3. When fewer goods are **made** available to consumers while prices are being **raised** by inflation, the rate of inflation will be **accelerated** when consumers *hoard* goods that they most *need*.
4. The heat-resistant tiles had to be **redesigned** and **replaced** because their surfaces had been **bombarded** by micrometeorites.
5. The different planes of the painting are immediately **noticed,** because their colors are **set** against a background of subtle shades of gray that are **laid** on in thin layers that cannot be **noticed** unless the surface is **examined** closely.
6. Before Ann Richards was elected governor of Texas, she was attacked as a liberal Democrat with a background in which drugs may have been used, but her campaign was conducted in a way in which negative advertising was also used.
7. In this article, it is argued that the Vietnam War was fought to extend influence in Southeast Asia and was not ended until it was made clear that the United States could not defeat North Vietnam unless atomic weapons were used.
8. Science education cannot be improved to a level sufficient to ensure that American industry will be supplied with skilled workers and researchers until more money is provided to primary and secondary schools.
9. The tone in the first part of Bierce's "An Occurrence at Owl Creek Bridge" is presented in a dispassionate way. In the first paragraph, two sentinels are described in detail, but the line, "It did not appear to be the duty of these two men to know what was occurring at the center of the bridge" takes emotion away from them. In paragraph 2, a description is given of the surroundings and spectators, but no feeling is betrayed because the language used is neutral

and unemotional. This entire section is presented as devoid of emotion even though it is filled with details.

Exercise 4.4

Revise any paragraph in Lesson 1 so that all the active verbs are passive. Then exchange paragraphs with someone and see if you can each rewrite your revisions back into the original.

THE "OBJECTIVE" PASSIVE

In one context, the sciences, the passive has a special role: It allegedly contributes to an objective point of view. Here is an example:

> Based on the writers' verbal intelligence, prior knowledge and essay scores, their essays **WERE ANALYZED** for structure and evaluated for richness of concepts. The subjects **WERE** then **DIVIDED** into a high- or low-ability group. Half of each group **WAS** randomly **ASSIGNED** to a treatment group or to a placebo group.

In truth, despite the widespread belief that we should choose the passive to avoid the first-person *I* or *we* in academic writing, particularly in scientific writing, many highly regarded academic and scientific writers use *I* and *we* regularly. The "rule" against using *I* or *we* in academic writing is folklore. These next passages all come from the introductions of articles in respected journals:

✓ This paper is concerned with two problems. How can we best handle, in a transformational grammar certain restrictions that. . . . To illustrate, we may cite. . . . we shall show . . . .

✓ Since the pituitary-adrenal axis is activated during the acute phase response, we have investigated the potential role. . . . Specifically, we have studied the effects of interleukin-1 . . . .

✓ Any study of tensions presupposes some acquaintance with certain findings of child psychology. We may begin by inquiring whether. . . . We should next proceed to investigate . . . .

Here are the first few words from several consecutive sentences in an article from *Science,* a journal of considerable prestige:

✓   We examine. . . . We compare. . . . We have used. . . . Each has been weighted. . . . We merely take. . . . They are subject. . . . We use. . . . Efron and Morris describe. . . . We observed. . . . We might find. . . .

—John P. Gilbert, Bucknam McPeek, and Frederick Mosteller,
"Statistics and Ethics in Surgery and Anesthesia," *Science*

To be sure, some writers and editors resolutely avoid the first person everywhere. But they are wrong to claim that writers must always choose the impersonal third person. The passive does not make the science objective; it only makes the sentences reporting it seem so. We know that behind those sentences are flesh-and-blood researchers doing, thinking, and writing.

METADISCOURSE: WRITING ABOUT WRITING

When academic writers do use the first person, however, they use it in particular ways. Look at the verbs in the passages above. There are two kinds:

- One kind of verb refers to research activities: *study, investigate, examine, observe, use.* These verbs are predictably in the passive voice: *The subjects were observed.*
- The other kind refers not to the subject matter or the research, but to the writer's own writing and thinking: *handle, cite, show, inquire.* These verbs are quite often active and in the first person: *We will show . . .*

When we use this second kind of verb to refer to our own thinking and writing or to our readers' acts of reading and understanding, we are using a kind of language called *metadiscourse*, or discourse about discourse. We need that technical term, because we need some metadiscourse in everything we write. Metadiscourse helps us tell readers how to read what we've written. Without that word *metadiscourse* we couldn't explain how these next kinds of words and phrases work. They don't refer to the product of a person's thinking and writing, but to the process of thinking and explaining:

- Rhetorical actions: *explain, show, argue, claim, deny, suggest, contrast, add, expand, summarize*
- Parts of the discourse: *first, second, third; to begin, finally*
- Logical connections: *therefore, however, consequently, if so*
- Hedges and emphatics to beliefs: *it seems, perhaps, undoubtedly, I think*

- Guides for readers: *consider now the matter of, as you might recall*

We use metadiscourse most often in introductions, where we announce our intentions: *We claim that* . . . , *We shall show* . . . , *We begin by* . . . , If we use metadiscourse at the beginning, we are likely to use it again at the end, when we summarize: *We suggested* . . . , *I have shown* . . . , *We have claimed.*

On the other hand, academic and scholarly writers rarely use the first person to describe particular actions that they performed *in* their research. We rarely find passages like this:

> To determine if monokines elicited an adrenal steroidogenic response, *I* added a monocyte-conditioned medium and preparations of . . . .

The writer of the original sentence used the passive verb:

> To determine if monokines elicited a response, preparations . . . WERE ADDED . . .

But there is a lurking problem with this kind of passive sentence: When as that writer did you cast a sentence like that in the passive, you risk dangling your modifier. You dangle a modifier when you create an introductory phrase whose implied subject differs from the specific subject of the verb in the following clause. In that example, the implied subject of the infinitive verb *determine* is *I* or *we: I determine* or *we determine.*

> [So that I could] ~~to~~ determine if monokines elicited a response, preparations . . . WERE ADDED . . .

But that implied subject *I* or *we* differs from the explicit subject of the clause it attaches to—*preparations.* When the implied subject of your introductory phrase differs from the actual subject of the following clause, you dangle the introductory phrase.

Writers of scientific prose use this pattern so often, however, that it is now standard usage in their community. When editors with stern views reject both first person subjects and dangling modifiers, they put their authors into a predicament where they are damned if they do and damned if they don't.

As a small historical footnote, we might note that this impersonal "scientific" style is a modern development. In his "New Theory of Light and Colors" (1672), Sir Isaac Newton wrote this charming first-person account of an early experiment:

I procured a triangular glass prism, to try therewith the celebrated phenomena of colors. And for that purpose, having darkened my laboratory, and made a small hole in my window shade, to let in a convenient quantity of the sun's light, I placed my prism at the entrance, that the light might be thereby refracted to the opposite wall. It was at first a very pleasing diversion to view the vivid and intense colors produced thereby.

Here's the point: The first person *I* and *we* appear in much scholarly prose. Some critics nevertheless frown on its use, particularly the expressions *I think . . . , I feel . . . , I believe . . .* Most of them do that because they see inexperienced writers use those words to introduce too much expression of mere baseless opinion. But when you are referring to some act of your own writing or thinking, the first person is entirely appropriate.

Exercise 4.5

The verbs in sentences 1 through 4 below are all passive, but two of them could be active because they are metadiscourse verbs that frequently take first-person subjects. Change the verbs that should be changed. But when you finish doing that, go through each sentence again and revise nominalizations into verbs if you think those nominalizations are hiding important actions.

1. ~~It is concluded that instability~~ of the image is caused by a deterioration of the optical system.
2. The model has been subjected to statistical analysis.
3. Failure to export sufficient crude oil for hard currency is proposed here as the cause of the collapse of the Soviet economy.
4. The creation of a database is being considered, but no estimate has been made in regard to the potential of its usefulness.

The verbs in sentences 5 through 8 are active, but two of them should be passive because they are not metadiscourse verbs. Revise in other ways that you think appropriate.

5. In Section IV, I argue that the indigenous culture engaged in overcultivation of the land at the base of the mesa leading to its exhaustion as a viable food-producing area.
6. Our intention in this book is to help readers achieve an understanding not only of the differences in grammar between Arabic and English but also the differences in worldview as reflected by Arabic vocabulary.
7. To make an evaluation of changes in the flow rate, I made a comparison of the original flow rate on the basis of figures I had compiled with figures that Jordan had collected in a study of the diversion patterns of slow-growth swamps.
8. We performed the tissue rejection study on the basis of methods developed with our discovery of increases in dermal sloughing as a result of cellular regeneration.

Exercise 4.6

Revise these passages. Change passive verbs into actives only where you think doing so will improve the sentence. If necessary, invent a rhetorical situation to account for your choice of active or passive.

1. Your figures were reanalyzed to determine their accuracy. Results will be announced when it is judged appropriate.
2. Home mortgage loans now are made for thirty years. With the price of housing at inflated levels, those loans cannot be paid off in any shorter period of time.
3. The author's impassioned narrative style is abandoned and in its place a cautious treatment of theories of conspiracy is presented. But the moment the narrative line is picked up again, he invests his prose with the same vigor and force.
4. Many arguments were advanced against Darwinian evolution in the nineteenth century because basic assumptions about our place in the world were challenged by it. No longer were we defined as privileged creatures but rather as a product of natural forces.
5. For many years federal regulations concerning the use of wiretapping have been ignored. Only recently have tighter restrictions been imposed on the circumstances that warrant it.

In these sentences, change passives to actives where appropriate and edit nominalizations into a more direct agent-action style. Invent agents where necessary.

6. It is my belief that the social significance of smoking receives its clearest explication through an analysis of peer interaction among adolescents. In particular, studies should be made of the manner in which relational interactive behavior is conditioned by social class.
7. These directives are written in a style of maximum simplicity as a result of an attempt at more effective communication with employees with limited reading skills.
8. The ability of the human brain to arrive at solutions of human problems has been undervalued, because studies have not been done that would be considered to have scientific reliability.

Exercise 4.7

What follows is a slightly altered version of a letter from the chancellor of a state university to parents of students. Why is the first part so impersonal? The next more personal? Change the first part so that you make whoever performed the actions the specific subjects of verbs. Then change the second part so that no specific character appears. How do the two parts now differ? Revise passives into actives and nominalize where necessary.

As you probably have heard, the U of X campus has been the scene of a number of incidents of racial and sexual harassment over the last several weeks. The fact that similar incidents have occurred on campuses around the country does not make them any less offensive when they take place here. Of the ten to twelve incidents that have been reported since early October, most have involved graffiti or spoken insults. In only two cases was any physical contact made, and in neither case was anyone injured.

U of X is committed to providing its students with an environment where they can live, work, and study without fear of being taunted or harassed because of their race, gender, religion, or ethnicity. I have made it clear that bigotry and intolerance will not be permitted and that U of X's commitment to diversity is unequivocal. We are also taking steps to improve security in campus housing. We at U of X are proud of this university's tradition of diversity . . . .

NOUN + NOUN + NOUN

There is one more stylistic choice that can distort the match that readers expect between the syntax of an idea and the grammar of a sentence: It is the long COMPOUND NOUN phrase:

> Early <u>childhood thought disorder misdiagnosis</u> often results from unfamiliarity with recent <u>research literature</u> describing such conditions. This paper is a review of seven recent studies in which are findings of particular relevance to <u>pre-adolescent hyperactivity diagnosis</u> and to <u>treatment modalities</u> involving <u>medication maintenance level evaluation procedures</u>.

Some grammarians claim that we should never use one noun to modify another, but that would rule out common phrases such as *stone wall, student center, space shuttle,* and vast numbers of technical terms that we need.

But you should try revising a long series of nouns when it is not familiar to your readers, and especially when it includes nominalizations. To revise it, simply reverse the order of words and find prepositions to re-connect them. Here is the first compound in the example passage revised:

1	2	3	4	5
early	childhood	thought	disorder	misdiagnosis
misdiagnose	disordered	thought	in early	childhood
5	4	3	1	2

Now we can see an ambiguity in the original: What's early, the childhood, the disorder, or the diagnosis?

> Physicians misdiagnose[5] disordered[4] thought[3] in young[1] children[2] because they are unfamiliar with recent literature on the subject.

> *Here's the point:* Whenever you write a string of nouns that you haven't seen before, try revising them. Start from the last and reverse their order, linking them with prepositions. If one of the nouns is a nominalization, rewrite it into a full verb.

Exercise 4.8

Finish revising the passage about disordered thought. Then turn the compound noun phrases in 1 through 4 into prepositional phrases.

1. The plant safety standards committee discussed recent air quality regulation announcements.
2. Diabetic patient blood pressure reduction may be brought about by renal depressor medication.
3. The main goal of this article is to describe text comprehension processes and recall protocol production.
4. On the basis of these principles, we may now attempt to formulate narrative information extraction rules.

In these next sentences, unpack compound nouns and edit by placing characters and actions in subjects and verbs. Invent characters as needed.

5. This paper is an investigation into information processing behavior involved in computer human cognition simulation.
6. Enforcement of guidelines for new automobile tire durability must be a Federal Trade Commission responsibility.
7. The Social Security program is a monthly income floor guarantee for individuals whose benefit package potential is based on a determination of lifelong contribution schedule.
8. Based on training needs assessment reviews and on office site visits, there was the identification of concepts and issues that can be used in our creation of an initial staff questionnaire instrument.
9. Corporate organization under state law supervision has resulted in federal government failures in regard to the effective implementation of accident reduction measures.

THE PROFESSIONAL VOICE

Every group expects its members to demonstrate that they accept its values by adopting its voice and vocabulary. The apprentice banker must learn not only to think and look like one but to sound like one as well. Too often, though, aspiring professionals think they sound professional only when they communicate in ways that are complex and abstract. Or they fall into that style because they read so much of it.

Whatever the cause, when they complicate substantive complexity with an unfriendly prose style, they make it difficult, if not impossible, for the merely well-educated lay person to understand issues that might be significant to us all. And that exclusionary style erodes the trust that a civil society depends on, especially in a world where information and expert knowledge are increasingly the means to power and control. Information may be free, but if it is encrypted in language so complex that it is beyond our ability to understand it, it might as well be locked up.

It is true that some exotic research can never be clear to merely intelligent lay readers—but less often than many researchers believe. Here is an excerpt from Talcott Parsons, a social scientist who was as influential in shaping the way sociologists think as he was notorious for the opacity of his prose.

> Apart from theoretical conceptualization there would appear to be no method of selecting among the indefinite number of varying kinds of factual observation which can be made about a concrete phenomenon or field so that the various descriptive statements about it articulate into a coherent whole, which constitutes an "adequate," a "determinate" description. Adequacy in description is secured insofar as determinate and verifiable answers can be given to all the scientifically important questions involved. What questions are important is largely determined by the logical structure of the generalized conceptual scheme which, implicitly or explicitly, is employed.

We can make that clearer to moderately well-educated readers:

> When scientists lack a theory, they cannot select from everything they could say about a subject only that which they can fit into a coherent whole and be "adequate" or "determinate." Scientists describe something "adequately" only when they can verify answers to questions they think are important, and they decide what questions are important based on their implicit or explicit theories.

And we could make even that more concise:

> Whatever you describe, you need a theory to fit its parts into a whole. You need a theory not only to verify answers, but even to decide what questions to ask.

This most concise version loses the nuances of Parsons's style. But his excruciating style numbs all but the most masochistically dedicated reader.

In short, to be a responsible writer, you owe a civil duty to your intended readers: Without compromising the intrinsic complexity of your ideas, you are ethically obliged not to impose on them gratuitous difficulty, and nothing complicates prose more gratuitously than nominalizations where verbs would do as well, or better.

Finally, I want to emphasize again that these principles of analysis and revision are not intended to reduce mature prose to a kind of Dick-and-Jane primer style intended for those who do not read much or well. They are intended to help you identify gratuitously complex prose, either your own or that of someone else, and then to help you change it if you can, and if you cannot, at least to understand why you are struggling with it.

Here's the point: Whether you are a reader or a writer, you must understand three things about a style that seems complex:

- Such a style may needlessly complicate simple ideas.
- Such a style may be necessary to express complex ideas precisely.
- Such a style may needlessly complicate already complex ideas.

As a reader, your task is to discriminate among these kinds of complexity so that you can know when a passage is needlessly complex and, if not condemn it, at least not blame yourself for failing to understand it. As a writer, your task is to recognize when you have committed that gratuitous complexity and, if you can, to revise it into something more accessible. It is just one more example of the Writer's Golden Rule: Write to others as you would have others write to you. If you don't like reading abstract, indirect, impersonal complex prose, don't write it.

SUMMING UP

1. Your readers are most likely to judge your prose clear when subjects of sentences are agents of actions and those actions are verbs.

Fixed	Subject	Verb	———
Variable	Character	Action	———

2. If you decide to tell stories in which you make abstract nominalizations main characters, use as few other nominalizations as you can:

   A _nominalization_ IS a **transformation** of a verb into a noun, often resulting in **displacement** of characters from subjects by nouns.

   ✓ When **_a nominalization_** TRANSFORMS a verb into a noun, _that nominalization_ often DISPLACES characters from subjects.

3. Use a passive if the agent of an action is self-evident:

   The voters REELECTED the president with 54 percent of the vote.

   ✓ _The president_ WAS REELECTED with 54 percent of the vote.

4. Use a passive if it lets you replace a long subject with a short one:

   Research that demonstrated the soundness of our reasoning and the need for action SUPPORTED this decision.

   ✓ This decision WAS SUPPORTED BY research that demonstrated the soundness of our reasoning and the need for action.

5. Use a passive if it gives your readers a coherent sequence of subjects:

   ✓   By early 1945, _the Axis nations_ had BEEN essentially DE-FEATED; all that remained was a bloody climax. _The German borders_ had BEEN BREACHED, and both _Germany and Japan_ were being bombed around the clock. _Neither country,_ though, had BEEN so DEVASTATED that _it_ could not RESIST.

6. Use an active verb if it is a metadiscourse verb:

   The terms of the analysis must BE DEFINED.

✓ *We* must **DEFINE** the terms of the analysis.

7. When convenient, rewrite long compound noun phrases:
   We discussed the **board[1] candidate[2] review[3] meetings[4] schedule[5]**.

✓ We discussed the **schedule[5]** of **meetings[4]** to **review[3] candidates[2]** for the **board[1]**.

HE or SHE

LESSON FIVE

Cohesion and Coherence

If he would inform, he must advance regularly from Things known to things unknown, distinctly without Confusion, and the lower he begins the better. It is a common Fault in Writers, to allow their Readers too much knowledge: They begin with that which should be the Middle, and skipping backwards and forwards, 'tis impossible for any one but he who is perfect in the Subject before, to understand their Work, and such an one has no Occasion to read it.
BENJAMIN FRANKLIN

The two capital secrets in the art of prose composition are these: first, the philosophy of transition and connection; or the art by which one step in an evolution of thought is made to arise out of another: all fluent and effective composition depends on the connections; secondly, the way in which sentences are made to modify each other; for the most powerful effects in written eloquence arise out of this reverberation, as it were, from each other in a rapid succession of sentences.
THOMAS DE QUINCEY

"Begin at the beginning," the King said, gravely, "and go on till you come to the end; then stop."
LEWIS CARROLL

LOCAL VERSUS GLOBAL CLARITY

So far, we've talked about clarity almost as if we could achieve it by mechanically mapping CHARACTERS and ACTIONS onto SUBJECTS and VERBS. But we need more than the local clarity of individual sentences. These passages, for example, say much the same thing, but they feel different, for reasons having little to do with abstract nouns:

> 1a. Since the discovery that one factor in Alzheimer's disease might be genetic, great strides in its early and accurate diagnosis have occurred in recent years. Senility in an older patient who seemed to be losing touch with reality, an entirely different condition, was often confused with Alzheimer's not too long ago. Blood chemistry and genetic clues are new and more reliable tests to diagnose it in the past few years, however. The risk of human tragedy of another kind, though, has resulted from the increasing accuracy of these procedures: Long before the appearance of any of its overt symptoms, physicians may be able to predict Alzheimer's. At that point, an apparently healthy person could be devastated by such an early diagnosis.

> ✓   1b. In recent years, since the discovery that one factor in Alzheimer's disease might be genetic, researchers have made great strides in its early and accurate diagnosis. Not too long ago, when a physician examined an older patient who seemed out of touch with reality, she had to guess whether that person had Alzheimer's or was senile, an entirely different condition. In the past few years, however, new and more reliable tests have focused on blood chemistry and genetic clues. But in the accuracy of these new tests lies the risk of human tragedy of another kind: Physicians may be able to predict Alzheimer's long before its overt appearance, but such an early diagnosis could psychologically devastate an apparently healthy person.

The passages differ in how we feel their sentences "hang together."

We look for that sense of "hanging together" to distinguish passages that seem coherent from those that do not.

- Readers must feel that they move easily from one sentence to the next, that each "coheres" with the one before and after.
- They must also feel that sentences are not just individually clear but constitute a unified passage focused on a coherent *set* of characters.

We have a problem discussing cohesion and coherence, though, that is the same as the problem describing clarity. Like the

word *clarity*, the words *cohesion* and *coherence* don't refer to anything "in" a passage. Like most other words that characterize the
qualities of prose—*flowing* or *disjointed*, *focused* or *disorganized*—
they refer not to what is on the page, but to how the writing on the
page makes us feel. Cohesion and coherence refer to what's going
on in our minds as we read. In fact, so powerful is our own ability—and desire—to create coherent sense of what we read, that we
can count on readers to go more than halfway toward creating
that experience of coherence for themselves, if we give them just a
bit of help.

The object of this lesson is to explain how you can use certain
features of style that your readers see *on the page* to help them feel
they are reading prose that is not just clear, but both flowing (cohesive) and well-formed (coherent). We'll deal with cohesion first,
then coherence.

COHESION: A SENSE OF FLOW

In Lesson 4, we devoted a few pages (78–86) to that widely repeated advice, "Avoid PASSIVES." If you followed the standard advice, you would choose the ACTIVE verb in sentence (2a) below over
the PASSIVE in (2b):

2a. The collapse of a dead star into a point perhaps no larger than a
marble CREATES$_{active}$ a Black Hole.

2b. A Black Hole IS CREATED$_{passive}$ by the collapse of a dead star into a
point perhaps no larger than a marble.

But the passive has its uses, including helping readers create that
sense of flow that characterizes a cohesive passage.

Imagine either of those two sentences between these two:

[1]Some astonishing questions about the nature of the universe have
been raised by scientists studying black holes in space. [2a/b][   ]. [3]So
much matter compressed into so little volume changes the fabric of
space around it in puzzling ways.

Which sentence creates a better flow between sentences (1) and
(3)—the active (2a) or the passive (2b)? Try the active sentence
first:

1a. [1]Some astonishing questions about the nature of the universe
have been raised by scientists studying black holes in space. [2a]The

collapse of a dead star into a point perhaps no larger than a marble **creates**$_{active}$ a black hole. [3]So much matter compressed into so little volume changes the fabric of space around it in puzzling ways.

Now try the passive:

> 1b. [1]Some astonishing questions about the nature of the universe have been raised by scientists studying black holes in space. [2b]A black hole **is created**$_{passive}$ by the collapse of a dead star into a point perhaps no larger than a marble. [3]So much matter compressed into so little volume changes the fabric of space around it in puzzling ways.

Our sense of "flow" should tell us that this passage calls not for (2a), the sentence with the active verb, but for sentence (2b), the one with the passive.

And the reason is clear: The last four words of the first sentence in the passage introduce an important new character—*black holes in space:*

> [1]Some astonishing questions about the nature of the universe have been raised by scientists studying **black holes in space.**

Follow that sentence with (2a), the sentence with the active verb:

> [1] . . . universe have been raised by scientists studying **black holes in space. [2a]The collapse of a dead star into a point perhaps no larger than a marble** creates$_{active}$ a black hole.

In sentence (2a), the first concept that we hit after black holes is collapsed stars and marbles, information that seems to come out of nowhere. The first familiar information that we recognize, *black holes,* doesn't appear until the end of that sentence.

But now after sentence (1) try (2b) with the passive verb; note how it opens:

> [1] . . . studying **black holes in space. [2b]A black hole** is created$_{passive}$ by the collapse of a dead star into a point perhaps no larger than a marble. [3]So much matter compressed into so little volume changes the fabric of space around it in puzzling ways.

We move from sentence (1) to (2b) more easily than from (1) to (2a) because we begin (2b) with *a black hole,* a familiar concept that helps us tie the two sentences together.

Note too that by using the passive, we have located at the end of sentence (2b) words that the reader can easily connect to the beginning of sentence (3):

> [1] . . . black holes in space. [2b]A black hole is created by the collapse of a dead star into **a point perhaps no larger than a marble.** [3]**So much matter compressed into so little volume** changes the fabric of space around it in puzzling ways

And that's what our sense of cohesion depends on: feeling that as we read, we see in each sentence something that connects it to the one before and to the one after. How we help readers create that sense of flow is the problem—and the challenge—of English prose.

> *Here's the point:*   In every *sequence* of sentences you write, you have to balance the principles that make individual sentences clear and the principles that give a sequence of sentences a sense of a cohesive flow. *But in that compromise, you must give priority to helping readers create a sense of cohesion.* Readers may understand individual sentences, but if they cannot see how that series of sentences "hangs together," then no matter how clear individual sentences are, readers will not feel that they add up to a cumulatively coherent passage.

THE FIRST PRINCIPLE OF COHESION: OLD-TO-NEW

That example about black holes helps us formulate two more principles of writing and revision; they are mirror images of each other. Here's the first:

1. Begin your sentences with information familiar to your readers.

Readers get that familiar information from two sources:

• They see it in the sentence or two just before the one they are reading. That's why sentence (2b) about black holes cohered with (1) and why (3) cohered with (2b).

> [1]Some astonishing questions about the nature of the universe have been raised by scientists studying **[black holes in space. [2b]A black**

hole] is created by the collapse of a dead star into **[a point perhaps no larger than a marble. ³So much matter compressed into so little volume]** changes the fabric of space around it in puzzling ways.

- They bring that familiar information with them in their general knowledge of a topic. We would not have been surprised if sentence (3) in that series about black holes had begun like this:

    1b. . . . changes the fabric of space around it in puzzling ways. ³**Astrophysicists have recently reported,** for example, that . . .

The words *Astrophysicists have recently reported* did not appear in the previous sentence as *black holes* did, but given that we are reading about black holes, we ought not be surprised by a reference to astrophysicists. It fits the context.

The second principle is the flip side of the first:

2. End your sentences with information your readers cannot anticipate.

It is easier to see how those two principles work—or don't—in the writing of others than in our own. We will always be our own worst editors because by the time we write a final draft, everything we write seems old—to us. But our readers must think that at least some of it is new (why else read it?).

So even though you will probably find it difficult to distinguish old information from new in your own writing, you must try, because you have to begin sentences from your readers' point of view, with what they know, either from information you provided in previous sentences or from knowledge they bring with them and would not be surprised to see in the context you've created.

Here's the point: These two principles about old and new information cooperate with the principles we discussed in Lessons 3 and 4 about characters as subjects. Once you mention your characters, they become familiar information to your readers. So when you get characters up front, you also get up front familiar information.

Exercise 5.1

Revise these two passages to improve their old-new flow.

1. Two aims—the recovery of the American economy and the restoration of America into a military superpower—were in Reagan's mind when he assumed the office of the presidency. The drop in unemployment figures and inflation, and the increase in the GNP testifies to his success in the first. But our increased involvement in international conflict without any clear set of political goals indicates less success with the second. Nevertheless, vast increases in the military budget and a good deal of saber rattling pleased the American voter.

2. The various components of Abco's current profitability, particularly growth in Asian markets, will be highlighted in our report to demonstrate its advantages versus competitors. Revenue returns along several dimensions: product type, end-use, distribution channels, distributor type, etc. will provide the basis for this analysis. Likely growth prospects of Abco's newest product lines will depend most on its ability in regard to the development of distribution channels in China, according to our projections. A range of innovative strategies that will be needed to support the introduction of new products.

COHERENCE: A SENSE OF FOCUS

When we create what readers feel is a cohesive flow, however, we take only the first of two steps toward helping them create a sense of a unified whole. They must feel that our writing is not only cohesive but coherent, a different quality from cohesion. This next passage, for example, has great cohesive "flow," because we move from each sentence to the next without a hitch:

> Saner, Wisconsin, is the snowmobile capital of the world. The buzzing of snowmobile engines fills the air, and their tanklike tracks crisscross the snow. The snow reminds me of Mom's mashed potatoes, covered with furrows I would draw with my fork. Mom's mashed potatoes usually made me sick, that's why I play with them. I like to make a hole in the middle of the potatoes and fill it with melted butter. This behavior has been the subject of long chats between me and my analyst.

But while this passage may seem cohesive, we surely judge it to be incoherent. We can connect each sentence to the one before and after, but we cannot see how the whole passage "hangs together"; it has no "focus": Each sentence begins with a different subject—first with Saner, then snowmobiles, then snow, then Mom's mashed potatoes, finally with behavior. (The passage was created by six different writers, one of whom wrote the first sentence, with the other five sequentially adding one sentence to fit just the immediately preceding one.) It's like that story that began with Little Red Riding Hood and ended up with the mother of the wife of the brother of the mayor of the village the woodsman lived in. These varying ways of starting a sentence scatter our attention across a random set of concepts.

To help readers feel our writing is coherent, we have to understand not just how readers move from one sentence to just the next. We also have to understand what makes them think that several sentences in a row "hang together" to form a *coherent* passage, a segment of discourse more than the sum of its individual sentences. Readers make that judgment based on what words they see toward the beginning of each sentence in the series of those sentences. If those words refer to a consistent set of ideas, they are more likely to judge that passage as coherent; if not, they are less likely to.

GRAMMATICAL SUBJECTS, PSYCHOLOGICAL SUBJECTS, AND TOPICS

The first thing readers want to know about a sentence is what it is "about," its *topic*. We ordinarily name the topic of a sentence and of each clause in it in their subjects (we will double underline topics; they are regularly, but not always, subjects):

> And therefore, politically speaking, in Eastern states since 1980, <u>acid rain</u> has become a serious concern.

That sentence is in some general sense about politics, the East, and 1980, but its real topic, what it is centrally "about," is its subject/topic, *acid rain.*

Readers judge a whole passage coherent to the degree that in a string of sentences, they can see two things about their topics:

- They can quickly identify the topics of individual sentences and clauses.
- They can see how those topics constitute a related but relatively limited set of ideas.

Compare the coherence of those two substantively identical passages (topics are double-underlined):

1a. <u>The particular ideas toward the beginning of sentences</u> define what <u>a passage</u> is "about" for a reader, so a<u> sense of coherence</u> depends on topics. <u>Moving through a paragraph from a cumulatively consistent point of view</u> is made possible by a sequence of topics that seem to constitute this coherent sequence of topicalized ideas. <u>A seeming absence of context for each sentence</u> is one consequence of making random shifts in topics. <u>Feelings of dislocation, disorientation, and lack of focus</u> will occur when that happens.

In that passage, the string of topics is inconsistent, scattered, diffuse:

The particular ideas toward the beginning of sentences

a sense of coherence

Moving through a paragraph from a cumulatively consistent point of view

A seeming absence of context for each sentence

Feelings of dislocation, disorientation, and lack of focus

And so we judge that passage to be out of focus, even disorganized. Now compare this revision (I double-underline topics in MAIN CLAUSES and single-underline topics of subordinate clauses to show how consistent the topics are throughout):

✓   1b. <u>Topics</u> are crucial for readers because <u>they</u> depend on topics to focus their attention on particular ideas toward the beginning of sentences; <u>topics</u> tell them what <u>a whole passage</u> is "about." If <u>readers</u> feel that <u>a sequence of topics</u> is coherent, then <u>they</u> will feel <u>they</u> are moving through a paragraph from a cumulatively coherent point of view. But if through that paragraph <u>readers</u> feel that <u>its topics</u> shift randomly, then <u>they</u> have to begin each sentence out of context, from no coherent point of view. When <u>that</u> happens, <u>readers</u> feel dislocated, disoriented, out of focus.

In that passage, the string of topics focuses on variations of just two concepts: *topics* and *readers,* and so we judge this passage to be more focused, more coherent, and therefore easier to read and remember. This matter is so important to how your readers read that it deserves some detailed attention.

SUBJECTS, TOPICS, AND GRAMMAR

For 500 years, English teachers have defined *subject* in two ways:

1. The subject of a sentence is the "doer" of the action.
2. The subject of a sentence is "what the sentence is about."

In Lessons 3 and 4, we saw why that first definition is not always reliable:

> <u>Our</u> analysis of the data led to our discovery of a new principle.

The "doer" in that sentence is not its subject, *analysis,* but its modifier, *our.*

But if that definition about subject as "doer" is not true for all sentences, it implies some good advice: In prose we judge to be clear, subjects usually are in fact "doers"—that is, characters who are AGENTS of actions represented by verbs. Revised:

✓   When <u>we</u> analyzed the data, <u>we</u> discovered a new principle.

SUBJECTS, TOPICS, AND PSYCHOLOGY

Also flawed but useful is that second schoolbook definition: A subject is what a sentence is "about." In this sense, "about" does not mean the gist of a sentence, but rather just the first main idea that we read and that the rest of the sentence "comments" on. In this sense, the idea of *topic* is part of the "psychological geography" of a sentence. That geography defines a space or position near the beginning of each sentence where we expect to see the concept that the rest of the sentence says something about. That place is usually the subject of a clause, but not always.

For example, this next sentence is "about" its topic, *international cooperation.* In this case, that phrase is indeed the subject of the verb:

> <u>International cooperation</u> is still the goal of most countries.

Often, though, the subject of a sentence does not announce what its sentence is "about"; that function can be performed by other elements:

- The subject of this sentence, for example, is *it,* but the sentence is about *your claims,* the OBJECT of the PREPOSITION *for:*
  > <u>It</u> is impossible for <u>your claims</u> to be proved conclusively.
- The subject of this next sentence is *I,* but the sentence is about *these questions,* the object of *to.*

In regard to <u>these questions</u>, I believe there is a need for more research.

- The subject of this sentence is *it*, but the sentence is about *our proposals*, the subject of a SUBORDINATE CLAUSE.

  <u>It</u> is likely that <u>our proposals</u> will be accepted.

- The subject of this next sentence is *no one*, but it is about *results like these*, a direct object shifted to the front for emphasis.

  <u>Results like these</u> <u>no one</u> could have predicted.

So when we use the term *topic* to mean what a sentence is "about," we don't mean its grammatical subject, but rather its "psychological" subject. That psychological subject is usually its grammatical subject, but not always, as these examples show. Nevertheless, the topic of a sentence will usually be one of its first few words—or at least that's where we want it to be, because we depend on these psychological subjects to understand what the rest of the sentence is about. More important, we depend on seeing in a sequence of topics in a sequence of sentences what a whole passage is about.

Here's the point: You can help readers feel a passage is coherent in two ways:

1. You help them identify the topics of individual sentences quickly.
2. You make those topics a connected set.

This does *not* mean that you should begin every sentence with the same topic. It means only that to your readers, your string of topics must seem to be related.

DIAGNOSIS, ANALYSIS, AND REVISION

You can use those two principles of reading to help you diagnose, analyze, and revise your writing to make it coherent.

1. Diagnosis:
   a. Underline the first five or six words of every sentence in a whole passage, ignoring short introductory phrases such as *In the beginning,* or *For the most part.*

    b. If you can, underline the first five or six words of every CLAUSE.

2. Analysis:
    a. Read what you have underlined to be certain that it consists of a series of related topics.
    b. Even if you do see connections among those topics, think hard about whether your readers will.
    c. Decide what characters you want to focus on. Those characters, real or abstract, should provide most of your topics.
    d. Imagine the passage has a title. The words in that title are likely to identify what should be the topics of most of the sentences.

3. Revision:
    a. In most of your sentences, signal those topics by making them subjects of verbs.
    b. Locate most of those subjects close to the beginning of your sentences. Avoid obscuring topics by opening sentences with long introductory clauses or phrases.

THE SYSTEM OF SYSTEMS

We can integrate principles about old and new and a consistent topic string with the principles we offered about characters, subjects, actions, and verbs (I'll fill in the empty box in Lesson 6):

Fixed	Topic		
Variable	Short, simple, familiar	New, long, complex	
Fixed	Subject	Verb	————
Variable	Character	Action	————

That graphic structure says this: If you begin sentences and even clauses with information familiar to your readers, with phrases that are short, simple, and familiar, your readers are more likely to think you write both clearly and coherently. And no two units of information are shorter and simpler than the name of a character as a subject and that character's specific actions as verbs. If you focus on a limited set of familiar characters, real or abstract, you create a sequence of topics that your readers will think is consistent and therefore coherent. It's a mechanical principle, but it works.

Exercise 5.2

Revise these passages to give them consistent TOPIC STRINGS. First determine the characters, then their actions. Then start each sentence with a character, and let the sentence take you where it wants to go. In (1), words that could be consistent subject/topics are boldfaced.

1. **Vegetation** covers the earth, except for those areas continuously covered with ice or utterly scorched by continual heat. Richly fertilized plains and river valleys are places where **plants** grow most richly, but also at the edge of perpetual snow in high mountains. The ocean and its edges as well as in and around lakes and swamps are **densely vegetated.** The cracks of busy city sidewalks have **plants** in them as well as in seemingly barren cliffs. Before humans existed, the earth was covered with **vegetation,** and the earth will have **vegetation** long after evolutionary history swallows us up.

2. The power to create and communicate a new message to fit a new experience is not a competence animals have in their natural states. Their genetic code limits the number and kind of messages that they can communicate. Information about distance, direction, source, and richness of pollen in flowers constitutes the only information that can be communicated by bees, for example. A limited repertoire of messages delivered in the same way, for generation after generation, is characteristic of animals of the same species, in all significant respects.

3. The importance of language skills in children's problem-solving ability was stressed by Jones (1985) in his paper on children's thinking. Improvement in nonverbal problem solving occurred as a result of improvements in language

skills. The use of previously acquired language habits for problem articulation and activation of knowledge previously learned through language was the cause of better performance. Therefore, systematic practice in the verbal formulation of nonlinguistic problems prior to attempts at their solution might be an avenue for exploration in the enhancement of problem solving in general.

Exercise 5.3

Distort the topic strings in any paragraph in this book. Exchange your revision with someone who did the same, then rewrite each other's revisions back to the original.

Exercise 5.4

Find an old paper of yours and analyze its topic strings. Or exchange old papers with someone and critique each other's topics.

THE DIFFICULT CRAFT OF BEGINNING A SENTENCE WELL

How you begin a sentence affects how your readers read it. But beginning a sentence well is hard to do. In its first few words you may have to juggle several elements that delay your readers from getting to its topic, that element crucial to whether they judge your writing to be coherent. Here are some traits of prose that prevent readers from achieving that sense of coherence. Avoid them.

 ### Throat-clearing

We often start a sentence with METADISCOURSE that connects that sentence to the previous one, with transitions such as *and, but, therefore:*

And therefore . . .

We then add a second kind of metadiscourse that expresses our attitude toward what is coming, words such as *fortunately, perhaps, allegedly, it is important to note, for the most part, politically speaking:*

And therefore, politically speaking . . .

Then we might indicate time, place, or manner:

> And therefore, politically speaking, in Eastern states since 1980 ...

Only then do we get to the topic/subject:

> And, therefore, politically speaking, in Eastern states since 1980, <u>acid rain</u> has become a serious problem.

This kind of "throat-clearing" hinders readers from understanding not just what individual sentences are "about," but cumulatively what a whole passage is about. When you find a sentence with several words before its topic, revise:

✓   Since 1980, therefore, <u>acid rain in Eastern states</u> has become a serious political problem.

This next passage appeared in a college curriculum review that some thought quite good—at least those willing to slog through it. But it went largely unread because its style was so thick with metadiscourse at the beginnings of sentences that few of us could struggle past the first few pages. Here is an example (I have italicized metadiscourse):

> *We think it useful to provide some relatively detailed illustration* of the varied ways "corporate curricular personalities" organize themselves in programs. *We choose to feature as a central device in our presentation what are called* "introductory," "survey," or "foundational" courses. *It is important, however, to recognize* the diversity of what occurs in programs after the different initial survey courses. *But what is also suggested is that if one talks about* a program simply in terms of the intellectual strategies or techniques engaged in, *when these are understood in a general way,* it becomes difficult to distinguish many programs from others.

We get a more coherent passage if (1) we excise the metadiscourse from the beginnings of sentences, (2) constitute the topics out of just two central characters *curricula* and *programs,* and (3) most important, get those topic/subject/characters closer to the beginnings of their sentences:

✓   *We can understand* how <u>curricula</u> organize themselves into programs through their "introductory," "survey," or "foundational" courses.

After these introductory courses, <u>programs</u> seem to offer diverse curricula, but <u>they</u> are actually alike because <u>they</u> employ such similar
intellectual strategies that <u>they</u> become hard to distinguish.

Alleged Monotony

At this point, you may recall some advice about avoiding monotony—"Vary the way you begin your sentences." That's not bad advice, but if you follow it mechanically, you do more harm to your
style than good. To be sure, readers will feel that your prose is monotonous if you repeat the same topic relentlessly. The writer of
this next passage mistook advice about consistent topics not as a
diagnostic principle, but as an iron rule:

> "<u>Moral climate</u>" is created when an objectivized moral standard for
> treating people is accepted by others. <u>Moral climate</u> results from
> norms of behavior which are accepted by society whereby if people
> conform they are socially approved of, or if they don't they are
> shunned. In this light, <u>moral climate</u> acts as a reason to refrain
> from saying or doing things that the community does not support. <u>A
> moral climate</u> encourages individuals to conform to a moral stan-
> dard and apply that standard to their own circumstances.

That goes over the top in consistency.

The topics of most of your paragraphs will vary naturally, because most stories have more than one character. But even if you
do repeat the same topic a few times in the same paragraph, readers are less likely to find that repetition monotonous than will you.
When you reread your own prose, you are more likely to think
that a sequence of the same topics is monotonous, because you
will notice it. But readers are rarely bored by consistent topics,
unless they are so unvaryingly identical that they feel mechanical,
like that example above.

> ***Here's the point:*** If you find that through several consecu-
> tive sentences you have used exactly the same words for the
> same topic in the same position, your readers may in fact feel
> you have created a topic string that is too consistent. If so,
> revise: Use pronouns, paraphrase the topic, move it into
> a prepositional phrase. Be cautious though: most writers
> change topics too often.

Exercise 5.5

Now explain why the snowmobile-snow-mashed potatoes passage seems so incoherent.

Exercise 5.6

Revise these passages so that they have more consistent topic strings. Before you begin, decide who you think the main characters should be, then make those characters the subjects of as many sentences as you can. In the first example, I have underlined topics so that you can see how inconsistent they are.

1. Some potential threats exist in the modern mass communications media, though there are many significant advantages. If a powerful minority should happen to control it, public opinion could be manipulated through biased reporting. And while a wide knowledge of public affairs is a great advantage that results from national coverage, divisiveness and factionalism can be accentuated by connecting otherwise isolated, local conflicts into a single larger conflict as a result of showing that conflicts about the same issues are occurring in different places. It will always be true, of course, that human nature produces differences of opinion, but the threat of faction and division may be reinforced when national coverage publicizes uninformed opinions. According to some, education can suppress faction when the true nature of conflicts reaches the public through the media, but history has shown that as much coverage is given to people who encourage conflict as to people who try to remove conflict.

2. Some sort of palace revolt or popular revolution plagued seven out of eight reigns of the Romanov line after Peter the Great. In 1722, achievement by merit was made the basis of succession when the principle of heredity was terminated by Peter. This resulted in many tsars' not appointing a successor before dying, including Peter. Ivan VI was less than two months old when appointed by Czarina Anna, but Elizabeth, daughter of Peter the Great, defeated Anna and ascended to the throne in 1741. Succession not

dependent upon authority resulted in the boyars' regularly disputing who was to become sovereign. Male primogeniture became the law in 1797 when Paul I codified the law of succession. But conspirators strangled him, one of whom was probably his son, Alexander I.

3. Many issues other than science, domestic politics in particular, faced Truman when he was considering the Oppenheimer committee's recommendation to stop the hydrogen bomb project. A Sino-Soviet bloc had been proclaimed by Russia and China, so the Cold War was becoming an issue. Support for Truman's foreign policy was shrinking among Republican leaders in Congress. And the first Russian atom bomb test made the public demand a strong response from him. Truman's conclusion that he could not afford letting the public think that Russia had been allowed to be first in developing the most powerful weapon yet was inevitable. In retrospect, the risk in the Oppenheimer recommendation was worth taking according to some historians, but the political issues that Truman had to face were too powerful to ignore.

Exercise 5.7

Revise the "moral climate" passage (p. 112). First, cut redundancy. Then revise topics so that the passage does not repeat exactly the same topic in the same position in every sentence.

Exercise 5.8

At the beginning of this passage from his essay, "Stranger in the Village," James Baldwin makes the cathedral at Chartres the topic and metaphorical agency. Here is his first sentence:

> **The cathedral at Chartres,** I have said, says something to the people of this village which **it** cannot say to me, but it is important to understand that **this cathedral** says something to me which **it** cannot say to them.

But in the second sentence, he switches the topic/subjects to the villagers and then to himself:

Perhaps **they** are struck by the power of the spires, the glory of the windows; but **they** have known God, after all, longer than **I** have known him, and in a different way, and **I** am terrified . . . .

Revise this passage so that you change the sequence of topics in a variety of ways. Here is one new version:

I have said that **I** hear something from the cathedral at Chartres that **the people** of this village do not hear, but it is important to understand that . . . .

How do they differ? What are the consequences? Here is the whole passage:

The cathedral at Chartres, I have said, says something to the people of this village which it cannot say to me, but it is important to understand that this cathedral says something to me which it cannot say to them. Perhaps they are struck by the power of the spires, the glory of the windows; but they have known God, after all, longer than I have known him, and in a different way, and I am terrified by the slippery bottomless well to be found in the crypt, down which heretics were hurled to death, and by the obscene, inescapable gargoyles jutting out of the stone and seeming to say that God and the devil can never be divorced. I doubt that the villagers think of the devil when they face a cathedral because they have never been identified with the devil. But I must accept the status which myth, if nothing else, gives me in the West before I can hope to change the myth.

What does this exercise suggest about any "natural" connection between characters and topics? What implications does this have for how we understand who's responsible for what actions?

ILLUSORY COHESION

I've described what we can call *organic cohesion*—the movement readers feel when they move easily from one sentence to the next, without their ever noticing how consistently the information in each sentence carries them from old to new to old to new. Of course, they must also see some logical connection between the sentences as well: premise and conclusion, coordination, statement and contradiction, and so on.

Some writers try to create that kind of logical cohesion by lacing their prose with logical conjunctions like *thus, therefore, however,* and so on, regardless of whether those words signal any genuine logical connections. Here is one such passage:

Because the press is the major medium of interaction between the president and the people, how it portrays him influences his popularity. *Therefore,* it should report on the president objectively. Both reporters and the president are human, *however,* subject to error and favoritism. *Also,* people act differently in public than they do in private. *Hence,* to understand a person, it is important to know the whole person, his environment, upbringing, and education. *Indeed,* from the correspondence with his family, we can learn much about Harry S. Truman, our thirty-third president.

Those connectors are virtually meaningless, creating only the illusion of cohesion. The writer dropped them in because he thought they would make the passage hang together more tightly. They don't.

Experienced writers rely more on the intrinsic logical flow of their prose than on connecting devices like these. They are particularly careful not to depend on connecting words like *and, also, moreover, another,* and so on, words that say simply *Here's one more thing.* You need a *but* or *however* when you contradict or qualify what you just said, and you can use a *therefore, consequently,* or *as a result* to wind up a line of reasoning. But you will not go far wrong if you avoid beginning more than a few sentences a page with words like these. If the logic of your ideas is sound, your readers probably don't need them.

SUMMING UP

We can sum up this chapter in this model:

Fixed	Topic	
Variable	Short, simple, familiar	New, long, complex
Fixed	Subject	Verb	———
Variable	Character	Action	———

And from it, we can derive these two principles:

1. Begin sentences with short simple words and phrases communicating information that appeared in previous sentences, or with knowledge that you can assume you and your reader share.

The number of dead in the Civil War exceeded all other wars in American history. <u>A reason for the lingering animosity between North and South today</u> is <u>the memory of this terrible carnage</u>.

✓   Of all the wars in American history, none has exceeded the Civil War in the number of dead. <u>The memory of this terrible carnage</u> is <u>one reason for the lingering animosity between North and South today</u>.

Example

2. Through a series of sentences that you want your readers to understand as a coherent, focused passage, keep your topics short and reasonably consistent:

✓   In the first phase of this study, <u>we</u> will examine how <u>Asian companies</u> compete with American companies in the Pacific region. <u>We</u> will examine in particular labor costs and their ability to introduce new products quickly. <u>We</u> will develop from this study a <u>plan that</u> will show <u>American industry</u> how to restructure its facilities.

LESSON SIX

Emphasis

In the end is my beginning.
T. S. ELIOT

The end of a matter is better than its beginning.
ECCLESIASTES 7:8

Beginning and end shake hands with each other.
GERMAN PROVERB

All's well that ends well.
WILLIAM SHAKESPEARE

One of the most difficult things is the first paragraph. I have spent many months on a first paragraph, and once I get it, the rest just comes out very easily. In the first paragraph you solve most of the problem with your book. The theme is defined, the style, the tone.
GABRIEL GARCIA MARQUEZ

If we can write sentences with short SUBJECT/TOPICS that name a few central CHARACTERS and then join them to strong VERBS, we stand a good chance of getting everything else in a sentence in the right place. But just as *choosing* the first few words of a sentence wisely is important, so is our choice of the last few, because how we end a sentence determines how readers' judge not only the clarity of our prose, but its emphasis and strength. In this lesson, we'll address clarity first, then emphasis, then how emphasis can contribute to a kind of cohesion even more global than the cohesion we gain from consistent topics.

CLARITY

Reading a sentence is like jumping a ditch: If you have to leap from a dead stop, you have a problem, but if you can get a running start, you have a better chance of clearing it. In the same way, if readers can get up some momentum in the beginning of a sentence, they can get through complicated material at the end more easily. Compare these two sentences:

> 1a. A sociometric and actuarial analysis of Social Security revenues and disbursements for the last six decades to determine possible changes in deficit projection methods is the motivation for this study.

> ✓   1b. In this study, we analyze Social Security's revenues and disbursements for the last six decades, using sociometric and actuarial criteria to determine possible changes in how to project deficits.

When we start (1a), we struggle with the first five words, and then we have to go nineteen more before we get to a verb, making the whole sentence an effort. On the other hand, after we start the second sentence, we are sixteen words into it before we hit a word that might slow us up, but by that time we have enough reading momentum to get through it. In the first sentence, we hit all the complexity—both syntactic and semantic—at the beginning; in the second, we don't hit real complexity until close to the end.

There are two kinds of complexity that we ought to put at the end of a sentence:

- Long and complicated PHRASES and CLAUSES
- New information, particularly technical terms that readers might find unfamiliar

Syntactic Complexity

Which of these two passages do you prefer?

> 1a. Lincoln's claim that the Civil War was God's punishment of both North and South for slavery appears in the last part of the speech.
>
> ✓ 1b. In the last part of his speech, Lincoln claims that God gave the Civil War to both North and South as punishment for slavery.

We prefer (1b) because even those words at the beginning are individually easy to understand, we don't like to start a sentence like (1a) with something as complex as that sixteen-word subject. We can deal with the same information more easily when it is parceled out into smaller, more easily comprehended pieces, with the most complicated ones at the end.

We can integrate that principle with the others we've worked on. Recall that the variable boxes reflect the *quality* of information (we'll fill in that upper-right box in a few pages):

Fixed	Topic	
Variable	Short, simple, familiar	New, long, complex

Fixed	Subject	Verb	———
Variable	Character	Action	———

Units of information that are short and simple go first; units of information that are long and complex go last.

Unfamiliar Language

Readers have a problem with a second kind of complexity that has less to do with unpacking long complicated phrases and clauses than with the mental effort of dealing with unfamiliar technical terms. Compare these next two passages:

> 1a. The role of calcium blocker drugs in the control of cardiac irregularity can be seen through an understanding of the role of calcium in the activation of muscle groups. The regulatory proteins

actin, myosin, tropomyosin, and troponin make up the sarcomere, the basic unit of muscle contraction. Its thick filament is made up of ATPase, an energy-producing protein myosin, while actin, tropomyosin, and troponin make up its thin filament. Interaction of myosin and actin trigger muscle contraction.

✓ 1b. When a muscle contracts, it uses calcium. We must therefore understand how calcium influences contraction to understand how cardiac irregularity is controlled by drugs called calcium blockers. The basic unit of muscle contraction is the sarcomere. It has two filaments, one thin and one thick, consisting of four proteins that regulate contraction: actin, myosin, tropomyosin, and troponin. Muscles contract when the protein in the thin filament, actin, interacts with the protein in the thick filament, the energy-producing or ATPase protein myosin . . . .

Both passages have the same technical terms, but if you don't know much about muscle chemistry, you can read (1b) more easily than you can (1a).

They differ in two ways. First, some information that is only implicit in (1a) is explicitly stated in (1b):

1a. . . . and troponin make up the sarcomere, the basic unit of muscle contraction. Its thick filament is made up of . . . .

✓ 1b. The basic unit of muscle contraction is the sarcomere. It has two filaments, one thick and one thin . . . .

But I revised (1a) in one more important way: I moved the unfamiliar technical terms at the beginnings of their sentences closer to their ends (the new information is boldfaced):

1a. The role of **calcium blocker drugs** in the control of **cardiac irregularity** can be seen through an understanding of the role of calcium in the activation of muscle groups. **The regulatory proteins actin, myosin, tropomyosin, and troponin** make up the **sarcomere,** the basic unit of muscle contraction.

1b. When a muscle contracts, it uses **calcium.** We must therefore understand how calcium influences muscle contraction in order to understand how **cardiac irregularity is controlled by drugs called calcium blockers.** The basic unit of muscle contraction is the **sarcomere.** It has two filaments, one thin and one thick, consisting of four proteins that regulate contraction: **actin, myosin, tropomyosin, and troponin.**

These principles apply to prose intended not just for rank novices, but even for the most advanced professional readers, as this next passage from the *New England Journal of Medicine* suggests. The writer begins the first sentence with technical terms, but he had used them before, so they were familiar. He then constructed the second sentence specifically to get a new technical term at its end:

> The incubation of peripheral-blood lymphocytes with a lymphokine, interleukin-2, generates lymphoid cells that can lyse fresh, noncultured, natural-killer-cell-resistant tumor cells but not normal cells. *We term these cells* **lymphokine-activated killer (LAK) cells.**

(Note also in that last sentence the first-person *we:* **We** *call these cells . . . .*)

> *Here's the point:*   When you use an unfamiliar technical term for the first time, especially one that your readers might find difficult, put that term not at the beginning of its sentence, in its topic, but at the end.

EMPHASIS AND STRESS

We look at the last few words in a sentence for new and complex information, but those last words also determine whether we feel that prose is not just clear, but emphatic. In the last lesson, we said that an important position in the psychological geography of a sentence was its first few words, because they announce the topic of a sentence, its psychological subject (see pp. 104–05).

Another important "position" in the psychological geography of a sentence is at its end. You can sense that position when you hear your voice naturally rise and fall on the last word or two of a sentence as you stress one syllable more strongly than you do the others:

> . . . more strongly than you do the $^{6-}$-thers.

You have the same experience when reading silently: Just as you imagine the content of a sentence in your "mind's eye," so you hear the sound of a sentence in your "mind's ear." And what you want to hear at the ends of sentences is an emphasis that falls on the words that deserve it.

We'll call this climactic part of a sentence its STRESS. We can now add that element to our last box.

Fixed	Topic		Stress
Variable	Short, simple, familiar	New, long, complex	
Fixed	Subject	Verb	———
Variable	Character	Action	———

How you manage the words in that concluding stress position goes a long way toward establishing the voice your readers hear.

Compare these synonymous passages. One of them was written to blame an American president for failing to deal effectively with the former Soviet Union on the issue of arms control. The other is mine; I revised it to make it seem to blame instead the then-Soviet Union. You can tell which is which if you imagine thumping your finger on your desk as you read the boldface words at the ends of the sentences:

1a. The administration has blurred an issue central to arms control, **the issue of verification.** Irresponsible charges, innuendo, and leaks have submerged **serious problems with Soviet compliance.** The objective, instead, should be not to exploit these concerns in order to further poison our relations, repudiate existing agreements, or, worse still, terminate arms control altogether, but to **insist on compliance and clarify questionable Soviet behavior.**

1b. The issue of verification—so central to arms control—has been **blurred by the administration.** Serious problems with Soviet compliance have been submerged in **irresponsible charges, innuendo, and leaks.** The objective, instead, should be to clarify questionable Soviet behavior and insist on compliance—not to exploit these concerns in order to **further poison our relations,**

repudiate existing agreements, or, worse still, terminate arms control altogether.

Here's the point: Readers assign special emphasis to the words they hear under this final stress, at the end of a sentence, and what they hear emphasized, they take to be rhetorically significant. So just as readers look for topics, so do they listen for stress. Just as you look at the first few words of a sentence to evaluate its topical coherence, look at the last few words of your sentences to see whether you have in fact ended them on the words and phrases that deserve the most rhetorical emphasis.

MANAGING ENDINGS FOR EMPHASIS

If you decide you didn't get the right words under the right stress, you have to revise. Here are some ways.

Three Tactical Revisions

1. Trim the end.

   Sociobiologists now make the provocative claim that our genes control our social behavior in the way we act in situations we find **around us every day.**

   Since *social behavior* means *the way we act,* we can drop everything after *behavior:*

   ✓ Sociobiologists now make the provocative claim that our genes **control our social behavior.**

2. Shift peripheral ideas to the left.

   The data offered to establish the existence of ESP are too weak to make us believers **for the most part.**

   ✓ **For the most part,** the data offered to establish the existence of ESP are too weak to **make us believers.**

   Particularly avoid ending with anticlimactic METADISCOURSE: Job opportunities are good and getting better in computer programming, **it must be remembered.**

   ✓ **It must be remembered** that job opportunities in computer programming are **good and getting better.**

3. Shift important ideas to the right.

A more common way you can manage what you stress is by moving rhetorically salient information to the right, into the stress of a sentence.

Questions relating to the ethics of withdrawing intravenous fluid are **more important** [than something else just mentioned].

More important [than something else just mentioned] are **questions relating to the ethics of withdrawing intravenous fluid.**

Seven Syntactic Devices

1. Passives (for the last time)

The passive voice exists to let you move elements around in a sentence so that you can get the words you want into topics and stresses. If in the sentences following either of these next two, you wanted to develop the concept of *genes influencing behavior,* readers would judge the second to be more helpful than the first, because it ends with that concept:

Sociobiologists now make the provocative claim that our **genes** influence$_{active}$ aspects of our behavior that we think are learned. **Our genes,** for example, seem to **determine** ...

In this next pair of passages, the passive would let us move *by our genes* to the end of one sentence so that it connects closely to *our genes* in the next.

✓ Sociobiologists now make the provocative claim that aspects of our behavior that we think are learned are in fact influenced$_{passive}$ by our **genes. Our genes,** for example, seem to determine ...

2. *There*

Some editors discourage *there is/there are* constructions. But if you avoid them entirely, you lose a device that lets you shift a phrase toward the end of its sentence and thereby emphasize it:

Several syntactic devices let you manage where in a sentence you locate units of new information.

✓ **There are** several syntactic devices that let you manage where in a sentence you locate units of new information.

You can use this device at the beginning of a paragraph to introduce concepts that you develop in sentences that follow (see p. 62).

3. *What-shift*

    This is another device that lets you shift a part of the sentence to the right:

    We need **a monetary policy** that will end wild fluctuations in money supply, unemployment, and high rates of inflation.

✓ *What* we need *is* a **monetary policy** that will end wild fluctuations in money supply, unemployment, and high rates of inflation.

4. *It*-shift 1

    This device simultaneously singles out a topic and throws added weight on the stress. Compare:

    In 1933 we experienced a depression that almost wrecked our democratic system of government.

✓ *It was* **in 1933** *that* we experienced a depression that almost wrecked our democratic system of government.

5. *It*-shift 2

    When you create a subject out of a long and complex introductory clause, you can move that clause to the end of the sentence by starting with an *it:*

    That oil prices must eventually rise to a level that could be dictated by OPEC once seemed inevitable.

✓ *It* once seemed inevitable **that oil prices must eventually rise to a level that could be dictated by OPEC.**

    The cost to the reader of these five devices is a few extra words, so use them sparingly.

6. *Not only X, but Y,* (as well)

    In this next pair, note how the *but* emphasizes the last element of the pair:

    We must clarify these issues and **develop trust.**

✓ We must *not only* clarify these issues, *but* **develop trust** *as well.*

Unless you have reason to emphasize the negative, end with the positive:

The point is to highlight our success, **not to emphasize our failures.**

The objective is not to emphasize our failures but **to highlight our success.**

7. Repeated words and pronoun substitution

    This is a fine point: Sometimes a sentence will end flatly if you repeat a word that you used just a few words before. When you repeat that word at the end of a sentence, your voice carries less emphasis, and it drops at the end of a sentence. You can hear that drop if you read aloud those last two sentences and this one. In that case, instead of repeating the noun use a pronoun so that the reader will hear emphasis on at least the word before the pronoun. And that sentence is a candidate for revision.

> Sometimes a sentence will seem to end flatly because you can't avoid using a word at the end of a sentence that you used just a few words before or even at the end of the **previous** *one*. But when you repeat that word there, your voice carries less emphasis, and it **drops.** In that case, if instead of repeating the noun you use a pronoun, the reader will at least hear emphasis on the word just **before** *it*.

Exercise 6.1

Revise these sentences so that the concepts that deserve emphasis appear at the end of the sentence, in the stressed position. Then eliminate wordiness, unnecessary nominalization, etc. In the first five, I have boldfaced elements that I think should be stressed.

1. The judiciary's tendency **to rewrite the Constitution** is the biggest danger to the Republic, in my opinion, at least.
2. A new political philosophy that could affect our society **well into the twenty-first century** may emerge from these studies.
3. There are **limited** opportunities for teachers to work with individual students in large American colleges and universities.
4. As used in the industry, "turnkey" means responsibility for **the satisfactory performance of a piece of equipment** in addition to the manufacture and installation of that equipment, according to everyone who understands the matter.
5. **Several upper and lower eyelid reconstruction evaluation studies** are presented with the aforementioned summary discussions for your general information.
6. Building suburban housing developments in floodplains has led to the existence of extensive and widespread flooding and economic disaster in parts of our country in recent years, it is now clear.

7. The teacher who makes an assignment of a long final term paper at the end of the semester and who then gives only a grade at the end and nothing else such as a critical comment is a common complaint among students at the college level.

8. Renting textbooks rather than buying them for basic required courses such as mathematics, foreign languages, and English, whose textbooks do not experience change from year to year, is feasible, however, economically speaking.

9. The outcome of the war was changed as a result of an event that occurred at about this same point in time, on the other hand.

10. Guidelines in the MLA style sheet and the NCTE guidelines for the nonsexist use of language should be adhered to by speakers and writers, to the best of their ability.

Exercise 6.2

Revise these passages so that their sentences begin with appropriate topics and end with appropriate emphasis.

1. The story of King Lear and his daughters was a popular one during the reign of Queen Elizabeth. At least a dozen available books offered the story to anyone wishing to read it, by the time Elizabeth died. The characters were undeveloped in most of these stories, however, making the story a simple narrative that stated an obvious moral. When he began work on Lear, perhaps his greatest tragedy, Shakespeare must have had several versions of this story available to him. He turned the characters into credible human beings with complex motives, however, even though they were based on the stock figures of legend.

2. Whether the date an operation intends to close down might be part of management's "duty to disclose" during contract bargaining is the issue here, it would appear. The minimization of conflict is the central rationale for the duty that management has to bargain in good faith. In order to allow the union to put forth proposals on behalf of its members, companies are obligated to disclose major

changes in an operation during bargaining, though the case law is scanty on this matter.

3. Athens' catastrophic Sicilian Invasion is the most important event in Thucydides' *History of the Peloponnesian War.* Three-quarters of the history is devoted to setting up the invasion because of this. Through the step-by-step decline in Athenian society that Thucydides describes, we can see how Thucydides chose to anticipate the Sicilian Invasion. The inevitability that we associate with the tragic drama is the basic reason for the need to anticipate the invasion.

This next passage will seem difficult because it deals with a strange subject. But even if you don't understand the words, you can still make it more readable.

4. Mucosal and vascular permeability altered by a toxin elaborated by the vibrio is a current hypothesis to explain this kind of severe condition. Changes in small capillaries located near the basal surface of the epithelial cells, and the appearance of numerous microvesicles in the cytoplasm of the mucosal cells is evidence in favor of this hypothesis. Hydrodynamic transport of fluid into the interstitial tissue and then through the mucosa into the lumen of the gut is believed to depend on altered capillary permeability.

Revise this next passage so that the most important data appear consistently at the ends of their sentences.

5. Changes in revenues are as follows. An increase to $56,792 from $32,934, a net increase of approximately 73 percent, was realized July 1–August 31 in the Ohio and Kentucky areas. In the Indiana and Illinois areas there was in the same period a 10 percent increase of $15,370, from $153,281 to $168,651. However, a decrease to $190,580 from $200,102, or 5 percent, occurred in the Wisconsin and Minnesota regions in almost the same period of time.

Exercise 6.3

Find a famous speech or other highly charged piece of rhetoric and read it aloud, thumping your finger on the last few words of every sentence. Do the words you thump feel like the words that should be thumped? If not, revise the sentence so that you do thump on the words that should receive the most emphasis. Try it on a speech by Martin Luther King, who understood how to end a sentence well.

TOPICS, STRESS, AND THEMES

There is one more function that the stress of certain sentences performs, a rather specialized one, but important to helping readers sense the coherence of a whole passage. As we saw in the last lesson, readers take the clearest topic to be a short noun phrase that comes early in a sentence, usually as its subject. That's why most of us judge this next paragraph to be out of focus: Its sentences do not open from any consistent point of view. Before you read this passage, just skim the underlined topics. Then read it (I double underline topics of main clauses, single underline topics of subordinate clauses):

> Since the discovery that <u>one factor in Alzheimer's disease</u> might be genetic, <u>great strides in its early and accurate diagnosis</u> have occurred in recent years. <u>Senility in an older patient who seemed to be losing touch with reality, an entirely different condition</u>, was often confused with Alzheimer's not too long ago. <u>Blood chemistry and genetic clues</u> have become new and more reliable tests to diagnose it in the past few years, however. <u>The risk of human tragedy of another kind</u>, though, has resulted from the increasing accuracy of these procedures: Long before the appearance of any of its overt symptoms, <u>physicians</u> may be able to predict Alzheimer's. At that point, <u>an apparently healthy person</u> could be devastated by such an early diagnosis.

If I revise that passage to make the topics more consistent, I make it more coherent:

> In recent years, since the discovery that <u>one factor in Alzheimer's disease</u> might be genetic, <u>researchers</u> have made great strides in its early and accurate diagnosis. Not too long ago, when <u>a physician</u> examined an older patient <u>who</u> seemed out of touch with reality, <u>she</u> had to guess whether <u>that person</u> had Alzheimer's or was senile, an entirely different syndrome. In the past few years, however, <u>new and more reliable tests</u> have focused on blood chemistry and genetic clues. In <u>the accuracy of these new tests</u>, however, lies the risk of human tragedy of another kind: <u>Physicians</u> may be able to predict Alzheimer's long before its overt appearance, but <u>such an early diagnosis</u> could psychologically devastate an apparently healthy person.

Those topics now focus on researcher/physicians and testing.

But I did something else that was a bit more subtle, but nevertheless crucially important to making that revision seem more coherent. I managed the form of the first sentence so that its stress introduced words that captured what the rest of the whole paragraph was globally about: *identifying Alzheimer's disease.* It's a small change with large consequences:

> In recent years, since the discovery that one factor in Alzheimer's disease might be genetic, researchers have made **great strides in its early and accurate diagnosis.**

In fact, those last words could have been the title of that paragraph, because they introduce the key concepts around which the whole passage is organized.

Look at the passage again: First look at just the boldface words; they are all associated with testing. Then look at the italicized words; they all refer to concepts associated with Alzheimer's (the topics are still single and double underlined):

> In recent years, since the discovery that <u>one factor in Alzheimer's disease</u> might be genetic, <u>researchers</u> have made **great strides in** *its* **early diagnosis.** Not too long ago, when <u>a physician</u> **examined** <u>an older patient who</u> seemed *out of touch with reality,* <u>she</u> **had to guess** whether <u>that person</u> had *Alzheimer's* or was *senile,* an entirely different *syndrome.* In the past few years, however, <u>new and more reliable</u> **tests** have focused on blood chemistry and genetic clues. In <u>the accuracy of these new</u> **tests**, however, lies the risk of *human tragedy* of another kind: <u>Physicians</u> may be able to **predict** *Alzheimer's* long before its overt appearance, but <u>such an early and accurate</u> **diagnosis** could psychologically *devastate* an otherwise *healthy person.*

This passage now "hangs together" not for just one reason, but for three:

- It has a consistent topic string consisting of patients, physicians, and tests.
- Running through it are two other strings of words that focus our attention on tests and on concepts related to Alzheimer's disease.
- And no less important, the opening sentence prepares us to notice those concepts by emphasizing them in its stress position.

And that's a third seemingly minor but actually quite important function of the stress position: You can use the stress positions of sentences that introduce a passage to highlight words that you want your readers to notice in what follows. This principle applies not just to sentences that introduce individual paragraphs, but also to introductions to passages of any length: Locate at the end of those sentences the words that announce the key concepts that you intend to develop in the rest of the passage.

We need a general term to name concepts that run through a whole passage. We will call them THEMES. Themes are the related sets of key concepts that run throughout a passage, a section, or a whole. Topics are one kind of theme; the other kind consists of related words other than topics.

Here's the point: Readers depend on your themes to create a sense of coherence in a passage. You can help them identify these themes in two ways:

- Repeat them as topics of sentences, usually as subjects.
- Repeat them elsewhere in a passage, as nouns, verbs, and adjectives.

Readers notice those themes if in the sentence by which you introduce a passage, you locate them toward its end, close to its stress position.

Exercise 6.4

In Lesson 5, you were asked to revise a few passages according to the old/new principle (p. 103, 109, and p. 113). Look at your revisions again from the point of view of the two principles of cohesion and coherence. Look particularly at the opening sentences of those passages and if necessary revise them.

Exercise 6.5

Here are three opening sentences and the rest of a paragraph that each of those sentences might introduce. Which introductory sentence best sets up the ideas that follow? In this case, assume that the reader would be familiar with the characters—Russian rulers. The best of the three sentences will in its last ten or so words highlight the new concepts that you should associate with those rulers. You'll have to read the passage to identify the key concepts that hold it together.

1. The next century the situation changed, because disputes over succession to the throne caused some sort of palace revolt or popular revolution in **seven out of eight reigns of the Romanov line after Peter the Great.**

2. The next century the situation changed, because after Peter the Great seven out of eight reigns of the Romanov line were **plagued by turmoil over disputed succession to the throne.**

3. Because turmoil over disputed succession to the throne plagued seven out of eight reigns of the Romanov line after Peter the Great, **the situation changed in the next century.**

The problems began in 1722, when Tsar Peter the Great passed a law of succession that terminated the principle of succession by heredity and required the sovereign to appoint a successor when he died. But because many of the Tsars, including Peter, died before they named successors, those who aspired to rule had no authority by appointment, and so their succession was often disputed by the boyars, lower-level aristocrats. There was turmoil even when successors were appointed. In 1740, Ivan VI was adopted by Czarina Anna Ivanovna and named as her successor at age two months, but his succession was challenged by Elizabeth, daughter of Peter the Great. In 1741, she defeated Anna and ascended to the throne herself. In 1797 Paul tried to eliminate these disputes by codifying a law: primogeniture in the male line. But turmoil continued. Paul was strangled by conspirators, one of whom was probably his son, Alexander I.

THE SYSTEM OF SYSTEMS

We are beginning to see the complexity of an ordinary English sentence. Each one is more than the sum of its parts; it is a system of systems whose parts we can match or mismatch, to the benefit or detriment of our readers' understanding. That system of systems implies this set of principles for diagnosing and revising sentences:

Fixed	Topic			Stress
Variable	Short, simple, familiar		New, long, complex	
Fixed	Subject	Verb	———	
Variable	Character	Action	———	

To the degree that your sentences reflect these patterns, your readers will judge you to be a clear and direct writer. But again, do not try to apply these principles *as* you write; use them to diagnose and revise *what* you have written.

But after you do that, step back from the details and *listen* to your prose. Have someone read it to you. Try to hear the voice it projects, because the voice your readers hear helps define your character. Some teachers of writing want to make that voice a moral choice between insincerity and authenticity. But we all speak in many voices, no one of which is more or less authentic or real. When you want to be authoritative and aloof, then that's the voice you should choose to project. When you want to be businesslike and direct, then choose that voice. Your job as a writer is to choose the voice that you want your readers to hear. That's no more insincere than choosing how you dress and behave. Some writers learn to make those choices naturally, without thought or instruction. The rest of us have to work at it.

SUMMING UP

1. Use the stress position of a sentence to introduce long, complex, or otherwise difficult to process material, particularly unfamiliar technical terms and new information.

> **A determination of involvement of lipid-linked saccarides in the assembly of the oligasaccharide chains**

of ovalbumin in vivo was the principal aim of this
study. *In vitro* **and** *in vivo* **studies utilizing oviduct
membrane preparations and oviduct slices and the
anitibiotic tunicamycin** were undertaken to accomplish this.

✓   The principal aim of this study was to determine how
**lipid-linked saccarides are involved in the assembly
of the oligasaccaride chains of ovalbumin** *in vivo*.
To accomplish this, studies were undertaken *in vitro*
and *in vivo*, **utilizing the antibiotic tunicamycin on
preparations of oviduct membrane and on oviduct
slices.**

2. Use the stress position of a sentence to put rhetorical emphasis on words that you want your readers to hear emphasized
   in their minds' ear.

   The administration has blurred an issue central to arms
   control, **the issue of verification.** Irresponsible
   charges, innuendo, and leaks have submerged **serious
   problems with Soviet compliance.**

   The issue of verification—so central to arms control—
   has been **blurred by the administration.** Serious problems with Soviet compliance have been submerged in **irresponsible charges, innuendo, and leaks.**

3. Use the end of the sentence that introduces a passage to
   announce the key concepts that the rest of the passage will
   develop:

   In recent years, since the discovery that <u>one factor in
   Alzheimer's disease</u> might be genetic, <u>researchers</u> have
   made **great strides in its early and accurate diagnosis.** Not too long ago, when <u>a physician</u> **examined** <u>an
   older patient who</u> seemed *out of touch with reality,* <u>she</u>
   had to guess whether <u>that person</u> had *Alzheimer's* or
   was *senile,* an entirely different *syndrome.* In the past
   few years, however, <u>new and more reliable</u> **tests** have focused on blood chemistry and genetic clues. In <u>the accuracy of these new</u> **tests**, however, lies the risk of *human
   tragedy* of another kind: <u>Physicians</u> may be able to **predict** *Alzheimer's* long before its overt appearance, but
   <u>such an early</u> **diagnosis** could psychologically *devastate*
   an otherwise *healthy person.*

PART III

Grace

There are two sorts of eloquence; the one indeed scarce deserves the name of it, which consists chiefly in laboured and polished periods, an over-curious and artificial arrangement of figures, tinseled over with a gaudy embellishment of words.... The other sort of eloquence is quite the reverse to this, and which may be said to be the true characteristic of the holy Scriptures; where the eloquence does not arise from a laboured and farfetched elocution, but from a surprising mixture of simplicity and majesty.

LAURENCE STERNE

LESSON SEVEN

Concision

I believe more in the scissors than I do in the pencil.
TRUMAN CAPOTE

Often I think writing is sheer paring away of oneself leaving always something thinner, barer, more meager.
F. SCOTT FITZGERALD

If you require a practical rule of me, I will present you with this: Whenever you feel an impulse to perpetrate a piece of exceptionally fine writing, obey it—wholeheartedly—and delete it before sending your manuscript to press. Murder your darlings.
ARTHUR QUILLER-COUCH

I write for those who judge of books, not by the quantity, but by the quality of them: who ask not how long, but how good they are? I spare both my reader's time and my own, by couching my sense in as few words as I can.
JOHN WESLEY

The ability to simplify means to eliminate the unnecessary so that the necessary may speak.
HANS HOFMANN

To a Snail: If "compression is the first grace of style," you have it.
MARIANNE MOORE

CLARITY, GRACE, AND CONCISION

We are a long way toward clarity when we can match CHARACTERS and ACTIONS to SUBJECTS and VERBS, and even further when we get the right characters into topics and can STRESS the right words. But even when we can do all that, readers may still think that prose is a long way from graceful if they read this:

> In my personal opinion, it is necessary that all of us not ignore the opportunity to think over in a careful manner each and every suggestion that others offer us.

That writer matched agents and actions with subjects and verbs, but in more words than needed: Every opinion is personal, so we don't need *personal.* And since this statement is opinion, we don't need *in my opinion,* either. *It is necessary* means *should. We* implies *all. Think over* means *consider. In a careful* manner means *carefully. Each and every* is redundant. A suggestion is by definition offered, so neither do we need *that others offer us.* And since the negative *not ignore* negates itself, why not express the same idea affirmatively? What's left is more concise:

✓   We must consider each suggestion carefully.

Though not elegant, that sentence has, at least according to Marianne Moore, style's first grace—that of compression, or as we'll call it, concision. Concision, though, is only the first grace of style. Once a sentence is concise, we can see its shape, and only if its shape is satisfying can clarity and grace give us—and our readers—great pleasure. In this lesson, we focus on this first grace of style—concision; in the next, on shape; in Lesson 9, on elegance.

When I edited that sentence about suggestions, I used five principles of concision:

1. Delete words that mean little or nothing.
2. Delete words that repeat the meaning of other words.
3. Delete words whose meaning a reader can infer.
4. Replace a phrase with a word.
5. Change negatives to affirmatives.

Unfortunately, though these principles are easy to state, they are hard to follow, because we can prune wordiness only by inching our way through every sentence, word by word, cutting here, compressing there, and that's labor-intensive. These five principles, though, can guide us in that work.

1. DELETE MEANINGLESS WORDS

Some words are verbal tics that we use as unconsciously as we clear our throats:

kind of	actually	particular	really	certain	various
virtually	individual	basically	generally	given	practically

> Productivity **actually** depends on **certain** factors that **basically** involve psychology more than **any particular** technology.

✓ Productivity depends on psychology more than on technology.

Leave yourself time to skim for words like these.

2. DELETE DOUBLED WORDS

Early in the history of English, writers began to pair a borrowed French or Latin word with a native English one, because borrowed words sounded more learned. Now they are just redundant. Among the common pairs:

full and complete	hope and trust	any and all
true and accurate	each and every	basic and fundamental
hopes and desires	first and foremost	various and sundry

Leave yourself time to skim for words like these, as well, and delete one of them.

3. DELETE WHAT READERS CAN INFER

This is the most common redundancy and the hardest to identify, because it comes in many forms.

Redundant Modifiers

Often, the meaning of a word implies its modifier:

> Do not try to *anticipate* **in advance** those events **that will completely** *revolutionize* **society** because **past** *history* shows that it is the

eventual *outcome* of minor events that **unexpectedly** *surprises* us more.

✓ Do not try to anticipate revolutionary events because history shows that the outcome of minor events surprises us more.

Some common redundancies:

completely finish	past history	various different
basic fundamentals	future plans	personal beliefs
final outcome	true facts	consensus of opinion
terrible tragedy	free gift	each individual

A common redundancy is a preposition implied by its verb:

continue **on**   return back **to**   penetrate **into**   circle **around**

Redundant Categories

Every word implies its general category, so you can usually cut a word that names its category. Compare:

During that *period* **of time,** the *membrane* **area** became *pink* **in color** and *shiny* **in appearance.**

✓ During that *period,* the *membrane* became *pink* and *shiny*.

Sometimes, when you eliminate the category, you have to change an ADJECTIVE into an ADVERB:

The holes must be aligned in an *accurate* **manner.**

✓ The holes must be aligned *accurately*.

Sometimes you must change an adjective into a NOUN:

The *educational* **process** and *public recreational* **activities** are the responsibility of the *county* **government.**

✓ The *county* is responsible for *education* and *public recreation*.

Here are some general nouns (boldface) often used redundantly:

large in **size**	round in **shape**	honest in **character**
unusual in **nature**	of a strange **type**	**area** of mathematics
of a bright **color**	at an early **time**	in a confused **state**

General Implications

This kind of wordiness is even harder to spot because it can be so diffuse:

> Imagine someone trying to learn the rules for playing the game of chess.

Learning implies *someone trying, playing a game* implies *rules, chess* is a kind of *game.* So more concisely,

> Imagine learning the rules of chess.

Unnecessary Explanation

In writing to an informed audience, professionals assume their readers know the meanings of technical terms:

> The basic type of verb stem results from rearrangement of the phonemic content of polysyllabic forms so that the initial CV of the first stem syllable is transposed with the first CV of the second stem syllable.

The writer didn't define *verb stem, phonemic content, stem syllable,* or *CV* because she assumed that anyone reading the journal in which that sentence appeared would know. On the other hand, if you were reading your first linguistics textbook, you would probably need a definition even of *phonetic transcription:*

> To study language scientifically, we need some kind of phonetic transcription, a system to write a language so that visual symbols consistently represent segments of speech.

4. REPLACE A PHRASE WITH A WORD

This redundancy is difficult to prune, because you need a big vocabulary and the wit to use it. For example,

> As you carefully read what you have written to improve wording and catch errors of spelling, punctuation, and so on, the thing to do before anything else is to see whether you could use sequences of subjects and verbs instead of the same ideas expressed in nouns instead of verbs.

That is,

✓   As you edit, first replace nominalizations with clauses.

I compressed six phrases into six words:

carefully read what you have written	→	edit
the thing to do before anything else	→	first
see whether	→	find
use X instead of Y	→	replace
sequences of subjects and verbs	→	clauses
nouns instead of verbs	→	nominalizations

I can offer no principle to tell you when you can replace a phrase with a word, much less give you the word. I can point out only that you often can, and that you should be alert for opportunities to do so—all of which is to say, try.

Here are some common phrases to watch for. Note that some of these also let you revise a nominalization into a verb:

the reason for due to the fact that owing to the fact that in light of the fact that considering the fact that on the grounds that this is why	because, since, why

We must explain **the reason for** the *delay* in the meeting.

✓ We must explain **why** the meeting is *delayed*.

despite the fact that regardless of the fact that notwithstanding the fact that	although, even though

Despite the fact that the data were checked, errors occurred.

✓ **Even though** the data were checked, errors occurred.

in the event that if it should transpire / happen that under circumstances in which	if

In the event that the information is ready early, contact this office.

✓ **If** the information is ready early, contact this office.

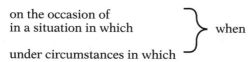

on the occasion of
in a situation in which

under circumstances in which

} when

In a situation in which a class is closed, you may petition for admission.

✓   **When** a class is closed, you may petition for admission

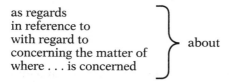

as regards
in reference to
with regard to
concerning the matter of
where . . . is concerned

} about

I should now like to say a few words **concerning the matter of money.**

✓   I should now like to say a few words **about** money.

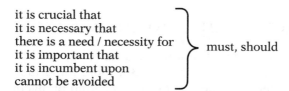

it is crucial that
it is necessary that
there is a need / necessity for
it is important that
it is incumbent upon
cannot be avoided

} must, should

There is a need for more careful *inspection* of all welds.

✓   You **must** *inspect* all welds more carefully.

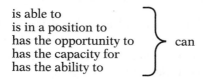

is able to
is in a position to
has the opportunity to
has the capacity for
has the ability to

} can

We are in a position to make you a firm offer.

✓   We **can** make you a firm offer.

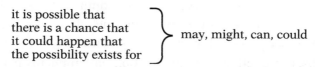

it is possible that
there is a chance that
it could happen that
the possibility exists for

} may, might, can, could

It is possible that nothing will come of these preparations.

✓   Nothing **may** come of these preparations.

prior to
in anticipation of
subsequent to } before, when, as, after
following on
at the same time as
simultaneously with

Prior to the *end* of the training, you should apply for your license.

✓ **Before** your training *ends,* you should apply for your license.

increase in } more/less/fewer, better/worse
decrease in

There has been an **increase in** the number of university *applications.*

✓ **More** people are *applying* to universities.

We have noted a **decrease in** the number of errors.

✓ We have noted *fewer* errors.

5. CHANGE NEGATIVES TO AFFIRMATIVES

When you express an idea in its negative form, you have to use an extra word: *same → not different.* But more important, you force readers to infer your meaning through a kind of algebraic factoring. These two sentences, for example, mean much the same thing, but the affirmative is more direct:

Do not write in the negative. → Write in the affirmative.

Do not translate a negative into an affirmative if you want to emphasize the negative. (Is that such a sentence? I could have written, *Keep a negative sentence when . . . .*) But you can rewrite most negatives, some almost formulaically:

not different	→	similar	not many	→	few
not the same	→	different	not often	→	rarely
not allow	→	prevent	not admit	→	deny
not notice	→	overlook	not include	→	omit
not remember	→	forget	not consider	→	ignore

Some verbs, conjunctions, and prepositions are implicitly negative:

Verbs   *preclude, prevent, lack, fail, doubt, reject, avoid, deny, refuse, exclude, contradict, prohibit, bar*

Conjunctions   *except, unless*
Prepositions   *without, against, lacking, but, for*

Multiple negatives can be difficult, but you baffle your readers if you combine them with these implicitly negative words. Compare these:

> **Except** when applicants have **failed** to submit applications **without** complete documentation, benefits will **not** be **denied.**

✓   You will receive benefits only if you submit all your documents.

✓   To receive benefits, submit all your documents.

And you thoroughly baffle your readers when you combine negatives and negative words with passives and nominalizations:

> There should be **no** submission of payments **without** notification of this office, **unless** the payment does **not** exceed $100.

This sentence relates two events, one a precondition for the other. To revise, first change nominalizations into verbs and passives into actives:

> Do not **submit** payments if you have not **notified** this office, unless you are **paying** less than $100.

Now revise the negatives into affirmatives:

✓   If you submit more than $100, notify this office first.

Which goes first in these condition-consequent sentences, the condition or its outcome? That depends on what you think your reader knows or is thinking about. Readers of these sentences would have in mind the idea of submitting payments, but would not know how to do it. So in these cases, we began with what readers knew, then moved to what they did not.

Here's the point: To be concise

1. Delete words that mean little or nothing.
2. Delete words that repeat the meaning of other words.
3. Delete words whose meaning a reader can infer.
4. Replace a phrase with a word.
5. Change negatives to affirmatives.

Exercise 7.1

Here are two actual sentences attached to two allegedly "free" offers.

> You will not be charged our first monthly fee unless you don't cancel within the first thirty days.

> To avoid being charged your first monthly fee, cancel your membership before your free trial ends.

Which one did you have to read twice? We have no way of knowing what motivated the person who wrote the less clear one, but what interpretation does that person risk? Revise the less clear one.

Exercise 7.2

Prune the redundancy from these sentences.

1. Critics cannot avoid employing complex and abstract technical terms if they are to successfully analyze literary texts and discuss them in a meaningful way.
2. Scientific research generally depends on fully accurate data if it is to offer theories that will allow us to advance into the future in a safe and secure way.
3. In regard to desirable employment in teaching positions, prospects for those engaged in graduate school level studies are at best not certain.
4. Those various agencies and offices that provide aid and assistance to those who participate in our program activities have reversed the policy that they recently announced to return to the earlier original policy.
5. In spite of the fact that the educational environment is a very significant facet to each and every one of our children in terms of his or her future development, some groups do not support reasonable and fair tax assessments that are required for providing an educational experience at a high level of quality.
6. Most likely, a majority of all patients who appear at a public medical clinical facility do not expect special medical

attention or treatment, because their particular health problems and concerns are often of a minor nature and for the most part can usually be adequately treated with minimal time, effort, and attention.

7. Notwithstanding the fact that all legal restrictions on the use of firearms are the subject of heated debate and argument, it is necessary that the general public continue carrying on discussions pro and con in regard to them.

8. Under circumstances in which people with financial resources anticipate the possibility that goods and services may continue to increase in price, those individuals will ordinarily put a majority of their discretionary resources into objects of artistic value.

9. In the event that governors have the opportunity to gather and discuss matters of economic needs and issues in their respective states, it is possible that they will find a way to overcome the major problem of specifying exactly how to divide up federal resources to their different states.

10. Those engaged in the profession of teaching have for a long time had an interest in significantly improving how individuals learn and commit to memory information from written sources. The first problem in doing this is identifying common and different features among comparable passages of writing. The second addresses the complex matter of assigning some kind of value to the quality and quantity of information that a reader retains in memory after that person reads a passage.

Exercise 7.3

What single words can you find for the negative phrases in these sentences? Each was in an early draft of this book.

1. While the standard definition of a verb as an action word is not reliable, it is in fact not bad advice.

2. A second set of rules includes those whose observance we do not notice, and whose violation we do not notice either.

3. But we ought not accept the argument that we do not need the word *finalize,* or that it is ugly because of the *-ize.*

4. While it is not clear what counts as "too many" prepositions, it is clear that when you do not use abstract nouns, you do not need most of the prepositional phrases.
5. These choices among points of usage let those among us who wish to do so express our sense of linguistic decorum, a decorum that many of us believe testifies to our precision. It is an impulse we ought not scorn, so long as it is not ignorant or thoughtless.

Exercise 7.4

Where appropriate, change the following negatives to affirmatives. Do any additional editing you think useful.

1. There is no possibility in regard to a reduction in the size of the federal government if reductions in federal spending are not introduced.
2. Do not discontinue medication unless symptoms of dizziness and nausea are not present for six hours.
3. No one should be prevented from participating in cost-sharing educational programs without a full hearing into the reasons for his or her not being accepted.
4. No agreement exists on the question of an open or closed universe, a dispute about which no resolution is likely as long as a computation of the total mass of the universe has not been done.
5. So long as taxpayers do not engage in widespread refusal to pay taxes, the government will have no difficulty in paying its debts.
6. No alternative exists in this country to the eventual development of tar sand, oil shale, and coal as sources of fuel, if we wish to stop being energy dependent on imported oil.
7. Not until a resolution between Catholics and Protestants in regard to the authority of papal supremacy is reached will there be a start to a reconciliation between these two Christian religions.
8. Except when such expenses do not exceed $250, the Insured may not refuse to provide the Insurer with all relevant receipts, checks, or other evidence of costs, when requested.

9. It seems to me that in looking at the nature of advertising, it is not illogical to start out with a statement that defines the term. This will establish a common point of reference so that we will not be subjective in our approach to a subject matter that is often the topic of emotional discussion. There is, however, no single definition or agreement for the word advertising, making the chances for possible objectivity not likely.

10. Regardless of the fact that we cannot not know with any degree of certainty whether or not there are life forms in the universe other than our own, evidence of a statistical nature makes it highly unlikely that life does not exist somewhere among the large number of planetary systems scattered throughout the universe as we know it.

A PARTICULAR KIND OF REDUNDANCY: METADISCOURSE

In Lesson 4, I described METADISCOURSE as the language we use to refer to:

- Our intention: *to sum up, candidly, I believe, therefore, however*
- The reader's response: *note that, consider now, as you see*
- The structure of our text: *first, second, finally*

We need metadiscourse in everything we write. But some writers bury their ideas in it:

> The last point I would like to make is that in regard to men-women relationships, it is important to keep in mind that the greatest changes have occurred in the way they now work with one another.

Only a few words in that sentence address men-women relationships:

> men-women relationships . . . greatest changes . . . the way they work with one another.

The rest is metadiscourse:

> The last point I would like to make is that in regard to . . . it is important to keep in mind that . . . .

If we prune the metadiscourse, we can tighten the sentence:

> The greatest changes in men-women relationships have occurred in the way that they work with one another.

Now that we see what the sentence says, we can make it yet more direct:

> ✓ Men and women have changed their relationships most in the way they work with one another.

Some teachers and editors urge us to cut all metadiscourse, but some successful writers use a lot; others, equally successful, little. You have to read with an eye to how it is used in your field by writers who you think are clear and concise, and then do likewise. There are, however, some types that you can usually cut.

Metadiscourse that Attributes Your Ideas to a Source

You might announce that something has been anonymously *observed* or found to *exist,* or *seen, noticed, noted,* etc., but it is more direct just to state the fact:

> High divorce rates **have been observed** to occur in areas that **have been determined to have** low population density.
> ✓ High divorce rates occur in areas with low population density.

Metadiscourse that Announces Your Topic

The boldface phrases tell your reader what your sentence is "about":

> **This section introduces** another problem, that of noise pollution. **The first thing to say about it is** that noise pollution exists not only . . .

You help readers catch a topic more easily if you do not bury it in metadiscourse:

> ✓ Another problem is noise pollution. First, it exists not only . . .

Look especially closely at a sentence opening with a metadiscourse subject and verb that merely announce a topic:

> In this essay, **I will discuss** Robert Frost's bird imagery.

I usually write that kind of sentence when I have little idea where I am going, saying in effect, "I have a topic to write about and hope

I eventually think of something to say about it." If at that point someone asked "So what?", I'd be hard-pressed for an answer. On the other hand, that kind of sentence in a professional journal expresses not a hope, but a real promise to develop that topic and at the end offer a claim based on its development.

Metadiscourse for Emphasis

There is one device of metadiscourse that just about all writers use to emphasize phrases. Contrast that sentence with

> One metadiscourse device is used by just about all writers to emphasize phrases.

When you begin a sentence with *there is / are / was / were*, you throw greater stress on the words that follow. Some teachers disparage this construction, but like the passive, it has its uses. You can use *there is / are* to stress a new idea that you elaborate in the next few sentences (as I did in this paragraph). Try revising it, however, if you find yourself using *there* more than two or three times a page.

You can use two other constructions to call similar attention to a word or phrase, usually mentioned at least once before:

> **In regard to** a vigorous style, the most important feature is a short, concrete subject followed by a forceful verb.
>
> **So far as** China's industrial development **is concerned,** it will take decades to equal that of Japan.

But you can usually maneuver that topic into the body of a sentence with a short subject:

✓ The most important feature of a vigorous style is a short, concrete subject followed by a forceful verb.

✓ China will take decades to equal Japan's industrial development.

Hedging and Intensifying

This kind of metadiscourse significantly influences what your readers infer about your character because it signals your confidence, your certainty, your caution. It is also a candidate for excision, but be cautious because each profession has its own idiom of caution and confidence. How successfully you tread the rhetorical line between timidity and arrogance depends a good deal on how you manage phrases like *a good deal*, a phrase that a few words ago allowed me to pull back from what I would have felt was too dogmatic:

> How successfully we tread the rhetorical line between timidity and arrogance depends on how we manage phrases like *a good deal*.

But this would have been too timid:

> How successfully we tread the rhetorical line between timidity and arrogance **often seems to** depend **at least to some degree** on how we manage **certain** phrases like *a good deal*.

Between hedging and intensifying, you have to find the middle way.

Hedges   Some readers think all hedging is not just redundant, but mealymouthed. And it is true that some writers qualify so often that their hedges seem like verbal tics:

> There **seems to be** some evidence that **may suggest** that **certain** differences between Japanese and Western rhetoric **could** derive from historical influences **possibly** traceable to Japan's long cultural isolation and Europe's equally long history of cross-cultural contacts.

That claim sounds so uncertain that we might wonder whether it is worth making. On the other hand, only a fool or someone with massive historical evidence would make an assertion as flatly confident as this:

> This evidence **shows** that Japanese and Western rhetorics differ because of Japan's long cultural isolation and Europe's equally long history of cross-cultural contacts.

In thoughtful academic writing, we more often state claims closer to this (and look closely at that clause you just read for my own hedging):

> ✓   This evidence **suggests** that **aspects** of Japanese and Western rhetoric **may** differ because of Japan's long cultural isolation and Europe's equally long history of cross-cultural contacts.

This next paragraph introduced the article announcing the most significant breakthrough in the history of genetics, the discovery of the double helix of DNA. If anyone was entitled to be positive, it was Crick and Watson. But they chose to be diffident; note too the first person **we** (hedges are boldface):

> We **wish to suggest a** [note: not *the*] structure for the salt of deoxyribose nucleic acid (D.N.A.). . . . A structure for nucleic acid has already been proposed by Pauling and Corey. . . . **In our opinion,** this structure is unsatisfactory for two reasons: (1) **We believe** that the material which gives the X-ray diagrams is the salt, not the free acid. . . . (2) **Some** of the van der Waals distances **appear** to be too small.
>
> —J. D. Watson and F. H. C. Crick, "Molecular Structure of Nucleic Acids"

Without the hedges, their claim would be more concise, but more aggressive, as in my revision. I boldface my stronger words, but most of the more aggressive tone comes from the absence of hedges:

> We **announce** here the [note: not **a**] structure for the salt of deoxyribose nucleic acid (D.N.A.). . . . A structure for nucleic acid has already been proposed by Pauling and Corey. . . . Their structure is unsatisfactory for two reasons: (1) The material which gives their X-ray diagrams is the salt, not the free acid. . . . (2) Their van der Waals distances **are** too small.

Your hedges say to your readers, "I stand behind my claims, but I understand they can be only tentative, and even if I am sure of them, I don't want to seem arrogant." And you hope your readers will think "There's someone who is thoughtful." That takes a few extra words, but they are worth it.

Some common hedges:

Adverbs	*usually, often, sometimes, almost, virtually, possibly, perhaps, apparently, in some ways, to a certain extent, somewhat, in some / certain respects*
Adjectives	*most, many, some, a certain number of*
Verbs	*may, might, can, could, seem, appear, suggest, indicate*

You can use the verbs *suggest* and *indicate* to make a claim about which you are less than 100 percent certain, but confident enough to propose:

✓ The evidence **indicates** that some of these questions remain unresolved.

✓ These data **suggest** that further studies are necessary.

Intensifiers   Confident writers use intensifiers less often than hedges because they do not want to sound smug. If readers think you use too many, they may feel you are in fact insecure:

> For a century now, **all** liberals have argued against **any** censorship of art, and **every** court has found their arguments so **completely** persuasive that **not a** person **any** longer remembers how they were countered. As a result, today, censorship is **totally** a thing of the past.

Inexperienced writers often think that this kind of aggressive style is the most persuasive. Quite the opposite: If we state claims moderately, our readers are likely to hear them thoughtfully:

> For **about** a century now, **many** liberals have argued against censorship of art, and **most** courts have found their arguments persuasive **enough** that **few** people **may** remember **exactly** how they were countered. As a result, today, censorship is **virtually** a thing of the past.

Some will claim that a passage hedged so much is both wordy and weak-kneed. Perhaps. But it does not come at the reader like a bulldozer. It leaves room for a reader to question, think, and imagine a reasoned and equally moderate response. In fact, in some academic areas, readers adopt the rule of thumb that if you open a sentence with *It is clear . . . .* or *It is obvious . . . ,* then you are about to claim something that is at least questionable.

A few common intensifiers:

Adverbs	*very, pretty, quite, rather, clearly, obviously, undoubtedly, certainly, of course, indeed, inevitably, invariably, always, literally*
Adjectives	*key, central, crucial, basic, fundamental, major, principal, essential*
Verbs	*show, prove, establish, as you / we / everyone knows / can see, it is clear / obvious that*

And of course, the most common intensifier is the absence of any hedge at all. In this case, less is more. The first sentence below has no intensifiers where the _____'s appear, but neither does it have any hedges there, and so it seems like a strong claim:

> _____ Americans believe that the federal government is _____ intrusive and _____ authoritarian.
>
> **Many** Americans believe that **certain branches** of the federal government are **often** intrusive and **increasingly** authoritarian.

Having urged you to prune metadiscourse, I must now say that all writers need some. Readers need help through prose of just about all kinds: Metadiscourse tells them how many points to expect, how certain you are, that a conclusion is coming, that you want them to recall something.

Exercise 7.5

Here are sentences that announce a topic rather than state a thesis. Delete the metadiscourse and rewrite what remains into a full statement. Then decide whether the full statement seems to make an interesting and contestable claim. For example:

> In this study, I examine the history of Congressional legislation regarding the protection of children in the workplace.

First, delete the metadiscourse:

> . . . the history of Congressional legislation regarding the protection of children in the workplace.

Then rewrite what is left into a full sentence:

✓ Congress has legislated the protection of children in the workplace.

That appears to be a self-evident or not particularly interesting claim—in short, banal.

1. This essay will survey recent research in schemata theory as applied to the pedagogy of mathematical problem solving.
2. I will analyze Frost's use of imagery of seasons in his longer poems published at the end of his career.
3. The methodological differences between English and American histories of the War of 1812 that resulted in radically differing interpretations of the cause of the conflict are the topic of this study.
4. This study will discuss the traditional but self-contradictory values that once showed us how to be good mothers and wives.
5. We will consider scientific thinking and its historical roots in connection with the influence of Egypt on Greek thought.

6. In this study, I analyze the mistaken assumption underlying Freud's interpretation of dreams.
7. This chapter discusses needle sharing among drug users.
8. The relationship between birth order and academic success will be explored.
9. I intend to address the problem of the reasons for the failure and success of trade embargoes in this century.

Exercise 7.6

Edit these for both unnecessary metadiscourse and redundancy.

1. On the other hand, however, we can perhaps point out that there may always be TV programming to appeal to our most prurient and, therefore, lowest interests.
2. In this particular section, I intend to discuss my position about the possible need to dispense with the standard approach to plea bargaining. I believe this for two reasons. The first reason that it is necessary to overhaul plea bargaining is that there is the possibility that it lets hardened criminals not receive their just punishment. The second reason is the following: Plea bargaining seems to encourage a growing lack of respect for the judicial system.
3. Turning now to the next question, there is in regard to the subject of wilderness area preservation activities one basic principle when attempting to formulate a way of approaching decisions about unspoiled areas that should be set aside as not open to development for commercial exploitation.
4. It is my belief that in regard at least to terrestrial-type snakes, an assumption can be made that there are probably none in unmapped areas of the world surpassing the size of those we have knowledge of.
5. Depending on the particular position that one takes on this question, the educational system has taken on a degree of importance that may be equal to or perhaps even exceed the family as a major source of transmission of social values.
6. I think that in regard to the current interest in life stages, most investigators in the area take the position that midlife is the most critical period or stage in a person's de-

velopment from a mental health point of view; that is to say, at that point in our development, we are in a position to know whether or not we are going to be on the winning side of the game of life or on the losing side.

Exercise 7.7

Find a passage that seems moderate in tone. Then revise it twice, adding hedges to one, emphatics to the other. Then exchange your revisions with someone else who has done the same thing to see if you can revise each other's work back to the original.

PRODUCTIVE REDUNDANCY

Learning by Writing

Some teachers and editors look upon redundancy as an unqualified bane. But in our development into competent writers, we inevitably fall into some redundancy. When we are outsiders to a community, we don't know what not to say, and so we inevitably say some things those in the community think we don't have to. We signal membership in a community of professionals by what we say and how we say it. But a surer sign is what we know to leave unsaid, because what we do not say is our community's common knowledge.

Here, for example, is a paragraph written by a student who had been correctly judged to be a good undergraduate writer (I checked). But this was his first paper in a new community of discourse, his law school:

> It is my opinion that the ruling of the lower court concerning the case of *Haslem* v. *Lockwood* should be upheld, thereby denying the appeal of the plaintiff. The main point supporting my point of view on this case concerns the tenet of our court system which holds that in order to win his case, the plaintiff must prove that he was somehow wronged by the defendant. The burden of proof rests on the plaintiff. He must show enough evidence to convince the court that he is in the right.

To this person's legal writing teacher, everything after the first sentence was redundant, self-evident: *Obviously* if a court upholds a ruling, it denies the appeal; *obviously* a plaintiff can win only if he proves a defendant has wronged him; *obviously* a plaintiff has the burden of proof; *obviously* a plaintiff has to provide evidence. But at this earliest stage in his career, this writer was an outsider still learning his community's tacit common knowledge, and so could not resist stating it.

 You may hear another version of this criticism, that your paper is all "summary." But as you learn a new subject, you will, like all others learning it, belabor the obvious. In fact, when you write out material you are learning, you master it just so that you can leave it unsaid later. It may be that before some of us—probably most of us—can analyze anything new and complex, we have to make it our own by articulating it in writing. And that often is in the form of a summary.

Autobiographical Metadiscourse

Just as "belaboring the obvious" may signal a writer just starting out in a field, so may some metadiscourse. When you are comfortable thinking through familiar problems, you suppress the narrative of your mental processes. But when you are inexperienced in a subject, you often feel compelled to give a running commentary about what you thought and did:

> **I was concerned with** the structural integrity of the supports, so **I proceeded** to test the weight that the beams would carry. **I have concluded** after numerous tests that the beams can carry the prescribed weight, but no more. **I think that it is important** that we notify every section using the storage facility of this finding.

If we eliminate the narrative and focus attention on what the reader needs to know, we make the passage more pointed:

> ✓ Every section using the storage facility must be notified not to exceed the prescribed kilogram-per-square-meter floor weight. Although tests have established the structural integrity of the beams, they are strong enough to carry only the prescribed weights.

Look again at that paper by the first-year law student. Not only did he "belabor the obvious," he made the machinery of his thinking too visible. I boldface metadiscourse, italicize the self-evident, and underline what is left:

It is my opinion that *the ruling of the lower court concerning the case of* <u>*Haslem v. Lockwood*</u> <u>should be upheld,</u> *thereby denying the appeal of the plaintiff.* **The main point supporting my point of view on this case concerns** *the tenet of our court system which holds that in order to win his case, the plaintiff must prove that he was somehow wronged by the defendant. The burden of proof rests on the plaintiff. He must show enough evidence to convince the court that he is in the right.*

When we delete autobiographical narrative and commonplaces that knowledgeable readers assume, we are left with something leaner:

> *Haslem* should be affirmed because plaintiff failed to meet his burden of proof.

The difference between experienced and inexperienced writers is that experienced writers know that summarizing is a good idea and do it deliberately, but they also know when to cut it from the final draft. They also know when to suppress the record of their thinking and offer only its product.

Having emphasized concision so relentlessly as the first grace of style, I must now qualify what I have urged: To be sure, readers dislike graceless redundancy. But neither do they like a style so concise, so tight, so compact that it is all sharp edges. Here, for example, is a paragraph of good advice from the most widely sold book on style, Strunk and White's, *The Elements of Style:* (I recommend it.)

> Revising is part of writing. Few writers are so expert that they can produce what they are after on the first try. If the work merely needs shortening, a pencil is the most useful tool, but quite often the writer will discover, on examining the completed work, that there are serious flaws in the arrangement of the material, calling for re-arrangement. When that is the case, he can save himself much labor and time by using scissors on his manuscript, cutting it to pieces and fitting the pieces together in a better order. Do not be afraid to seize whatever you have written and cut it to ribbons; it can always be restored to its original condition in the morning, if that course seems best. Remember, it is no sign of weakness or defeat that your manuscript needs major surgery. This is a common occurrence in all writing, and among the best writers.

If we run that paragraph through the style-compactor, we can squeeze a lot out, including its amiable charm:

> Writers always revise, because few are so expert they write perfect first drafts. If you want only to shorten a draft, erase, but if you mis-arranged its parts, then cut and reorder; it can always be restored. Even great writers revise, so if your manuscript needs surgery, it signals no weakness or failure.

That says just about everything the original did, but curtly. I can't tell you how to know when that happens. That's why you have to pay close attention to what your readers say, because they know something you never can: They know how it feels to read your prose.

Exercise 7.8

Pick a respectable journal in your field and in its lead article, pick out every word and phrase that either hedges or emphasizes its claims. Examine it for metadiscourse. Then compare it with a recent piece of your own writing.

SUMMING UP

Concision alone does not guarantee grace, but it clears away dead-wood so that you can see the shape of a sentence more clearly.

1. Redundant pairs

   If and when we can define our final aims and goals, each and every member of our group will be ready and willing to offer aid and assistance.

   ✓ If we define our goals, every member will be ready to help.

2. Redundant modifiers

   In the business world of today, official governmental red tape is seriously destroying initiative among individual businesses.

   ✓ Government red tape is destroying business initiative.

3. Redundant categories

   In the area of education, tight financial conditions are forcing school boards to cut nonessentials expenses.

✓   Tight finances are forcing school boards to cut nonessentials.

4. Meaningless modifiers

Most students generally find some kind of summer work.

✓   Most students find summer work.

5. Obvious implications

Energy used to power industries and homes will in years to come cost more money.

✓   Energy will eventually cost more.

6. Excessive detail

A microwave oven that you might buy in any department store uses less energy that is so expensive than a conventional oven that uses gas or electricity.

✓   Microwave ovens use less energy than conventional ones.

7. A phrase for a word

[A sail-powered craft] [that has turned on its side or completely over] must [remain buoyant enough so that it will bear the weight of] [those individuals who were aboard].

✓   A capsized sailboat must support its passengers.

8. Excessive metadiscourse

It is almost certainly the case that totalitarian systems cannot allow a society to have what we would define as stable social relationships.

✓   Totalitarianism cannot allow stable social relationships.

9. Indirect negatives

There is no reason not to believe that engineering malfunctions in nuclear energy systems cannot be anticipated.

✓   Malfunctions in nuclear energy systems will surprise us.

10. Hedges and emphatics

The only principle here is the Goldilocks rule: Not too much, not too little, but just right. Not much help, but this is a matter where you have to develop and then trust your ear.

Too certain:	Research **proves** that people with a gun in their home use it to kill themselves or a family member instead of to protect themselves from an intruder.

Too uncertain: **Some** recent research **seems** to **suggest** that there **may** be a **risk** that **some** people with a gun in their homes **could** be **more prone** to use it to kill themselves or a family member than to protect themselves from **possible** intruders.

Just right?   Recent research **suggests** that people with a gun in their homes **are more likely** to use it to kill themselves or a family member than they are to protect themselves from an intruder.

LESSON EIGHT

Shape

The structure of every sentence is a lesson in logic.
JOHN STUART MILL

Sentences in their variety run from simplicity to complexity, a progression not necessarily reflected in length: a long sentence may be extremely simple in construction—indeed must be simple if it is to convey its sense easily.
SIR HERBERT READ

A long complicated sentence should force itself upon you, make you know yourself knowing it.
GERTRUDE STEIN

You never know what is enough until you know what is more than enough.
WILLIAM BLAKE

Long sentences in a short composition are like large rooms in a little house.
WILLIAM SHENSTONE

Something that looks like a bad sentence can be the germ of a good one.
LUDWIG WITTGENSTEIN

165

CLARITY IN COMPLEXITY

Those who can write individually clear and concise sentences have achieved a good deal, and much more if they can assemble them into coherent passages. But a writer who can't write clear sentences longer than twenty words or so is like a composer who can write only short jingles. No one can communicate complex ideas in short sentences alone, so you have to know how to assemble a sentence long and complex enough to express complex ideas, but still clear enough to be read easily. You can do that, if you know some principles of sentence construction that go beyond SUBJECTS and VERBS, CHARACTERS and ACTIONS. Those principles are the subject of this lesson.

Consider, for example, (1a):

1a. In addition to differences in ethnicity or religion that have for centuries plagued Bosnians, Serbs, and Croats, explanations seeking causes of their hatred must include all of the other social, economic, and cultural conflicts that have plagued them that are rooted in their troubled history that extends 1000 years into the past.

Even if that idea needs all fifty-three of those words, they surely don't have to be assembled into a sentence so ungainly.

We can start revising if we edit the abstractions into character/subjects and action/verbs and then break the sentence into shorter ones:

1b. Historians have tried to explain why Bosnians, Serbs, and Croats hate one another today. Many have claimed that the sources of conflict are age-old differences in ethnicity or religion. But they must also study all of the other social, economic, and cultural conflicts that have plagued them through the 1000 years of their troubled history.

But if (1a) is shapeless, (1b) is, though clear, simplistic and fragmented. We need something closer to this:

✓ 1c. To explain why Bosnians, Serbs, and Croats hate one another today, historians must study not only age-old differences of ethnicity and religion, but all the other social, economic, and cultural conflicts that have plagued them through their 1000 years of troubled history.

That sentence is long, but it does not slouch. So it is not length alone that makes a sentence ungainly, but its form.

DIAGNOSING TWO KINDS OF PROBLEMS

It's easier to recognize ungainliness in the writing of others than in our own because we all read our own prose too easily. To diagnose your own prose, start by putting a slash mark after every PUNCTUATED SENTENCE. / Then pick out sentences longer than two typed lines and read them aloud, pausing where it feels natural to do so. / If in reading one of your long sentences you get the feeling that you are about to run out of breath before you come to a place where you can pause to integrate all of its parts into a whole that communicates a single conceptual structure (breathe), you have identified a sentence your readers are likely to wish you had revised, like this one. / Or if, as you read aloud, your sentences, because of one interruption after another, seem repeatedly to stop and start, your readers are, if they are typical readers, likely to make a judgment that your sentences, as this one does, lurch from one idea to the next. Those two characteristics undermine clarity in complexity: They are interruptions and sprawl.

Revise such sentences in two steps: First, revise in all the ways we've suggested—CHARACTERS as SUBJECTS, ACTIONS as VERBS, old before new, the right emphasis, no redundancy. Then if you still see a problem, revise them following either or both of these two principles of construction:

* At the start of a sentence, get to the MAIN subject quickly, then quickly connect that subject to its verb, and then again the verb to its object.
* After the verb and its OBJECT, extend the sentence in either or both of two ways that we will describe in detail below.

STARTING A SENTENCE BRISKLY

Readers have a problem when they begin sentences with long windups because they have to hold in mind a lot of grammatical structure before they reach the main subject of the sentence. It is only then that they can they "download" the information in that introductory segment from their short-term memory and start figuring out the MAIN CLAUSE. For example, suppose I had written the preceding two sentences like this:

> When readers begin a sentence with a long windup that forces them
> to hold in mind a lot of grammatical structure before they reach the

main subject of the sentence, because only when they reach the subject, can they "download" the information in that introductory segment from their short-term memory so that they can start figuring
out the main clause, readers have a problem.

You help readers get through a sentence most easily if you
keep in mind that they look for three points to help them assemble
the core of its meaning:

1. They look for the first word of the subject of the main clause.
2. Then they look for a verb that they can connect to that subject.
3. Then they look for an object that they can connect to that
   verb.

Schematically, it looks like this:

(Introductory elements) 〉1 〈Subject〉 2 〈Verb〉 3 〈Object〉 (Rest of Sentence)

If readers can't find those three points quickly and surely, they
have to work harder to understand the structure of the sentence.
Here are three rules of thumb about how to help readers see
that structure.

Rule of Thumb 1: Start with Subjects.

Readers expect most sentences to start with their main subjects,
so avoid starting more than a few sentences with long introductory CLAUSES and PHRASES. As readers work their way through introductory phrases and clauses, they have to hold in mind that the
subject and verb of the main clause are still coming, a suspension
that frustrates easy understanding. Compare these:

1a. Since most students change their majors at least once during
    their undergraduate careers, if you are a freshman and not cer-
    tain about the program of studies you want to pursue, you
    should not load up your schedule with requirements for a partic-
    ular program.

✓ 1b. Most students change their majors at least once during their un-
    dergraduate careers, so if you are a freshman, you should be
    certain about the program of studies you want to pursue before
    you load up your schedule with requirements for a particular
    program.

As we read the first thirty-one words in (1a), we have to hold in
mind that the subject of the main clause is still coming:

> Since most students change their majors at least once during their undergraduate careers, if you are a freshman and not 100% certain about the program of studies you want to pursue,
>> you should not load up your schedule with requirements . . .

In (1b), the most we have to hold in mind at any one time is five words: *if you are a freshman.*

Rule of Thumb 2: Get to the Verb Quickly.

Readers like to get past the subject to its verb quickly.
   That means

- keep subjects short,
- don't interrupt the subject⟩⟨verb connection with long interrupters.

Short Subjects   If you have a long subject consisting of NOMINALIZATIONS, you can revise it as I've suggested earlier:

> **Abco Inc.'s understanding of the drivers of its profitability in the Midwest market for small electronics** helped it pursue oppportunities on the West Coast.
>
> ✓ **Abco** was able to pursue opportunities on the West Coast because **it** understood what drove profitability in the Midwest market for small electronics.

Sometimes subjects also grow long from RELATIVE CLAUSES. When that happens, break the relative clause out into an introductory SUBORDINATE CLAUSE or into its own INDEPENDENT CLAUSE:

> A musical group **that specializes in early music that insists on using either authentic period instruments or instruments constructed according to historical standards**_{subject} produces a sound that is markedly different from that of groups playing early music on modern instruments.
>
> ✓ **When early music groups specializing in early music insist on using either authentic period instruments or instruments constructed according to historical standards,'**_{subordinate clause} **they**_{subject} produce a sound that is markedly different from that of groups playing early music on modern instruments.
>
> ✓ **Some groups specializing in early music**_{subject} **insist on using either authentic period instruments or instruments constructed according to historical standards.**_{independent clause} **They** produce a

sound that is markedly different from that of groups playing early music on modern instruments.

No Interruptions   You also frustrate readers if you interrupt the grammatical connection between subject and verb:

> 1a. A semantic theory, if it is to represent on-line cognitive behavior, must propose more neurally plausible psychological processes than those described here.

> ✓ 1b. If a semantic theory is to represent on-line cognitive behavior, it must propose psychological processes that are more neurally plausible than those described here.

In (1a), that long *if*-clause after the subject forces us to hold our mental breath until we reach the verb, *must propose*. The interruptions look like this:

> A semantic theory ⟩   ⟨ must propose
>   if it is to represent on-line cognitive behavior

The revised sentence (1b) lets us move from element to element uninterrupted:

> ✓ If a semantic theory is to represent on-line cognitive behavior, it ⟩ ⟨ must propose psychological processes more neurally plausible than those suggested here.

Readers do not hesitate over short interruptions:

> ✓ Some scientists⟩ **deliberately** ⟨write in a style that is impersonal and objective.

But they do over longer ones:

> Some scientists ⟩ **because they write in a style that is impersonal and objective,** ⟨do not easily communicate with laypeople.

To revise, move the phrase or clause to the beginning or end of its sentence, depending on how you can best tie the end of that sentence to what comes next (review pp. 99–101):

> ✓ Because some scientists write in a style that is impersonal and objective, they do **not easily communicate with laypeople. This lack of communication** damages . . .
> ✓ Some scientists do not easily communicate with laypeople because they write in **a style that is impersonal and objective. It is a kind of style** filled with passives and . . .

Rule of Thumb 3: Get to the Object.

Readers like to get past the verb to its object quickly, unlike this sentence:

> We must develop), **if we are to become competitive with other companies in our region,** ⟨ a core of knowledge regarding the state of the art in operationally effective industrial organizations.

You can move an interrupting element either to the beginning of its sentence or to the end, depending on what comes next:

✓ **To compete with other companies in our region,**⟩⟨we must develop⟩⟨ a core of knowledge regarding the state of the art in **operationally effective industrial organizations. Such organizations provide ...**

✓ **We** must develop⟩⟨ a core of knowledge regarding the state of the art in operationally effective industrial organizations **if we are to compete with other companies in our region. The increasing competition ...**

Here's the point: Readers read most easily when you get them quickly

- to the subject of your main clause,
- past your subject to its verb,
- past your verb to its object.

At that point, you can give your readers longer and more complicated material.

Exercise 8.1

These sentences have long subjects. Revise in whatever ways seem appropriate.

1. Explaining why Shakespeare decided to have Lady Macbeth die off-stage rather than letting the audience see her die has to do with understanding the audience's reactions to Macbeth's death.
2. An agreement by the film industry and by television producers on limiting how often characters are shown using

cigarettes, even if carried out, would do little to discourage young people from smoking.

3. The key components for an antiballistic missile system that could protect the United States from attack by a rogue nation such as North Korea or Libya or by accidental launches are available at the present time, but the political will for increased budgets to test and build such a system has not yet developed in Congress.

4. Software downloaded and copied into the memory of users' computers, whether they use it for commercial or entertainment purposes, is regulated by copyright laws, and any unauthorized copying for any purpose, whether commercial or not, constitutes a serious violation of the law.

5. A student's right to have access to his or her own records, including medical records, academic reports, and confidential comments by advisers, will generally take precedence over an institution's desire to keep those records private, except when limitations of those rights under specified circumstances were agreed to by the student during registration.

Exercise 8.2

These sentences have long subjects and long introductory elements. Revise in whatever ways seem appropriate.

1. Since workfare has not yet been shown to be a successful alternative to welfare because evidence showing its ability to provide meaningful and regular employment for welfare recipients is not yet available, those who argue that all the states should make a full-scale commitment to workfare are premature in their recommendations.

2. While grade inflation has been a subject of debate by teachers and administrators and even in newspapers, employers looking for people with high levels of technical and analytical skills have not had difficulty identifying desirable candidates.

3. Although one way to prevent foreign piracy of videos and CDs is in the criminal justice systems of foreign countries

and for cases to move faster through their systems and for stiffer penalties to be imposed, no improvement in the level of expertise of judges who hear these cases is expected any time in the immediate future.

4. Since school officials responsible for setting policy about school security have said that local principals may require students to pass through metal detectors before entering a school building, the need to educate parents and students about the seriousness of bringing on to school property anything that looks like a weapon can be made a part of the total package of school security.

5. If the music industry ignores the problem of how a rating system applied to offensive lyrics could be applied to music broadcast over FM and AM radio, then even if it were willing to discuss a system that could be used in the sale of music in retail stores, the likelihood of any significant improvement in its image with the public is nil.

Exercise 8.3

These sentences are unfortunately interrupted. First, eliminate wordiness, then correct the interruption.

1. The construction of the Interstate Highway System, owing to the fact that Congress, on the occasion when it originally voted funds for it, did not anticipate the rising cost of inflation, ran into serious financial problems.

2. Such prejudicial conduct or behavior, regardless of the reasons offered to justify it, is rarely not at least to some degree prejudicial to good order and discipline.

3. TV talk shows, because they have an appeal to our fascination with real life conflict because of our voyeuristic impulses, are about the most popular shows that are regularly scheduled to appear on TV.

4. The merit selection of those who are judges, given the low quality and character of elected officials, is an idea whose time came long ago.

5. The field of physics, using devices that can actually accelerate particles to a speed almost as fast as the speed of light, is exploring the ultimate nature and makeup of matter.

6. The continued and unabated emission of carbon dioxide gas into the atmosphere, unless there is a marked reduction prior to the end of the century, will eventually result in serious changes in the climate of the world as we know it today.

7. Insistence that there is no proof by scientific means of a causal link between tobacco consumption and various disease entities such as cardiac heart diseases and malignant growth, despite the fact that there is a strong statistical correlation between smoking behavior and such diseases, continues to be the officially stated position of cigarette companies.

CONTROLLING SPRAWL

Once readers make these Subject⟩⟨Verb⟩⟨Object core connections, they are ready to deal with longer, more complicated bundles of information that follow. But they expect that what follows your S-V-O core will not have a shape like this:

> Of the areas of science that are important not just to knowledge about life on this planet, few are more promising than genetic engineering, which is a new way of manipulating the elemental structural units of life itself, which are the genes and chromosomes that tell our cells how to reproduce to become the parts that constitute our bodies.

That sentence ignores another rule of thumb: A sentence starts to sprawl when it strings out one clause tacked on to another tacked on to another, especially when the clauses are the same kind. It looks like this:

> Of the areas of science
>   **that** are important to knowledge about life on this planet,
>   few are more promising than genetic engineering,
>   **which** is a new way of manipulating the elemental structural units of life itself,
>   **which** are the genes and chromosomes
>   **that** tell our cells how to reproduce to become the parts
>   **that** constitute our bodies.

You can diagnose this problem if you have someone read your prose aloud to you. If that person seems to run out of breath before getting to the end of a sentence, so will your silent reader. You can do some quick and reliable revising in two ways:

1. Try reducing some of the relative clauses to phrases by deleting *who / that / which + is / was, etc.:*

✓   Of the many areas of science ~~that are~~ important not just to the future of knowledge but to life on this planet, few are more promising than genetic engineering, ~~which is~~ a new way of manipulating the elemental structural units of life itself, ~~which are~~ the genes and chromosomes that tell our cells how to reproduce to become the parts that constitute our bodies.

Occasionally, you have to rewrite the remaining verb into an *-ing* form:

     The day is coming when we will all have numbers **that will identify** our financial transactions so that the IRS can monitor all activities **that involve** economic activity.

✓   The day is coming when we will all have numbers ~~that will~~ **identifying** our financial transactions so that the IRS can monitor all activities ~~that~~ **involving** economic activity.

2. If that doesn't work, break the subordinate clauses out into their own sentences.

✓   Many areas of science are important not just to the future of knowledge but to life on this planet, but few are more promising than genetic engineering. It is a new way of manipulating the elemental structural units of life itself, the genes and chromosomes that tell our cells how to reproduce to become the parts that constitute our bodies.

And if that doesn't work, then you have to do some major restructuring.

Two Ways to Write a Long but Clear Sentence

You can avoid a monotonous line of clauses clumping one after another but still write a long, clear sentence, in two ways: by RUNNING MODIFIERS and COORDINATION.

1. Running Modifiers: Resumptive, Summative, and Free

You are probably not familiar with those terms. But mature writers use what they name to extend the line of a sentence gracefully, so if you want to write as mature writers do, you have to know how those constructions work. And like everything else, it's easier to learn how something works if you know what to call it. We call these kinds of modifiers "running modifiers" because they keep the sentence running. There are three kinds: resumptive, summative, and free.

Resumptive Modifiers   These two sentences contrast a relative clause and a resumptive modifier:

> Since mature writers often use resumptive modifiers to extend a sentence, we need a word to name what I am about to do in this sentence that I could have ended after the word *sentence* but extended to show you a relative clause attached to a noun.

> ✓   Since mature writers often use resumptive modifiers to extend a sentence, we need a word to name what I am about to do in this sentence, **a sentence that I could have ended at that comma, but extended to show you how resumptive modifiers work**~resumptive modifier~•

The boldface resumptive modifier gives the reader a chance to take a breath, then repeats a key word and starts again.

When you feel that a sentence has gone on long enough, find a key word, usually a noun, then pause after it with a comma:

> Since mature writers often use resumptive modifiers to extend a sentence, we need a word to name what I am about to do in this **sentence,**

Then repeat it:

> Since mature writers often use resumptive modifiers to extend a sentence, we need a word to name what I am about to do in this **sentence,**
>
> **a sentence ...**

And then to that repeated word add a relative clause:

> Since mature writers often use resumptive modifiers to extend a sentence, we need a word to name what I am about to do in this sentence,
>
> a sentence **that I could have ended at that comma, but extended to show you how resumptive modifiers work.**

These resumptive modifiers usually begin with nouns, but you can resume with an ADJECTIVE or verb as well; in that case, you don't have to add the relative clause:

✓   It was American writers who found a voice that was both **true** and **lyrical,**

> **true** to the rhythms of the working man s speech and **lyrical** in its celebration of his labor.

✓   All who value independence should **resist** the trivialization of government regulation,

> **resist** its obsession with administrative tidiness and compulsion to arrange things not for our convenience but for theirs.

Summative Modifiers   Here are two sentences that contrast relative clauses and summative modifiers. Notice how the *which* in the first one feels "tacked on":

> Economic changes have reduced Russian population growth to less than zero **which will have serious social implications.**

✓   Economic changes have reduced Russian population growth to less than zero, **a demographic event that will have serious social implications**_{summative modifier·}

To create a summative modifier, end a grammatically complete segment of a sentence with a comma:

> Economic changes have reduced Russian population growth to less than zero,

Find a noun that sums up the substance of the preceding:

> Economic changes have reduced Russian population growth to less than zero,
>
> > **a demographic event . . .**

Then continue with a relative clause:

> Economic changes have reduced Russian population growth to less than zero,
>
> > a demographic event **that will have significant social implications.**

Free Modifiers   Compare these:

Socrates questioned the foundations of political behavior **and encouraged youth to question the authority of their elders while maintaining that he wanted only to puzzle out the truth.**

✓ Socrates questioned the foundations of political behavior,
    encouraging youth to question the authority of their elders,
    claiming all the while that he wanted only to puzzle out the
    truth_{free modifier}•

Like the other two kinds of modifiers, a free modifier can also appear at the end of a clause, but instead of repeating a key word or summing up what went before, it says something about the subject of the closest verb:

✓ Free modifiers resemble resumptive and summative modifiers, **letting you** [i.e., the free modifier lets you] **extend the line of a sentence while avoiding a train of ungainly phrases and clauses.**

Free modifiers most often begin with an *-ing* PRESENT PARTICIPLE, as these did, but they can also begin with a PAST PARTICIPLE form of the verb:

✓ Leonardo da Vinci was a man of powerful intellect,
    driven **by** [i.e., da Vinci was driven by] **an insatiable curiosity**
    and haunted by a vision of artistic perfection.

A free modifier can also begin with an adjective:

✓ In 1939, we began to assist the British against Germany,
    aware [i.e., we were aware] **that we faced another world war.**

We call these modifiers "free" because they can both begin and end a sentence:

✓ **Driven by an insatiable curiosity,** Leonardo da Vinci was . . .
✓ **Aware that we faced another world war,** in 1939 we began . . .

Exercise 8.4

In these sentences, create resumptive, summative, and free modifiers. In the first five, start a resumptive modifier with the word in italics. Then use the word in brackets to create another sentence with a summative modifier. For example:

✓ Within ten years, we could meet our energy needs with solar power.
[a possibility]

Resumptive:

✓ Within ten years, we could meet our *energy needs* with solar power,
needs that will soar as our population grows.

Summative:

✓ Within ten years, we could meet our energy needs with solar power, a
possibility that few anticipated ten years ago.

Free:

✓ Within ten years, we could meet our energy needs with solar power,
freeing ourselves of dependence on foreign oil.

But before you begin adding resumptive and summative modifiers, edit these sentences for redundancy, wordiness, nominalizations, and other problems.

1. Many different school systems are making a return back
   to traditional *education* in the basics. [a change]
2. Within the period of the last few years or so, automobile
   manufacturers have been trying to meet new and more
   stringent-type quality control *requirements*. [a challenge]
3. The reasons for the cause of aging are a *puzzle* that has
   perplexed humanity for millennia. [a mystery]
4. The majority of young people in the world of today cannot
   even begin to have an understanding of the *insecurity* that
   a large number of older people had experienced during the
   period of the Great Depression. [a failure]
5. The successful accomplishment of test-tube fertilization of
   embryos has raised many *issues* of an ethical nature that
   continue to trouble both scientists and laypeople. [an
   event]
6. Many who lived during the period of the Victorian era
   were appalled when Darwin put forth the suggestion that
   their ancestry might have included creatures such as apes.
7. The concept of systematic skepticism is in effect a kind of
   denial that there can ever be any kind of certain knowledge of reality so long as it goes on being screened and influenced by human perception.

8. The point when scientific inquiry began to develop is to be found in the individual observations of primitive peoples about the natural things that seemed to occur in a regular way.

9. In the period known to scholars and historians as the Renaissance, increases in affluence and stability in the area of political affairs had the consequence of allowing streams of thought of different kinds to merge and flow together.

10. In recent years, the field of journalism has to an increasing degree placed its focus on the kind of news stories and events that at one time in our history were considered to be only gossip of a salacious and sexual nature.

Exercise 8.5

Find sentences in a paper that you have already written and out of them create several resumptive, summative, and free modifiers.

2. Coordination

Of the two solutions to the problem of sprawl, coordination is more demanding on the writer, but when done well, more pleasing to the reader. Coordination is in fact the foundation of a gracefully shaped sentence. Compare these. My version is first; the original is second:

> The aspiring artist may find that even a minor, unfinished work which was botched may be an instructive model for how things should be done, while for the amateur spectator, such works are the daily fare which may provide good, honest nourishment, which can lead to an appreciation of deeper pleasures that are also more refined

✓ For the aspiring artist, the minor, the unfinished, or even the botched work, may be an instructive model for how things should—and should not—be done. For the amateur spectator, such works are the daily fare which provide good, honest nourishment—and which can lead to appreciation of more refined, or deeper pleasures.

—Eva Hoffman, "Minor Art Offers Special Pleasures"

My revision sprawls through a string of tacked-on clauses, mostly relative:

> The aspiring artist may find that even a minor, unfinished work
>> which was botched may be an instructive model for
>>> how things should be done,
>>>> while for the amateur spectator, such works are the daily fare
>>>>> which may provide good, honest nourishment,
>>>>>> which can lead to an appreciation of deeper pleasures
>>>>>>> that are also more refined.

Hoffman's original gets a shape from its multiple coordinations. Structurally, it looks like this:

For the aspiring artist,
$$\left\{ \begin{array}{c} \text{the minor,} \\ \text{the unfinished,} \\ \text{or} \\ \text{even the botched} \end{array} \right\} \text{work,}$$

may be an instructive model for how things
$$\left\{ \begin{array}{c} \text{should} \\ \text{and} \\ \text{should not} \end{array} \right\} \text{be done.}$$

For the amateur spectator, such works are

the daily fare
$$\left\{ \begin{array}{l} \text{which provide} \left\{ \begin{array}{c} \text{good,} \\ \text{honest} \end{array} \right\} \text{nourishment—} \\ \\ \text{and} \\ \\ \text{which can lead to appreciation of} \left\{ \begin{array}{c} \text{more refined,} \\ \text{or} \\ \text{deeper} \end{array} \right\} \text{pleasures.} \end{array} \right\}$$

That last sentence in particular shows how elaborate a coordination can get.

Some inexperienced writers mistake just adding on element after element with an *and* for careful coordination:

Grade inflation is a problem at many universities, **and** it leads to a devaluation of good grades earned by hard work **and** will not be solved simply by grading harder.

Those *and*'s obscure the real relationships among those claims:

✓ Grade inflation is a problem at many universities, **because** it devalues good grades that were earned by hard work, **but** it will not be solved simply by grading harder.

We should note a feature that distinguishes well-formed coordination from ill-formed. This passage, for example, has a problem in the way it ends. Read it aloud, and you will hear it:

We should devote a few final words to a matter that reaches beyond the techniques of research, to the connections between those subjective values that reflect our deepest ethical choices and objective research.

That sentence seems to end too abruptly with *objective research.* Structurally, it looks like this:

$$\text{between} \left\{ \begin{array}{c} \text{those subjective values that reflect our} \\ \text{deepest ethical choices} \\ \text{and} \\ \text{objective research.} \end{array} \right\}$$

Here is a revision that moves from shorter to longer by reversing the two coordinate elements and by adding a parallelism to the second one to make it longer. Read this one aloud:

We should devote a few final words to a matter that reaches beyond the techniques of research, to the ~~connections between objective research~~ and those values that reflect our deepest ethical choices and strongest intellectual commitments.

Structurally, it looks like this:

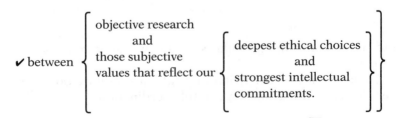

So a rule of thumb: When you coordinate, try to construct coordinate elements so that they move not from longer to shorter, but from shorter to longer. We'll return to coordination in the next lesson.

Exercise 8.6

The best way to learn how to manage coordination is by imitating it. Try imitating any of the passages laid out above. For example, imitating the Eva Hoffman passage, you might write this:

> For the serious student, the library sometimes provides a chance to be alone and to think through problems that may be too complex or too painful to think about in a noisy and crowded dormitory.

TROUBLESHOOTING LONG SENTENCES

Even when their internal structures are well managed, though, long sentences can still go wrong.

Faulty Coordination

Ordinarily, we coordinate elements only of the same grammatical structure: clause and clause, PREPOSITIONAL PHRASE and prepositional phrase, etc. When you coordinate different grammatical structures, readers may feel you have created an offensive lack of PARALLELISM. Careful writers avoid this:

The committee recommends {
revising the curriculum to recognize trends in local employment
and
that the division be reorganized to reflect the new curriculum.
}

They would correct that to this:

✔ . . . recommends {
that the curriculum be revised to recognize . . .
and
that the division be reorganized to reflect. . . .
}

But some nonparallel coordinations occur in well-written prose. For example, careful writers often coordinate a noun phrase with a *how*-clause, and careful readers do not blink:

✔ We will attempt to delineate

{
the problems of education among developing nations
and
how coordinated efforts can address them in economical ways.
}

Or an ADJECTIVE or ADVERB with a prepositional phrase:

✔ The proposal appears to have been written

{
quickly,
carefully,
and
with the help of many.
}

Readers respond to coordination most positively when the elements are coordinate not only in grammar but in thought. This seems "off":

Many voters [believe that elected officials are abusing their privileges], [are calling for term limits], **and** [in that way think that they can get rid of them].

While those three elements may be grammatically coordinate, they aren't coordinate logically. They are instead a sequence of cause-effect / cause-effect:

✓ Many voters believe **so** strongly that elected officials are abusing their privileges **that** they are calling for term limits **in order to** get rid of them.

Unfortunately, I cannot tell you how to recognize when elements coordinate in grammar are not coordinate in thought.

Unclear Connections

What bothers readers more than faulty parallelism is a coordination so long that they lose track of its internal connections and pronoun references:

> Teachers should remember that students are vulnerable, insecure, and uncertain about those everyday, ego-bruising moments that adults ignore, and that they do not understand that one day they will become as confident and as secure as the adults that bruise them.

Just enough to interrupt the flow of that sentence is a flicker of hesitation about where to connect:

> . . . and that they do not understand that one day they . . .

To revise a sentence like this, shorten the first half of the coordination so that the second half begins closer to the point where the coordination began:

> Teachers should remember that students are vulnerable to ego-bruising moments that adults ignore and that they do not understand that one day . . .

If you can't do that, repeat a word that reminds the reader where coordination began:

> ✓ Teachers should try to remember that students are vulnerable to ego-bruising moments that adults ignore, to remember that they do not understand that . . .

Dangling Modifiers

Again, a modifier "dangles" when its implied subject differs from the explicit subject of the clause it attaches to. Modifiers dangle most often at the beginning or end of a sentence. Free modifiers in particular risk dangling, so be sure that their implied subjects are identical to the explicit subjects:

> Hoping to find some cause of the flaw, the results of the tests were reviewed.

The modifier, *hoping to find*, dangles because its implicit subject (whoever hopes) differs from the explicit subject of the clause it attaches to (the results of the tests). To revise, make the implied and explicit subjects identical:

✓   **We** reviewed the results of the tests extensively, **hoping** to find . . .

The most common dangling modifier begins as if the writer intended to write a direct, ACTIVE sentence. This would be correct:

✓   **Realizing** the need for more time, **the agency** delayed its decision.

But before writing the subject of the main clause, the writer makes the verb PASSIVE or NOMINALIZES it, thereby changing the explicit subject so that it is no longer the same as the implicit subject of the introductory phrase. Now the modifier dangles:

> **Realizing** the need for time, **the decision** was delayed.
>
> **Realizing** the need for time, there was **a delay** in the agency's decision.

Readers ignore some dangling modifiers. Few notice, much less care, when the implied subject of the modifier is different from the explicit subject of the main clause when either is METADISCOURSE:

✓   **To summarize,** it is clear that . . .

✓   **Turning now to the question of financial resources,** our first question is . . .

Misplaced or "Squinting" Modifiers

Another problem with modifiers is that sometimes readers can't see which of two things they modify:

> Overtaxing oneself in physical activity too frequently results in injury.

What happens too frequently, overtaxing or injuries? We make its meaning unambiguous by moving *too frequently:*

✓   Overtaxing oneself too frequently in physical activity results in injury.

✓   Overtaxing oneself in physical activity results too frequently in injury.

An ambiguous modifier at the end of a clause can modify either a neighboring or a more distant phrase:

> Scientists have learned that their observations are as subjective as those in any other field **in recent years.**

We can move the modifier to a less ambiguous position:

✓   **In recent years,** scientists have learned that . . .
✓   Scientists have learned that **in recent years** their . . .

Exercise 8.7

These sentences suffer from a variety of problems. Revise as you see fit.

1. Having no previous familiarity with it, the metal detection device did not function as expected.
2. With every expectation of success, new efforts to resolve the differences that have resulted in interference with communication are necessary.
3. Realizing that the undergraduate curriculum must be completely reevaluated in the next few weeks, proposals have suddenly appeared on the agenda that had received earlier attention but were rejected.
4. After making an audit of all internal operations in the summer of 1996, a second audit examined the record of foreign affiliates that had not been previously audited by their local headquarters.

INTRINSIC SENSE

These devices can help you shape a long yet graceful sentence, but not even the best syntax can salvage it if its content is incoherent. This next sentence appeared one Sunday in the *New York Times* travel section. The sentence before had introduced the professional women of Amsterdam's red-light district:

> They are so unself-conscious about their profession that by day they can be seen standing naked in doorways, chatting with their neighbors in the shadow of the Oudekerstoren Church, which offers Saturday carillon concerts at 4 P.M. and a panoramic view of the city from its tower in summer.

This syntactically well-formed sentence opens with a coherent clause:

> They are so unself-conscious about their profession that by day they can be seen standing naked in doorways . . .

It continues with a free modifier:

> . . . chatting with their neighbors in the shadow of the Oudekerstoren Church . . .

then concludes with a relative clause containing a balanced pair of direct objects:

. . . which offers
{
Saturday carillon concerts at 4 P.M.
and
a panoramic view of the city from its tower in the summer.
}

But the movement of ideas is goofy (or evidence of a sly sense of humor).

SUMMING UP

Here are the principles for giving sentence a coherent shape:

1. Get to the first word of the subject, then to the verb, then to the object quickly. Specifically:

   a. Avoid long introductory phrases and clauses. Revise them into their own independent clauses:

   > **Since most students change their majors at least once during their undergraduate careers, if you are a freshman and not certain about the program of studies you want to pursue,** you should not load up your schedule with requirements for a particular program.

   ✓ **Most students change their majors at least once during their undergraduate careers,** so if you are a freshman, you should be certain about the program of studies you want to pursue before you load up your schedule with requirements for a particular program.

   b. Avoid long subjects. Revise a long subject either into an introductory subordinate clause, or better, into a sentence of its own:

   > **A musical group that specializes in early music that insists on using either authentic period instruments or instruments constructed according to historical standards**$_{\text{subject}}$ produces a sound markedly

different from that of groups playing early music on modern instruments.

✓ **When early music groups insist on using either authentic period instruments or instruments constructed according to historical standards,**_{subordinate clause} **they** produce a sound that is markedly different from that of groups playing early music on modern instruments.

✓ **Some early musical groups insist on using either authentic period instruments or instruments constructed according to historical standards.**_{independent clause} **They** produce a sound that markedly differs from that of groups playing early music on modern instruments.

   c. Avoid interrupting subjects and verbs. Move the interrupting element either to the beginning or end of the sentence, depending on what the next sentence is about:

Some scientists, **because they write in a style that is impersonal and objective,** do not easily communicate with laypeople.

✓ **Because some scientists write in a style that is impersonal and objective, they do not easily communicate with laypeople. This lack of communication** damages . . .

✓ Some scientists do not easily communicate with laypeople **because they write in a style that is impersonal and objective. It is a kind of style** filled with passives . . .

   d. Avoid interrupting verbs and objects. Move the interrupting element either to the beginning of the sentence or to the end, depending on the sentence that follows:

We must develop, **if we are to become competitive with other companies in our region,** a core of knowledge regarding the state of the art in operationally effective industrial organizations.

✓ **To compete with other companies in our region,** we must develop a core of knowledge regarding the state of the art in operationally effective industrial organizations.

✓ We must develop a core of knowledge regarding the state of the art in operationally effective industrial organizations **in order to compete with other companies in our region.**

 2. After the main clause, avoid adding one subordinate clause to another to another to another . . .

   a. Trim relative clauses and break the sentences into two:

Of the areas of science **that** are important to knowledge about life on this planet, few are more promising than genetic engineering, **which** is a new way of manipulating the elemental structural units of life itself, **which** are the genes and chromosomes **that** tell our cells how to reproduce to become the parts **that** constitute our bodies.

✓   Many areas of science are important to knowledge about life on this planet, but few are more promising than genetic engineering. It is a new way of manipulating the elemental structural units of life itself, **which** are the genes and chromosomes **that** tell our cells how to reproduce to become the parts that constitute our bodies.

✓   Of the many areas of science ~~that are~~ important to knowledge about life on this planet, few are more promising than genetic engineering, ~~which is~~ a new way of manipulating the elemental structural units of life itself, ~~which are~~ the genes and chromosomes that tell our cells how to reproduce to become the parts ~~that~~ constituting our bodies.

b.   Extend the line of a sentence with resumptive, summative, and free modifiers:

✓   **Resumptive:** When we discovered that the earth was not the center of the universe, it reshaped our understanding of who we are, **an understanding that was changed again by Darwin, again by Freud, and again by Einstein.**

✓   **Summative:** After a period of uncertainty, American productivity has risen to new heights, **an achievement that only a decade ago was considered an impossible dream.**

✓   **Free:** Global warming will become a central political issue of the 21st century, **raising questions whose answers will affect the standard of living in every Western nation.**

c.   Coordinate elements that are parallel not only in grammar but in sense:

Besides the fact that no civilization has experienced such rapid alterations in their spiritual and mental lives, the material conditions of their daily existence have changed greatly too.

✓   No civilization has experienced such rapid alterations in their spiritual and mental lives and in the material conditions of daily existence.

Lesson Nine

Elegance

In literature the ambition of the novice is to acquire the literary language; the struggle of the adept is to get rid of it.
GEORGE BERNARD SHAW

Anything is better than not to write clearly. There is nothing to be said against lucidity, and against simplicity only the possibility of dryness. This is a risk well worth taking when you reflect how much better it is to be bald than to wear a curly wig.
SOMERSET MAUGHAM

But clarity and brevity, though a good beginning, are only a beginning. By themselves, they may remain bare and bleak. When Calvin Coolidge, asked by his wife what the preacher had preached on, replied "Sin," and, asked what the preacher had said, replied "He was against it," he was brief enough. But one hardly envies Mrs. Coolidge.
FRANK L. LUCAS

Read over your compositions, and wherever you meet with a passage which you think is particularly fine, strike it out.
SAMUEL JOHNSON

TEACHING WHAT CANNOT BE TAUGHT

Anyone able to express complex ideas clearly should rejoice to have achieved so much. But while most readers prefer bald clarity to the density of institutional prose, they sometimes feel that the relentless simplicity of the plain style can eventually seem dry, even arid. The plain style has the spartan virtue of unsalted meat and potatoes, but such fare is rarely memorable. A touch of class, a flash of elegance can mark the difference between bland clarity and a thought so elegantly shaped that it not only fixes itself in the minds of readers, but gives them a flicker of pleasure every time they recall it.

This lesson is for those who aim at more than spartan plainness, who enjoy prose not as a transparent medium but an aesthetic experience, who take a special pleasure when they read a well-turned sentence, especially when it is one of their own.

I wish I could tell you how to write elegant sentences, but I can't. In fact, I am inclined to agree with the quotations from the previous page—the best eloquence is disarming simplicity—and so when we think we have written something quite fine, we should strike it out. Yet there are a few devices used by writers thought to be graceful, devices that express thoughts in ways that are both elegant and clear.

But I also know that listing them is about as useful as listing the ingredients in the bouillabaisse of a great cook and then expecting anyone to make it. Knowing the names of the ingredients and knowing how to combine them is the difference between reading cookbooks and Cooking. It's a matter of practice and taste, and maybe it's a gift.

BALANCE AND SYMMETRY

The feature of a style that more than any other makes a sentence graceful is a balance and symmetry among its parts that echo each other in sound, rhythm, structure, and meaning. The most common kind of balance depends on COORDINATION, but an accomplished writer can balance almost any pair of constructions, coordinate or not.

Balanced Coordination

I described in the last lesson how to extend the line of a sentence with simple coordination, a device that itself has the rhythm of repetition. When a writer makes that coordination more complex by balancing individual parts of one half of a coordination against parts of another, the passage rises above the ordinary. Here is a passage and my revision of it. Even a tin ear can identify which is which:

✓   1a.   The national unity of a free people depends upon a sufficiently even balance of political power to make it impracticable for the administration to be arbitrary and for the opposition to be revolutionary and irreconcilable. Where that balance no longer exists, democracy perishes. For unless all the citizens of a state are forced by circumstances to compromise, unless they feel that they can affect policy but that no one can wholly dominate it, unless by habit and necessity they have to give and take, freedom cannot be maintained.

—Walter Lippmann

1b.   The national unity of a free people depends upon a sufficiently even balance of political power to make it impracticable for an administration to be arbitrary against a revolutionary opposition that is irreconcilably opposed to it. Where that balance no longer exists, democracy perishes, because unless all the citizens of a state are habitually forced by necessary circumstances to compromise in a way that lets them affect policy with no one dominating it, freedom cannot be maintained.

In Lippmann's original, we hear CLAUSES echo one another and thereby reflect the architecture of his thought. In my version, the sentences limp from one uncoordinated PHRASE and clause to the next.

But Lippmann shapes his prose with more than simple coordination. Like other especially elegant writers, he balances the meanings and sounds of phrases against other phrases, the meanings and sounds of clauses against other clauses, giving the whole passage an intricate architecture of balanced and symmetrical members whose parts resonate against and with one another.

If we extend the concepts of TOPIC and STRESS from a whole sentence to its internal phrases and clauses, we can see how this kind of architectural elegance works even in relatively short segments. Note how each significant word balances another one in its corresponding coordinate phrase. (I boldface topics of phrases, italicize stresses.)

The national unity of a free people depends upon a sufficiently even balance of political power to make it impracticable

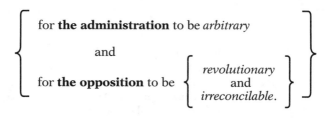

Lippmann first balances the opposing topics of *administration* and *opposition,* and closes by balancing the stressed meanings and sounds of *arbitrary, revolutionary,* and *irreconcilable.*

He follows with a short concluding sentence whose stressed words are not coordinated, but nevertheless balance each other (to indicate noncoordinated balance, I use square brackets):

Where [**that balance** *no longer exists,* **democracy** *perishes.*]

Then in an especially intricate design, he creates a complex balance of many sounds and meanings woven out of internal topics and stress:

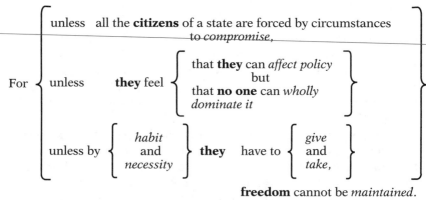

freedom cannot be *maintained.*

Here is what Lippmann does:

- He repeats references to *citizens* as the SUBJECT/topic of each clause (note that he had to use a passive in the first one: *citizens are forced*): *all the citizens, they, they.*
- He balances the sound and sense of *force* against *feel,* and the meaning of *affect policy* against the meaning of *dominate it.*
- In the last *unless*-clause, he balances the meaning of *habit* against *necessity,* and the stressed *give* against *take.*
- Then to parallel the clauses of that short preceding sentence, *balance no longer exists = democracy perishes,* he concludes this long sentence with an equally short clause whose balanced meaning and structure of topic and stress parallel that pair in the preceding sentence:

balance	no longer exists
democracy	perishes
freedom	cannot be maintained

To the reader who can learn to hear designs like this, it is an impressive achievement.

Uncoordinated Balance

Readers can hear the same balanced effect in grammatical structures that are not coordinate. In this example, the whole subject balances an OBJECT:

Scientists whose research	*creates revolutionary views of the universe*
	invariably upset
those of us who	*construct our vision of reality out of our common sense experience of it.*

In this next one, the PREDICATE of a RELATIVE CLAUSE in a subject balances the predicate of the whole sentence:

A government
> unwilling to *listen* to the *moderate* hopes of its *citizenry*
>
> must eventually *answer* to the *harsh* justice of its *revolutionaries*.

Here a direct object parallels the object of a PREPOSITION:

Those of us concerned with our school systems will not sacrifice

> the *intellectual growth* of our *innocent children*
> to
> the *social engineering* of *incompetent bureaucrats*.

Here is a more complicated example:

Were I trading[1a]
> scholarly principles[2a]
> for
> financial security,[2b]

I would not be writing[1b]
> short books[3a]
> on
> minor subjects[3b]
> for
> small audiences.[3c]

This sentence balances

- A SUBORDINATE CLAUSE (1a), *Were I trading,* against the MAIN CLAUSE (1b), *I would not be writing,*
- The object of that subordinate clause (2a) *scholarly principles,* against the object in the prepositional phrase (2b) *financial security,*
- The object in the main clause (3a) *short books,* against the objects of prepositions in two following prepositional phrases, (3b) *minor subjects,* and (3c) *small audiences.*

None of these phrases is coordinated, but each is balanced. Used to excess, these patterns can seem merely clever, but if you use them prudently, you can emphasize an important point or conclude the line of an argument with a flourish that careful readers notice.

But if these patterns might impress your reader, they can help you even more: Just trying to write a sentence like this encourages you to think of things you might not have thought otherwise. Suppose you begin a sentence like this:

> In his earliest years, Picasso was not only a master draftsman of the traditional human form, but a . . . .

Now you force yourself to wonder what else he might have been. Or not have been.

CLIMACTIC EMPHASIS

Light and Heavy Words

When readers get close to the end of a sentence, they expect words that deserve rhetorical emphasis (p. 122), so they may feel a sentence is anticlimactic if it ends on words with slight grammatical or semantic weight. At the end of a sentence prepositions feel light—one reason we sometimes avoid leaving one there. The rhythm of a sentence should carry readers toward strength. Compare:

> Studies into intellectual differences among races is a project that only the most politically naive psychologist is willing to give support to.

> ✓   Studies into intellectual differences among races is a project that only the most politically naive scientist is willing to support.

ADJECTIVES and ADVERBS are heavier than prepositions, but lighter than NOUNS. The heaviest words are NOMINALIZATIONS. Though readers may have problems with them at the beginning of a sentence, at the end, nominalizations provide a satisfyingly climactic thump, particularly when they are paired. Compare my version of a sentence from Winston Churchill's "Finest Hour" speech with the original. Always elegant and emphatic, Churchill ended his sentence with a parallelism climaxed by a balanced pair of heavy nominalizations:

> ✔   . . . until in God's good time, the New World,
>   with all its power and might, steps forth to
>
> $$\left\{ \begin{array}{c} \text{the } \textbf{rescue} \\ \text{and} \\ \text{the } \textbf{liberation} \end{array} \right\} \text{ of the old.}$$

He could have written more simply, and more banally:

> . . . until in God's good time, the New World rescues us.

Elegant Stress: Three Devices

If you want to end a sentence with special emphasis, here are three ways.

1. *of* + Nominalization. This one seems unlikely, but it's a fact: Writers looking for a grand effect combine nominalizations and coordination at the end of a sentence, particularly in prepositional phrases beginning with *of.* That pattern appears at the end of the Churchill quotation. The lightly stressed *of* (and an equally light *a* or *the*) quickens the rhythm just before it is brought down hard by the weight of the last monosyllable, *old:*

   > . . . the rescue and the liberation of the old.

   We associate this pattern with highly self-conscious elegance, as in the first few sentences of Edward Gibbon's *History of Decline and Fall of the Roman Empire:*

✓   In the second century of the Christian era, the Empire of Rome comprehended **the fairest part** *of* **the earth,** AND **the most civilized portion** *of* **mankind.** The frontiers of that extensive monarchy were guarded **by ancient renown** AND **disciplined valour.** The gentle but powerful influence of laws and manners had gradually cemented **the union** *of* **the provinces.** Their peaceful inhabitants enjoyed and abused **the advantages** *of* **wealth and luxury.** The image of a free constitution was preserved with decent **reverence:** the Roman senate appeared to possess the sovereign authority, and devolved on the emperors all **the executive powers** *of* **government.**

   In comparison, my revision is flat:

   > In the second century of the Christian era, the Roman Empire comprehended **the earth's fairest, most civilized part.** Ancient renown and disciplined valour guarded **its extensive frontiers.** The gentle but powerful influence of laws and manners had gradually **unified the provinces.** Their peaceful inhabitants enjoyed and abused luxurious wealth while decently preserving what

seemed to be **a free constitution.** Appearing to possess the sovereign authority, the Roman senate devolved on the emperors all **executive governmental powers.**

2. Echoing Salience. Readers hear special emphasis at the end of a sentence when they come to a word or phrase there whose meaning echoes or contrasts with an earlier one. (These examples are all from Peter Gay's *Style in History.*)

✓ I have written these essays to anatomize this familiar yet really strange being, **style the centaur;** the book may be read as an extended critical commentary on Buffon's famous saying that **the style is the man.**

When we hear the stressed words echo the sound of earlier ones, these balances feel even more emphatic

✓ Apart from a few mechanical tricks of rhetoric, **manner** is indissolubly linked to **matter; style shapes,** and in turn is **shaped** by, **substance.**

✓ It seems frivolous, almost inappropriate, to be **stylish** about **style.**

Gay echoes both the sound and meaning of *manner* in *matter, style* in *substance, shapes* in *shaped by,* and *stylish* in *style.*

3. Chiasmus. This is, admittedly, a rarefied way of creating emphasis, interesting, perhaps, only to those who have a taste for obscure matters of style. It is called *chiasmus,* from the Greek word for "crossing."

It is like parallelism in that it consists of two balanced parts, but contrasts with parallelism, in that the second half of the construction reverses the order of the elements in the first half. For example, this would be both coordinate and parallel, but not a chiasmus, because the two elements in the two balanced parts are in the same order (AB : AB):

$$
✔ \text{A concise style can improve both} \left\{ \begin{array}{l} \textbf{our own}^{A1} \ \textit{thinking}^{B1} \\ \text{and} \\ \textbf{our readers'}^{A2} \ \textit{understanding.}^{B2} \end{array} \right\}
$$

But a writer looking for special emphasis might reverse the order of elements in the second part so that they mirror those in the first half. That reversal throws a surprising emphasis on the last element in the pattern. This next would be a chiasmus because the pattern is not A1B1 : A2B2, but rather A1B1 : B2A2:

✔ A concise style can improve not only

$$\left\{ \begin{array}{l} \textbf{our own}^{A1} \textit{ thinking}^{B1} \\ \text{but} \\ \text{the } \textit{understanding}^{B2} \textbf{ of our readers.}^{A2} \end{array} \right\}$$

The next example is more complex. This is parallel because the balanced elements in each part appear in the same order: ABCDE : ABCDE.

$$\left[\begin{array}{l} \text{You}^{A} \quad \text{reveal}^{B} \quad \textbf{your own}^{C} \textit{ highest rhetorical}^{D} \text{ SKILL}^{E} \\ \qquad\qquad\qquad \text{by the way} \\ \text{you}^{A} \quad \text{respect}^{B} \quad \textbf{your reader's}^{C} \textit{ most deeply held}^{D} \text{ BELIEFS.}^{E} \end{array} \right]$$

In this next version, however, only the first two elements are parallel. The last three now mirror one another: AB CDE : AB EDC.

$$\left[\begin{array}{l} \text{You}^{A} \quad \text{reveal}^{B} \quad \textbf{your own}^{C} \textit{ highest rhetorical}^{D} \text{ SKILL}^{E} \\ \qquad\qquad\qquad \text{by the way} \\ \text{you}^{A} \quad \text{respect}^{B} \text{ THE BELIEFS}^{E} \text{ most deeply held}^{D} \textbf{ by your reader.}^{C} \end{array} \right]$$

To be sure, developing an appreciation for these patterns takes a bit of practice (and more to create them).

EXTRAVAGANT ELEGANCE

When writers combine *of* + nominalizations with balanced and parallel constructions, when they create RESUMPTIVE and SUMMATIVE MODIFIERS to extend the line of a sentence (review pp. 176–78), we know they are aiming at something special, as in this next passage by Joyce Carol Oates:

> Far from being locked inside our own skins, inside the "dungeons" of ourselves, we are now able to recognize that our minds

belong, quite naturally, to a collective "mind," a mind in which we share everything that is mental, most obviously language itself, and that the old boundary of the skin is not boundary at all but a membrane connecting the inner and outer experience of existence. Our intelligence, our wit, our cleverness, our unique personalities—all are simultaneously "our own" possessions and the world's.

—Joyce Carol Oates, "New Heaven and New Earth"

Here is the anatomy of that passage:

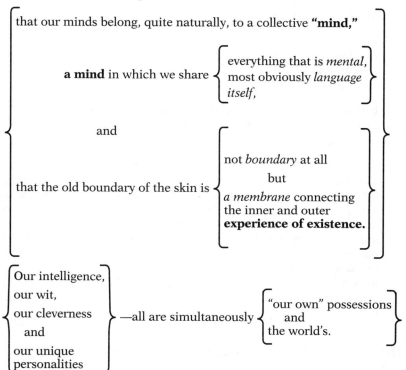

Far from being locked **inside** our own skins,

   inside the "dungeons" of ourselves,

we are now able to recognize

that our minds belong, quite naturally, to a collective **"mind,"**

a mind in which we share { everything that is *mental,* / most obviously *language itself,* }

and

that the old boundary of the skin is { not *boundary* at all / but / a *membrane* connecting the inner and outer **experience of existence.** }

Our intelligence, / our wit, / our cleverness / and / our unique personalities } —all are simultaneously { "our own" possessions / and / the world's. }

In addition to all the coordination, note the two resumptive modifiers:

> Far from being locked **inside** our own skins, **inside** the "dungeons" of ourselves, . . .
> our minds belong . . . to a collective "**mind,**" a **mind** in which we share . . .

Note too the doubled nominalization at the end of the first sentence and the coordinate nominalizations at the end of the second:

> . . . the inner and outer experience of existence.
> . . . "our own" possessions and the world's.

And in the second sentence, note the SUMMATIVE SUBJECT, *all:*

> Our intelligence, our wit, our cleverness, our unique personalities—*all* are simultaneously . . .

But such patterns can become more elaborate yet. This is the last sentence from Frederick Jackson Turner's *The Frontier in American History:*

> This then is the heritage of the pioneer experience—a passionate belief that a democracy was possible which should leave the individual a part to play in free society and not make him a cog in a machine operated from above; which trusted in the common man, in his tolerance, his ability to adjust differences with good humor, and to work out an American type from the contributions of all nations—a type for which he would fight against those who challenged it in arms, and for which in time of war he would make sacrifices, even the temporary sacrifice of individual freedom and his life, lest that freedom be lost forever.

Here is the elaborately balanced and parallel structure of that passage made visible:

This then is the heritage of the pioneer experience—

[free modifier]   a passionate belief that a democracy was possible

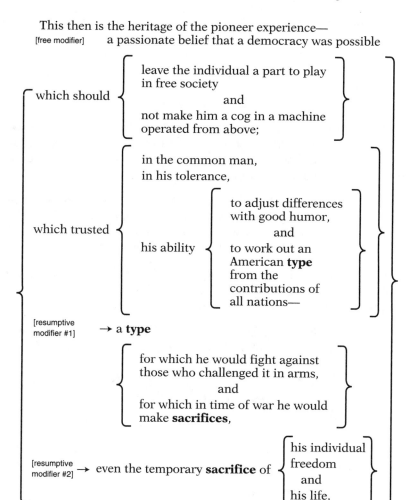

which should
- leave the individual a part to play in free society

  and

- not make him a cog in a machine operated from above;

which trusted
- in the common man,
- in his tolerance,

his ability
- to adjust differences with good humor,

  and

- to work out an American **type** from the contributions of all nations—

[resumptive modifier #1]   → a **type**

- for which he would fight against those who challenged it in arms,

  and

- for which in time of war he would make **sacrifices**,

[resumptive modifier #2]   → even the temporary **sacrifice** of
- his individual freedom
- and
- his life,

lest that freedom be lost forever.

This verges on the excessive. Note the quadruple chiasmus in the last 15 words:

the temporary[1]   sacrifice[2]   of   individual FREEDOM[3] and *his life*[4],
lest[4]   that FREEDOM[3] be   lost[2]   **forever**[1].

The meaning of *temporary* balances *forever; sacrifice* balances *lost; freedom* balances *freedom;* and the sound of *life* balances the sound of *lest* (not to mention the echo of *lest* in *lost*). It's not the kind of thing you see much any more.

Exercise 9.1

You can develop a knack for this kind of elegance in two ways: Practice writing balanced sentences from scratch or imitate them. Try imitating a few of the examples you've seen, not word for word, just the general pattern:

> Survival in the wilderness requires the energy and wit to overcome the brute facts of an uncooperative Nature but rewards the person who acquires that power with the satisfaction of having done it once and with the confidence of being able to do it again.

First, think of a subject close enough to the one in that sentence to make your imitation easy—the academic life. Then follow the outline of that sentence, creating something like this:

> Life as a college student offers a few years of intellectual excitement but imposes a sense of anxiety on those who look ahead and know that its end is in sight.

Exercise 9.2

Here are the first halves of some sentences. Finish them with balancing last halves. For example, given this:

> Those who keep silent over the loss of small freedoms . . .

finish with something like this:

> . . . will be silenced when they protest the loss of large ones.

1. Those who keep silent over the loss of small freedoms . . .
2. While the strong are often afraid to admit weakness, the weak . . .
3. We should pay more attention to those politicians who tell us how to make what we have better than to those . . .

4. When parents raise children who do not value the importance of hard work, the adults those children become will . . .
5. Some teachers mistake neat papers that rehash old ideas for . . .

You can find other models in dictionaries of quotations, sermons, and political speeches.

Exercise 9.3

These sentences end on weak adjectives and adverbs or clumsy possessives. Edit them for clarity and concision, then revise them so that they end on more heavily stressed words, particularly with prepositional phrases beginning with *of.* For example:

> Our interest in paranormal phenomena testifies to the fact that we have **empty spirits and shallow minds.**

✓　Our interest in paranormal phenomena testifies to **the emptiness of our spirits and the shallowness of our minds.**

In the first three, I have boldfaced words you might nominalize.

1. If we invest our sweat in these projects, we must avoid appearing to be working only because we are **interested** in ourselves.
2. The blueprint for the political campaign plan was concocted by those who were least sensitive to what we **needed** most critically.
3. Throughout history, science has made progress because dedicated scientists have gotten around a **hostile** public that is uninformed.
4. Not one tendency in our governmental system has brought about more changes in American daily life than federal governmental agencies that are very powerful.
5. In the year 1923 several representatives from the side of the victorious Allied nations went to Versailles with the intention of seeking to dismember Germany's economic potential and to destroy her armaments industry.

6. The day is gone when school systems' boards of education have the expectation that local taxpayers will automatically go along with whatever extravagant things that incompetent bureaucrats decide to do.

7. Irreplaceable works of folk art are progressing into slow deterioration in many of our most prestigious museums for the reason that their curators have no recognition of how extremely fragile even recent artifacts can be.

NUANCES OF LENGTH AND RHYTHM

Ordinarily, the length of a sentence is an issue only when a passage consists of series of them all ten or fifteen words long, or much longer. One twenty-word sentence after another is no ideal, but they will seem cumulatively less monotonous than an extended passage consisting of sentences all longer or shorter. But in artful prose, length is controlled and varied. Some stylists write a series of short sentences to strike a note of urgency:

> Toward noon Petrograd again became the field of military action; rifles and machine guns rang out everywhere. It was not easy to tell who was shooting or where. One thing was clear; the past and the future were exchanging shots. There was much casual firing; young boys were shooting off revolvers unexpectedly acquired. The arsenal was wrecked. . . . Shots rang out on both sides. But the board fence stood in the way, dividing the soldiers from the revolution. The attackers decided to break down the fence. They broke down part of it and set fire to the rest. About twenty barracks came into view. The bicyclists were concentrated in two or three of them. The empty barracks were set fire to at once.
>
> —Leon Trotsky, *The Russian Revolution*, trans. Max Eastman

Or terse certainty:

> The teacher or lecturer is a danger. He very seldom recognizes his nature or his position. The lecturer is a man who must talk for an hour. France may possibly have acquired the intellectual leadership of Europe when their academic period was cut down to 40 minutes. I also have lectured. The lecturer's first problem is to have enough words to fill 40 or 60 minutes. The professor is paid for his time, his results are almost impossible to estimate. . . . No teacher has ever failed from ignorance. That is empiric professional knowledge.

Teachers fail because they cannot "handle the class." Real education must ultimately be limited to men who INSIST on knowing, the rest is mere sheep-herding.

—Ezra Pound, *ABC of Reading*

Or passion. In this example, D. H. Lawrence invests his prose with urgency by breaking sentences into FRAGMENTS and what could have been longer paragraphs into quick, breathless utterances.

Let us look at this American artist first. How did he ever get to America, to start with? Why isn't he a European still, like his father before him?

Now listen to me, don't listen to him. He'll tell you the lie you expect. Which is partly your fault for expecting it.

He didn't come in search of freedom of worship. England had more freedom of worship in the year 1700 than America had. Won by Englishmen who wanted freedom and so stopped at home and fought for it. And got it. Freedom of worship? Read the history of New England during the first century of its existence.

Freedom anyhow? The land of the free! This the land of the free! Why, if I say anything that displeases them, the free mob will lynch me, and that's my freedom. Free? Why I have never been in any country where the individual has such an abject fear of his fellow countrymen. Because, as I say, they are free to lynch him the moment he shows he is not one of them. . . .

All right then, what did they come for? For lots of reasons. Perhaps least of all in search of freedom of any sort: positive freedom, that is.

—D. H. Lawrence, *Studies in Classic American Literature*

Self-conscious stylists can also write one long sentence after another. Here is just part of a single sentence describing a protest march:

In any event, up at the front of this March, in the first line, back of that hollow square of monitors, Mailer and Lowell walked in this barrage of cameras, helicopters, TV cars, monitors, loudspeakers, and wavering buckling twisting line of notables, arms linked (line twisting so much that at times the movement was in file, one arm locked ahead, one behind, then the line would undulate about and the other arm would be ahead) speeding up a few steps, slowing down while a great happiness came back into the day as if finally one stood under some mythical arch in the great vault of history, helicopters buzzing about, chop-chop, and the sense of America divided on this day now liberated some undiscovered patriotism in Mailer so that he felt a sharp searing love for his country in this moment and on this day, crossing some divide in his own mind wider than the Potomac, a love so lacerated he felt as if a marriage were being torn and children lost—never does one love so much as then, obviously, then—and an odor of wood smoke, from where you knew not, was also in the air, a smoke of dignity and some calm heroism, not unlike the sense of freedom which also comes when a marriage is burst—Mailer knew for the first time why men in the front line of battle are almost always ready to die; there is a promise of some swift transit . . .

—Norman Mailer, *The Armies of the Night*

This single PUNCTUATED SENTENCE consists of several GRAMMATICAL SENTENCES. But it does not sprawl.

- Mailer opens with staccato phrases to suggest the confusion of the scene, but he controls those phrases by coordinating them.
- He continues the sentence by coordinating free modifiers: *arms linked . . . (line twisting . . .) speeding up . . .*
- After several more free modifiers, he continues with a resumptive modifier: *a love so lacerated . . .*
- After another GRAMMATICAL SENTENCE, he adds another resumptive modifier: *a smoke of dignity and some calm heroism . . .*

A sentence like this makes us feel we are overhearing a writer thinking aloud, letting the shape of his sentence lead him from one insight to the next. But of course, such a sentence is the product of artful writing.

―――――――――――

Exercise 9.4

Combine some of Lawrence and Pound's short sentences into longer ones, like Mailer's. How do they sound? Break up Mailer's long sentence into shorter ones in the style of Lawrence and Pound. How do they differ? Imitate the style of Lawrence, Pound, and Mailer. Then transform your Lawrence imitation into a Mailer imitation, and your Mailer imitation into a Lawrence imitation. Only by seeing how you can express the same content in different styles can you see how different styles can seem to change content (a self-conscious chiasmus there).

METAPHOR

Clarity, vigor, symmetry, rhythm—prose so graced is a great achievement. And yet, while those virtues might encourage admiration for our craft, they do not excite anyone about the reach of our imagination. This next passage displays all these stylistic devices and graces, but it goes beyond craft. It reveals a truth about pleasure through a figure of speech embedded in a comparison that is itself metaphorical (I boldface the metaphors):

> The secret of the enjoyment of pleasure is to know when to stop. . . . We do this every time we listen to music. We do not seize hold of a particular chord or phrase and shout at the orchestra to go on playing it for the rest of the evening; on the contrary, however much we may like that particular moment of music, we know that its perpetuation would interrupt and **kill** the movement of the melody. We understand that the beauty of a symphony is less in these musical moments than in the whole movement from beginning to end. If the symphony tries to go on too long, if at a certain point the composer exhausts his creative ability and tries to carry on just for the sake of filling in the required space of time, then we begin to fidget in our chairs, feeling that he has denied the natural rhythm, has broken **the smooth curve from birth to death,** and that though **a pretense of life** is being made, it is in fact **a living death.**
>
> —Alan W. Watts, *The Meaning of Happiness*

Watts could have written this:

> . . . however much we like that moment, we know that its perpetuation would interrupt and spoil the movement of the melody. We begin to fidget in our chairs, feeling that he has denied the natural rhythm, has interrupted the regular movement from beginning to end, and that though a pretense of wholeness is being made, it is in fact a repeated end.

The two passages are equally clear, equally graceful. But the first shocks us with an insight into music—and pleasure, far beyond my revision. That metaphor of birth and of the smooth curve of life into death startles us with a flash of unexpected truth. The figure invites us to look at life, death, and music in a new way.

Similes do the same, but less intensely, because their *like* or *as* moderates the force of the comparison. Compare these:

> The schoolmaster is the person who takes the children off the parents' hands for a consideration. That is to say, he establishes a child prison, engages a number of employee schoolmasters as turnkeys, and covers up the essential cruelty and unnaturalness of the situation by torturing the children if they do not learn, and calling this process, which is within the capacity of any fool or blackguard, by the sacred name of Teaching.
>
> —George Bernard Shaw, *Sham Education*

> The schoolmaster establishes something **like** a child prison, engages a number of schoolmasters to act **like** turnkeys, covers up the essential cruelty and unnaturalness of the situation by doing things to children that are **like** torture if they do not learn, calling this process, which is within the capacity of any fool or blackguard, by the sacred name of Teaching.

That second passage says about the same thing, but less intensely. Metaphor can vivify all kinds of prose. Historians rely on it:

> This is what may be called the common-sense view of history. History consists of a corpus of ascertained facts. The facts are available to the historian in documents, inscriptions, and so on, like fish on the fishmonger's slab. The historian collects them, takes them home, and cooks and serves them in whatever style appeals to him. Acton, whose culinary tastes were austere, wanted them served plain . . . Sir George Clark, critical as he was of Acton's attitude, himself contrasts the "hard core of facts" in history with the "surrounding pulp of disputable interpretation"—forgetting perhaps that the pulpy part of the fruit is more rewarding than the hard core.
>
> —E. H. Carr, *What Is History?*

So do biologists:

> Some of you may have been thinking that, instead of delivering a scientific address, I have been indulging in a flight of fancy. It is a flight, but not of mere fancy, nor is it just an individual indulgence. It is my small personal attempt to share in the flight of the mind into new realms of our cosmic environment. We have evolved wings for such flights, in shape of the disciplined scientific imagination. Support for those wings is provided by the atmosphere of knowledge created by

human science and learning: so far as this supporting atmosphere extends, so far can our wings take us in our exploration.

—Julian Huxley, "New Bottles for Old Wine,"
Journal of the Royal Anthropological Institute

And philosophers:

Quine has long professed his skepticism about the possibility of making any sense of the refractory idioms of intentionality, so he needs opacity only to provide a quarantine barrier protecting the healthy, extensional part of a sentence from the infected part.

—Daniel C. Dennett, "Beyond Belief"

And even physicists, when they write about ideas for which no standard language exists:

Whereas the lepton pair has a positive rest mass when it is regarded as a single particle moving with a velocity equal to the vector sum of the motions of its two components, a photon always has zero rest mass. This difference can be glossed over, however, by treating the lepton pair as the offspring of the decay of a short-lived photonlike parent called a virtual photon.

—Leon M. Lederman, "The Upsilon Particle," *Scientific American*

These metaphors serve different ends. Shaw used the prison metaphor to invest his argument with an intensity that literal language could not express. Carr used fish and fruit to emphasize and to illuminate. He could have expressed his ideas more prosaically, but the literal statement would have been weaker. Dennett and Lederman required no heightened emphasis; they used their comparisons simply to explain, and maybe to play a bit.

But if a striking metaphor evidences imagination, it can betray those of us whose imagination fails its demands. Of metaphor, Aristotle wrote,

By far the greatest thing is to be a master of metaphor. It is the one thing that cannot be learned from others. It is a sign of genius, for a good metaphor implies an intuitive perception of similarity among dissimilars.

When that perception is not quite right, we create passages in which we confuse elegance with excess—Huxley's passage comes close with its wings of inquiry flapping in an atmosphere of knowledge.

Those of us short on genius can still use metaphor, but we have to be careful that it does not distort the idea that we want to express, like this:

> Societies give birth to new values through the osmotic flow of daily social interaction. Conflicts evolve when old values collide with new, a process that frequently spawns yet a new set of values that synthesize the conflict into a reconciliation of opposites.

We get the picture, but darkly. The birth metaphor suggests a traumatic event, but the values, it is claimed, result from osmotic flow, a process of invisibly small events. Conflicts do not "evolve"; they more often occur in an instant, as suggested by the metaphor of collision. The spawning image echoes the metaphor of birth, but by this point the image is collectively ludicrous.

Had the writer thought more carefully, he might have expressed himself more exactly—and even more gracefully—in literal language:

> ✓   As we interact in small ways, we gradually synthesize new social values. When we behave according to an old value and someone else according to a new one, our values may conflict, but they may also create a third value that reconciles the conflict.

Metaphors can even embarrass us if we aren't sensitive to how their literal meanings can unexpectedly revive, as in this student example:

> The classic blitzkrieg relies on a tank-heavy offensive force, supported by ground-support aircraft, to destroy the defender's ability to fight by running amuck [sic] in his undefended rear, after penetrating his forward defenses.

The risk of striving for elegance is that your failures can be so spectacular. And when you fail spectacularly, you will be reluctant to try again. I can only encourage you to accept with good humor those first awkward attempts and failures that we have all experienced.

THE RESPONSIBILITY OF METAPHOR

But metaphor is not limited to these figurative moments. It is so deeply ingrained in our everyday language that we are scarcely aware of it: We become *boiling* mad when we see no *headway* in the *war* against drugs, because we think the government is not *deeply* committed to *going as far* as it could to *stamp out* drug use among teenagers. Metaphor is at the heart (another metaphor) of our use of language.

But just because metaphors are so deeply entrenched in our language, typically below the level of our conscious use and understanding, they can mislead when their implications shape not only our own thinking, but those of our readers. They may create a network of implications that, taken unreflectively, imply what we do not intend. Consider these:

- A school official explains why a student was suspended from school for defending / condemning [take your pick] homosexuality:

  Homosexuality / homophobia [take your pick] is a disease that has to be isolated. We removed the student because we cannot let his beliefs infect others.

Beliefs are not communicable diseases.

- An environmentalist defends those who vandalize logging equipment:

  It is natural law that every living thing has a right to protect itself from those who would destroy it. If a living thing cannot defend itself, then those who love it have a duty to do so. That is natural law. The redwoods cannot defend themselves, so we who love them must defend them. We are only following the law.

Trees do not have natural rights established by natural law. Only people do.

- A law enforcement official comments on the accidental shooting of an innocent person in a drug raid:

  The war on drugs is no picnic. Every war has civilian casualties, but that doesn't stop us from fighting.

In the heat of battle, armed forces inadvertently kill innocent people. Governments deplore that fact, but rarely punish those who do it. Does that mean that law enforcement officers will be excused when they inadvertently kill innocent people in an activity they *call* "a war on drugs?" Metaphor is a powerful device of style, but that's exactly why it can mislead us.

> ***Here's the point*** We must take responsibility for the literal meaning of our words, but must also take responsibility for the effects of our figurative language. There is no poetic license to mislead. When we slip into metaphor as a way to heighten impact, we are ethically obligated to think about the consequences.

Abstractions vs. Characters as Causative Agents

We use language in another way that is almost metaphorical, but not quite, which makes it even more insidious: We make abstractions the seeming agents of actions:

> The environment demands our respect.
>
> Faith offers us more comfort than doubt.
>
> The truth will prevail, when evidence guides our thinking.

In those sentences, abstractions seem to perform actions that only humans can: *the environment **demands**, faith **offers**, truth **prevails**, evidence **guides**.* When we use abstractions as seeming agents of actions, we *reify* the abstractions, making them seem concrete. Ordinarily, we do no harm when we speak and write like this, because we know it is not abstractions that demand, offer, prevail, or guide, but people.

These seem less figurative, almost literal:

> Science has proven that the universe is finite.
>
> Your country expects the best of you.
>
> History proves the failure of economic sanctions.
>
> Your duty calls.

In each of these sentences, however, we have again made an abstraction the subject of a verb that represents an action that only a human can perform: *prove, expect, show, call.* But these abstractions feel more authoritative, larger, and more powerful than do mere individuals. But science proves nothing; only people do. A country can expect nothing; only people can. History proves nothing; only people do. Duty does not call; only people do.

It would be easy to claim that, well, this is just common quasi-metaphorical expression. But it is just because it feels so natural that we must be cautious when we read something like this:

> Natural law requires us to let these values guide our thought and actions.

The only thing that can demand and guide are people.

Of all the devices of language, metaphor is the most powerful, the most captivating (another metaphor), the most persuasive. It is so deeply a part of our language that we cannot choose not to use it. But that just makes us that much more responsible to know how we are using it and how it affects our readers thinking and our own.

SUMMING UP

The qualities that define elegance are so varied and subtle that no summary can capture it. Nevertheless, elegant passages typically have two characteristics that seem incompatible, but in fact are not; they may even be necessarily complementary:

- Balanced syntax, meaning, sound, and rhythm. I offered Walter Lippmann's passage as a good example:

  > The national unity of a free people depends upon a sufficiently even balance of political power to make it impracticable for the administration to be arbitrary and for the opposition to be revolutionary and irreconcilable. Where that balance no longer exists, democracy perishes. For unless all the citizens of a state are forced by circumstances to compromise, unless they feel that they can affect policy but that no one can wholly dominate it, unless by habit and necessity they have to give and take, freedom cannot be maintained.

- Simplicity of language. Walter Lippmann's elegance is partly a result of his simple vocabulary. Notice how few nominalizations he uses, only five: *balance* twice, and *unity, necessity,* and *freedom* once each.

So much of what we call elegant writing depends finally on the subject matter, the quality of thinking, the elevation of sentiments. The most elegantly constructed passage will seem foolish if its topic is tooth flossing. Maybe the only way to approach elegance is to read enough writing to get a sense of it in your nerves and bones. Only then will you be able to look at your own prose and know when it is elegant, or just inflated. The only reliable rule, I think, is "Less is more." Compression is the first grace of style.

PART IV

Ethics

Ethics is in origin the art of recommending to others the sacrifices required for cooperation with oneself.

BERTRAND RUSSELL

LESSON TEN

The Ethics of Prose

Loquacity and lying are cousins.
GERMAN PROVERB

There is no artifice as good and desirable as simplicity.
ST. FRANCIS DE SALES

Affected simplicity is refined imposture.
LA ROCHEFOUCAULD

Everything should be made as simple as possible, but not simpler.
ALBERT EINSTEIN

*Many a writer seems to think he is never profound except when he
can't understand his own meaning.*
GEORGE D. PRENTICE

*Everyone calls "clear" those ideas which have the
same degree of confusion as his own.*
MARCEL PROUST

*Essentially style resembles good manners. It comes of endeavouring
to understand others, of thinking for them rather than yourself—
or thinking, that is, with the heart as well as the head.*
SIR ARTHUR QUILLER-COUCH

*We believe thoughtful people more deeply and more quickly in general
but completely so when knowledge is inexact and there is room for
doubt.*
ARISTOTLE

219

In the last nine lessons, I have looked at so many fine details of style that I may have made it seem only a matter of craft, of a *techné* that tidies up sentences after finishing the more serious work of drafting them. If so, I have belied what I believe is a home truth: When we work hard to make our sentences work right, we do more than make them merely appealing to our readers. As we struggle to understand how best to arrange CHARACTERS and AC-TIONS into a coherent story, we engage in a process of discovery as important as the thinking we did before we got a word down on paper or up on a screen. It is not a small choice whether to write

> Serbs and Albanians demonize each other because they remember generation after generation of cultural conflict.
>
> Memories of cultural conflict for generation after generation have caused Serbs and Albanians to demonize each other.

Which better reflects where we think agency lies: with Serbs and Albanians or with history? What do we want to stress: the cause or the effect? Our choices even reflect a philosophy of human action: Do we choose to act, or do our circumstances incline us to?

But there is another, no less important principle running through these lessons, one that I mentioned in the first lesson, then left implicit. I want to focus on it here in this last lesson.

THE OBLIGATIONS OF WRITERS

We write and revise our earliest drafts to discover and express what we mean, but in the drafts thereafter, we write and revise to make it clear to our readers. At the heart of that process is a prin-ciple whose model you probably recall:

> Write for others as you would have others write for you.

When we do that, we do not impose on our readers more difficulty than our ideas warrant. But neither do we oversimplify and thereby misrepresent ideas that are genuinely complex: If we are responsible readers, we don't need condescension; we will work hard to understand what we read, but only if we think a writer is being straight with us, treating us not as eavesdroppers to his out-loud thinking, but rather as the other half of a working partner-ship. If we think that a writer hasn't given a thought to our prob-lems in understanding, if we think he hasn't spent time revising with us in mind, well, the number of our days is too brief to spend on the gratuitously complex prose of those indifferent to our best interests. Or, for that matter, on the prose of those who, by dumbing down their ideas, misrepresent their real complexity. Out of that principle of our reading falls a principle of writing: If we don't like to read either kind of prose, then we ought not write it.

Of the two extremes, over-complexity is the bigger risk. Few of us deliberately set out to baffle our readers (though as we shall see, some claim to see in complexity a political value, and in clarity an ideological risk). It's just that we are all inclined to think that our writing is so clear and our ideas so good that if our readers have to struggle to understand them, the problem is not ours but theirs.

But that indifference to readers risks more than their refusal to read what we've written. It risks what rhetoricians since Aristotle have called a writer's *ethos*. Your ethos is the character your readers infer from your prose: Does your writing makes them think you are thoughtfully tentative or arrogantly certain? amiably candid or impersonally aloof? Your *ethos* is crucial to your career because it is what your readers remember about you long after they've forgotten what you've written.

When criticized for the difficulty of his writing, for example, one writer said of his critic,

> Instead of admitting that he is not familiar with the range of concepts used in my sentences and does not wish to bother to acquire the knowledges necessary to comprehending the text, he proposes that the failure of communication is the result of the presence, beginning in the first sentence, of unusual punctuation and "buzzwords."
>
> —Donald Morton, *PMLA*

He has a point: Before abusing his prose, his critic should have learned something of his subject. But were we the object of that kind of dismissal, we would shrink up a little, and remember it. Even more important, when readers weigh competing claims that seem equally plausible (or equally uncertain), they rely on the writer who seems more thoughtful, more reliable, more aware of her readers. A writer's *ethos* is as important to her credibility as the quality of her reasons and evidence. So it's not just generous to go an extra step for your readers. It's smart.

Now to be sure, some readers read less well than others, and some expect more from a writer than their meager investment of time and effort earns them. In fact, just as writers have an obligation to us readers, so do we as readers have an obligation to writers: If we assume that writers work hard to say something important to us, then we should read thoughtfully and generously, at least until we decide they have given us good reason to stop.

Conversely, if we assume that our readers read as we do, responsibly and carefully, then as writers, we ought to go more than halfway to show them that what we offer is in fact worth their time. When all of us, both readers and writers, go more than halfway toward understanding the other, then every exchange will be more than fair to all.

Ethics and Style

What is finally at stake here is an ethics of prose. I have used economic metaphors to describe the partnership between readers and writers, but it has nothing to do with buying and selling. A thoughtful writer is not like a salesperson eager to foist off goods on a gullible buyer, nor is a thoughtful reader like a customer looking for the cheapest price. The social contract between thoughtful writers and readers implies a goodwill exchange fair to everyone and in the long-term best interests of both. If so, we should then not only write to others as we would have others write to us—in ways we judge to be clear and candid. But we should also read their writing as we would have them read ours—in ways that are equally careful and generous.

In this last lesson, I offer no definition of *ethical* beyond this: An action is ethical when as its agent, we would in principle be willing to trade places with the person who is its object, or vice versa. Writing in particular is ethical when as a matter of principle, we would be willing to trade places with our intended reader, to read prose of the same quality we produce, motivated by the same kind of intention, and then to experience what our reader does, with the same kind of result. Some writers unknowingly write prose complex beyond the needs of its substance, leaving us confused and frustrated. Others use language deliberately to hide their intentions, even to deceive us, leaving us scornful and angry. Since none of us would willingly submit ourselves to such writing, then none of us should willingly write that way. It's just a specific application of "Do unto others . . . ."

But it's not quite that simple. How, for example, do we think about those who write opaquely but don't know they do; or those who write that way on purpose; or those who know they write that way and defend it? Each of those situations raises an ethical question of a different kind. In the last part of this lesson, I spend some time on one of our great historical documents, Abraham Lincoln's Second Inaugural Address, because its style raises some of these same issues. As we'll see, maybe Honest Abe wasn't quite the candid writer we think he was.

Unintended Obscurity

In my experience, those who write in ways that we judge to be dense and convoluted rarely think they do, much less intend to. Far more often, writers draft something that makes sense to them, and then thinking that it will to others, they send it off to their intended readers. Then they are often surprised that their readers don't admire their writing as much as they do. Most of us admire our own prose too easily because as we read it, we know what we want to see—what we hoped to mean when we wrote it. And since most of us think we think well, that's what we see. But our readers don't have the advantage of knowing what we hoped to mean.

For example, I do not believe that the writers of this next passage intended to write it as they did:

> A major condition affecting adult reliance on early communicative patterns is the extent to which the communication has been planned prior to its delivery. Adult speech behaviour takes on many of the characteristics of child language, where the communication is spontaneous and relatively unpredictable.
>
> —E. Ochs and B. Schieffelin, *Planned and Unplanned Discourse*

That means (I think),

> Adults rely on forms of child language to the degree they speak spontaneously.

The authors might object that I have stated their position too bluntly, but those thirteen words express what I got out of their forty-four. That may seem like crass cost accounting, but we all have more to read than our days allow, so the more help we get from writers, the more time we have to read what we want to read, so I wish that's what they had written.

If there is an ethical issue here, it is certainly not bad intentions, not even willful indifference. Almost certainly, those two writers wrote to their colleagues as unselfconsciously as their colleagues write to them. They all have adopted practices and values that are no more evident to them than the air they breathe. In that case, the ethical burden falls less on such writers than on those readers who have the opportunity and standing to respond to them. In these circumstances, when writers don't know any better, it's up to readers who do to fulfill their half of the reader-writer contract: not just to read carefully, but when given the opportunity, to respond candidly.

I know that many of you reading this book think you are in no position to criticize the authors of what you have to read. But many of you are, and eventually, most of you probably will be. If you wrote in ways that vexed your readers, would you want to know? If so, then do for others what you would have others do for you: Let them know.

At this point, I should repeat something I said earlier: It is not possible to express genuinely complex ideas and relationships in one twenty-word sentence after another, all of them in the active voice. Moreover, we have to use the language that technical fields require. It would be impossible for an engineer to represent this in "ordinary" language:

> The drag force on a particle of diameter d moving with speed u relative to a fluid of density p and viscosity μ is usually modeled by $F = 0.5C_D u^2 A$, where A is the cross-sectional area of the particle at right angles to the motion.

But that does not relieve us of the obligation to consider whether our complexity is justified, a question that we can answer only when we think hard about our audience.

I also know that cost-accounting our time is inappropriate when we want the kind of intellectual pleasure that we can find only in patient reading. When we read slowly, generously, unpacking each phrase and sentence, we can take a leisurely pleasure in what we find. And it's just for that reason that I want those who write with more prosaic motives to use my time well.

> *Here's the point:*   Most of those who write in ways that are gratuitously dense and complex don't know they do so. When the opportunity arises, it is the responsibility of those who read such writing to say so.

Exercise 10.1

The next time you feel yourself struggling with something you are reading, stop and analyze it. Look at how the sentences begin; find a paragraph and start cutting unnecessary words. If it is a textbook, ask your instructor whether your revision represents what he thinks is the meaning.

INTENDED OBSCURITY

The ethical questions are starkly clearer when writers seem intent on deceiving us, or at least on deflecting our easy understanding. In some cases, the issues are not profound. For example, here is a letter from a natural gas utility telling its customers it was raising their rates. (The topic / subject in every clause, main or subordinate, is underlined; nominalizations are boldfaced.)

> The Illinois Commerce Commission has authorized a **restructuring** of our rates together with an **increase** in Service Charge revenues effective with service rendered on and after November 12, 1990. This is the first **increase** in rates for Peoples Gas in over six years. The **restructuring** of rates is consistent with the policy of the Public Utilities Act that rates for **service** to various classes of utility customers be based upon the cost of **providing** that **service.** The new rates move revenues from every class of customer closer to the cost actually incurred to provide gas service. This bill covers a period in which **proration** of Service Charges is occurring. **Proration** means that part of the bill is based on the former Service Charges, which are identified on your bill as "Old Rate," and part of the bill is based on newly authorized **service** charges, which are identified on your bill as "New Rate."

That notice is a model of indirectness: After the first sentence, the writer never begins a sentence with a character, least of all the reader, the character whose interests are centrally at stake. He (or perhaps she) mentions the reader only three times, in the third person, never as a topic / agent / subject:

> for services to various classes of utility **customers**
>
> move revenues from every class of **customer**
>
> **your** bill

In fact, the writer mentions the company only once, in the third person, and not as a topic / agent / subject:

increase in rates for **Peoples Gas** in over six years

Had the company wanted to make utterly clear who the real "doer" was and who was being done to, the notice could have begun like this:

> As authorized by the Illinois Commerce Commission, <u>we</u> will charge you more for gas service after November 12, 1990. <u>We</u> have not made you pay more in over six years. But under the Public Utilities Act, <u>we</u> can now charge you more . . .

If whoever wrote this notice in fact intended to deflect readers from understanding its meaning, then we can reasonably charge the writer with breaching the first Rule of Writing, for surely, he would not want his readers to write to him as he wrote to them, avoiding at every step a clear, direct, candid statement of what he meant.

Of course, we ought not confuse this kind of indirectness with the entirely human impulse to soften the edges of bad news. When a supervisor says to you

> I'm afraid the funding did not come through to continue your position

you know it means "You have no job here." But that kind of indirectness is not intended to deceive, but to seem less callous.

Here is a passage that raises ethical issues more consequential. Several years ago, the Government Accounting Office investigated why fewer than half the automobile owners who got recall letters complied with them. Its study found that owners did not bring their cars in for repair because they could not understand the letters or were left unmoved by them. I actually received the following. It illustrates how writers can meet legal obligations while ignoring ethical ones.

> [1]A defect which involves the possible failure of a frame support plate may exist on your vehicle. [2]This plate (front suspension pivot bar support plate) connects a portion of the front suspension to the vehicle frame, and [3]its failure could affect vehicle directional control, particularly during heavy brake application. [4]In addition, your vehicle may require adjustment service to the hood secondary catch system. [5]The secondary catch may be misaligned so that the hood may not be adequately restrained to prevent hood fly-up in the event the primary latch is inadvertently left unengaged. [6]Sudden hood fly-up beyond

the secondary catch while driving could impair driver visibility. [7]In certain circumstances, occurrence of either of the above conditions could result in vehicle crash without prior warning.

Look at the topics of the sentences; they are concise and consistent.

[1]a defect   [2]this plate   [3]its failure   [4]your vehicle
[5]the secondary catch   [6]sudden hood fly up   [7]occurrence of
either condition

This is a story not about drivers, much less about me in particular, but about car parts and impersonal events. The author—probably a committee of lawyers—NOMINALIZED some VERBS and made most others PASSIVE when they referred to actions that might make me anxious:

failure	vehicle directional control	heavy brake application
be misaligned	not restrained	hood fly-up
left unengaged	driver visibility	crash warning

Then they deleted all references to themselves and most references to me (in *your vehicle* twice and *driver* once), thereby creating a story not about me or them, but about my car:

> There is a car that might have defective parts. Its plate could fail and its hood fly up, and if they do, it could crash and nobody will warn it.

If we assume that the recall letter didn't just turn out like this, then we can raise the question of whether its writers violated their ethical duty to communicate with others as they would have others communicate with them, for surely they would be unwilling to swap places with readers not concerned enough to correct a condition that threatened their lives. If not, then by their prose style, they breached the ethical duty they owed their readers.

Finally, we must acknowledge that being candid can exact costs that some writers think that they can't pay. It would be naive to claim that we are all free to write as as we please, especially when our jobs depend on saying things in self-interested ways. As easy as it was to abuse that automobile recall letter, I don't know the circumstances that may have coerced its writers to write what they did. But that doesn't change the consequences of their choices. When any of us writes in ways that we would not want others to write to us, we at least abrade, if not tear, the fabric of trust that we would like to think a reasonable society needs. Whether those writers were coerced or not, we can't close our eyes to the consequences of such actions, because they have ethical consequences.

Exercise 10.2

Revise the rest of the gas rate notice, using *we* as a TOPIC / agent / SUBJECT wherever you can. Then revise a second time making the topic / agent / subject *you*. For example:

> As the Illinois Commerce Commission has authorized, <u>you</u> will have to pay us higher service charges after November 12, 1990. <u>You</u> have not had to pay higher rates in . . . .

Would the company resist sending either revision? Why? What ethical issues does the original raise? Was it "good" writing?

Exercise 10.3

Revise the recall letter, making the word *you* the subject of the driver's actions as often as you can. Certainly one of the sentences will read,

> If <u>you</u> brake hard and the plate fails, <u>you</u> will . . .

Why would the company have been reluctant to send out that version? What ethical issues are involved? Are they different from those in the gas company notice? Is the original letter "good" writing? Which of the following, if either, is closer to the "truth"? Is that even the right question?

> If the plate fails, you could crash.
> If the plate fails, your car could crash.

RATIONALIZED OBSCURITY

A more complicated matter is responding to those who know they write in ways that are difficult to understand, but claim they must, because they are breaking new intellectual ground. Is that a kind of self-indulgence verging on the unethical, or are they right? This is a vexing question not just because the only way to settle it is case by case, but because there are reasons we might not be able to settle it at all, at least not to everyone's satisfaction. We might try to find a "difficult" passage about groundbreaking ideas intended for an audience a bit wider than a writer's narrow circle of colleagues; then see if we can make it clearer without bleaching its meaning.

Here is a moderately difficult passage written by someone making a reasonably surprising claim: Clear writing discourages complex thinking (we quoted him in Lesson 1. The "homogenization and standardization" of language refers to clear language):

> In effect, what is missed in this analysis [of curricula] is that the homogenization and standardization of language in the mass media and the schools point to how language and power often combine to offer the general public and students subject positions that are cleansed of any complex thought or insight.

> —Stanley Aronowitz, *Postmodern Education*

I think that means (though I am not sure),

> These critics ignore how schools and the mass media use clear language to prevent students and the public from recognizing how [someone?] combines power and language to keep them from understanding their social and political circumstances.

Some (particularly the author) might claim that by ironing out his syntax, I have flattened the nuances of his thought, not the least by dropping one of his technical terms: *subject position* (it means, roughly, the sum of our socially created knowledge and understanding that allows us to understand our social circumstances).

And that objection would pose a difficult question, because while it would be easy (and predictable) to assert that I substantially changed his meaning, how would we decide whether in fact I have, or whether the writer were only defending nuances that, at least in the experience of the ordinarily competent reader, are just not there? Or at least not there given the amount of time I can devote to reading him?

Most of us think that what we have to say is worth our readers' time and that we have said it clearly, but we usually think we've said it more clearly than our readers think we have. So while we might create complex prose and defend its nuances, we can never be sure that our readers, even our best readers, will read slowly and carefully enough to notice them, or worse, keep reading.

This is a hard question: We owe our readers an ethical duty to write as exactly as we can, but each of us is also entitled to write exactly as we choose. What we ought not assume, however, is that we are also entitled to our readers' time, that they owe a duty to us to invest more time and effort than they think we have earned. If a writer chooses to write in ways that she thinks represent the full complexity of her nuanced thinking, knowing it will seem to her readers so dense and complex that it will put great burdens on their time—well, it's a free country. In the marketplace of ideas, truth is the most important value, but not the only one.

At the end of the day, I can suggest only that when writers claim their prose style must be dense because their ideas are new, they are, as a matter of simple fact, more often wrong than right. The philosopher of language Ludwig Wittgenstein said,

> Whatever can be thought can be thought clearly; whatever can be written can be written clearly.

I'd like to add a nuance of my own:

> Whatever can be thought can be thought *more* clearly; whatever can be written can be written *more* clearly.

All that means is that a few more minutes revising with the reader in mind is time well invested, at least for those who care about their readers.

SALUTARY COMPLEXITY/SUBVERSIVE CLARITY

There are two more defenses of complexity, one claiming that complexity can be good for us, the other that clarity can be bad.

As to the first claim, some argue that the harder we have to work to understand what we read, the more deeply we think. Everyone should be happy to know that there is not a shred of evidence to support such a claim, and substantial evidence that complex language impedes our reading, understanding, and memory. Inconvenient facts like these regularly embarrass our beliefs, but there you are.

As to the second claim, some argue that "clarity" as a value is a political device wielded by those in power to mislead us about the complex social arrangements that control our affairs. By making things deceptively simple, they say, those who feed us information render us unable to discover and understand the full complexity of our political and social circumstances. The author of the passage I revised on page 229, also wrote this:

> The call to write curriculum in a language that is touted as clear and accessible is evidence of a moral and political vision that increasingly collapses under the weight of its own anti-intellectualism. . . . [T]hose who make a call for clear writing synonymous with an attack on critical educators have missed the role that the "language of clarity" plays in a dominant culture that cleverly and powerfully uses "clear" and "simplistic" language to systematically undermine and prevent the conditions from arising for a public culture to engage in rudimentary forms of complex and critical thinking.
>
> —Stanley Aronowitz, *Postmodern Education*

And that writer I cited on page 221 who charged his reader with culpable ignorance of his subject went on to claim that clear language is the product of a class politics aimed at maintaining the ideological status quo.

> I leave aside the [author's] naiveté in regarding "clarity" as a "natural" given and not a historicopolitical construct, a systematic effect of class politics. . . . [The question my critics do not answer is] how do retrograde pedagogues masquerading as progressives use the defense of commonsensical language (from the street, clear to all) to perpetuate the rule of the dominant ideology?
>
> —Donald Morton, *PMLA*

Now both writers make a good point: Language is deeply implicated in politics and ideology. Through recorded history, the Ins have regularly used not just language, but its exclusionary qualities to manage the Outs. In our earliest history, the educated elite used writing itself to exclude the illiterate; then later in England, they used Latin and then French to exclude those who knew only English. In our more recent history, many of those defending authority of a variety of kinds have relied on a vocabulary thick with Latinate nominalizations and, as we saw in Lesson 2, on a Standard English that requires those aspiring to be one of the Ins to submit to a decade-long grammatical education, during which, it is hoped, they not only acquire the linguistic habits of the Ins, but give up the political and social values of the Outs, as well. We have not inherited these forms of linguistic "difficulty" as the natural by-products of complex thinking; they have been institutionally maintained.

And in the same way, clarity is not a prelapsarian virtue spoiled by fallen academics, bureaucrats, and others jealous to preserve their authority. Clarity as a value is something a society has to create and then work to maintain, because it is not just hard to be clear; it is close to being an unnatural act. To be sure, just as those who lie persuasively can achieve socially corrosive ends, so too can those who, by oversimplifying complexity, keep us from thinking clearly about our circumstances. But it is not the clarity that subverts; it is the unethical use of it. If we fail to insist that in principle, those who manage our affairs have a duty to tell the truth clearly, then we lose the trust that depends on shared understanding, a loss that no society aspiring to democracy can survive. That's idealistic, but the alternative is unacceptable.

So is "clarity" a value that reflects our political ideology? Of course, it is; how could it be otherwise? But those who attack clarity as part of an ideological conspiracy miss the same point missed by those who attack science: Neither science nor clarity is a threat; the threat is in their misuse.

Artful Misdirection

Those who wrote the notices about gas rate increases and hood flyup were, I think, trying to deflect us from understanding who was doing what to whom. By their nominalizations and passives, they signaled that they had moved actions and characters around in their sentences, eliminating most of the characters in the process. Once we see how they do it, the less likely they are to deceive us, because they betray themselves in all those PREPOSITIONAL PHRASES and nominalizations, those words ending in *-tion, -ment, -ence,* and so on.

The more interesting examples are more subtle, perhaps even unintended, and just because of that, even more insidious. They too have an ethical aspect that we ought to recognize.

Shaping Stories

Artful writers can shape their stories in ways that make it seem they had no choice but to focus on the agents they did. In Lesson 9, we considered some of those issues when we looked at sentences like these, in which we used reifications, abstractions, as seeming agents of actions:

> Science has proven that the universe is finite.
>
> Your country expects the best of you.
>
> History proves the failure of economic sanctions.
>
> Your duty calls.

Only humans can prove, expect, argue, or call. We can also contrast sentences like these, which arguably refer to the same event "out there," but shape our understanding of it in different ways, by assigning responsibility to different characters:

> You are not clear in this passage you wrote.
>
> This passage you wrote is not clear.
>
> I do not clearly understand this passage you wrote.

But now which of those sentences is closest to "the truth" and, if truth is ethical, then most ethical? Wrong question. The right question is why the writer wants us to think that one character rather than another is the responsible agent. Once we know that, we can ask the ethical question: In a similar situation, would the writer be willing to be manipulated in the same way?

Lawyers get a lot of practice doing that:

> Smith met Jones and sold him a gram of cocaine. He received $100 for it. Smith had responded to Jones's request that . . .
>
> Jones met Smith and bought a gram of cocaine. He paid $100 for it. Jones had requested that . . .

Both sentences refer to the same event, but if you were Smith (or Jones), which story would you want a jury to hear? Lawyers are obligated not to lie, but they are also obligated to tell the story that best represents their clients, and that means deciding how best to represent who was doing what to whom. And those are stylistic choices.

They are also the kinds of choices that skilled communicators make every day. A few years ago, the California attorney general's office accused the Sears Company of overcharging for automobile repairs. In response, Sears ran an ad that included these two sentences:

> With over two million automotive customers serviced last year in California alone, mistakes may have occurred. However, Sears wants

you to know that we would never intentionally violate the trust customers have shown in our company for 105 years.

In the first sentence, the writer could have avoided mentioning Sears as the party responsible for mistakes by using a passive verb:

> With over two million automotive customers serviced last year in California alone, mistakes **may have been made.**

But that would have encouraged readers to wonder "By whom?" Instead, the writers found another verb that moved Sears into the background by giving the mistakes a life of their own: they may have just "occurred." In the second sentence, though, the writer explicitly makes *Sears* the responsible agent, because in that sentence he wants to emphasize Sears as the agent of good actions.

> **Sears** wants you to know that **we** would never intentionally violate . . .

If we revise the first sentence so that it explicitly refers to Sears and the second so that it hides Sears, we get a rhetorical effect that would make its vice-president for public relations wince:

> When Sears serviced over two million automotive customers last year in California alone, we made mistakes. However, you should know that no intentional violation of 105 years of trust occurred.

In short, the character we make the topic / subject of a verb is not determined by the world but by us. The writer for Sears *chose* to deflect us from its responsibility for bad actions and to emphasize its responsibility for good ones.

But how unethical are those choices? Well, with every sentence we write we have to choose *some* point of view; we cannot not choose. These choices are forced on us by the nature of the English language, so their availability and our need to choose from among them is ethically neutral. The ethical quality of those choices depends on the motives that drive them. Only by knowing motives can readers know whether a writer would willingly be the object of such writing, to be influenced (or manipulated) in the same way, with the same result.

Exercise 10.4

Consider these versions of the "same" story. Invent three contexts in which one would be the right choice and the other two the wrong choices. Imagine first that the readers are from Abco, then that they are from Zorax. For example, if Abco were doing things satisfactorily, while Zorax were doing something new and different, which would be most effective if Abco were the audience?

Abco Incorporated is losing customers to Zorax Limited.

Zorax Limited is taking customers from Abco Incorporated.

Customers are leaving Abco Incorporated and moving to Zorax Limited.

An Extended Analysis

It's easy to abuse passages that are ethically challenged. What's more difficult is thinking about these matters when they appear in a document that seems above criticism, one written by a writer whom we would never charge with deceit. But it is just such a writer and document that force us to think hard about matters of style, clarity, and ethics. Such an analysis also lets us apply everything we've discussed not just to manage our own writing and that of others, but to analyze and understand prose that deserves our most careful attention.

Along with our Constitution, the most celebrated prose texts in American history are the Declaration of Independence, Abraham Lincoln's Gettysburg Address, and his Second Inaugural Address. These last three have not only the power of great thought, but the eloquence of powerful literature. In previous editions of this book, I have written about the style of the Gettysburg Address and the Declaration. Exercises at the end of this lesson ask you to look at some of their stylistic features. Here we examine the style of Lincoln's Second Inaugural.

Lincoln delivered this speech in March of 1865, a few weeks before Lee's surrender. He knew that the North would win, but worried that as victor, it would punish the South for both slavery and the carnage of the war. He was right to worry, as history demonstrated. Anticipating that outcome, Lincoln tried to reconcile North and South in words we all recognize:

> With malice toward none; with charity for all; with firmness in the right, as God gives us to see the right, let us strive on to finish the work we are in; to bind up the nation's wounds; to care for him who shall have borne the battle, and for his widow, and his orphan—to do all which may achieve and cherish a just, and a lasting peace, among ourselves, and with all nations.

We do not, however, commit to our civic memory the opening sentences of his speech because we are stirred by neither their language nor their thought:

> Fellow-countrymen: At this second appearing to take the oath of the presidential office, there is less occasion for an extended address than there was at the first. Then a statement, somewhat in detail, of a course to be pursued, seemed fitting and proper. Now, at the expiration of four years, during which public declarations have been constantly called forth on every point and phase of the great contest which still absorbs the attention and engrosses the energies of the nation, little that is new could be presented. The progress of our arms, upon which all else chiefly depends, is as well known to the public as to myself; and it is, I trust, reasonably satisfactory and encouraging to all. With high hope for the future, no prediction in regard to it is ventured.

Were that written by someone other than Lincoln, we might judge it at best pedestrian. It is abstract, indirect. The proportion of nominalizations to all words is not high: ten in 134 words, but most of them open sentences:

> At this second **appearing**
>
> Then a **statement**
>
> Now, at the **expiration** of four years, during which public **declarations**
>
> The **progress** of our arms
>
> With high **hope** for the future, no **prediction**

He could have written this:

> Fellow-countrymen: As **I appear** here for the second time to take the oath of the presidential office, I have less occasion to **address** you at length than **I** did at the first. Then **I** thought it fitting and proper that **I state** in detail the course to be pursued . . .

In fact, that is close to the style of his First Inaugural Address:

> Fellow-citizens of the United States: In compliance with a custom as old as the government itself, **I appear** before you to address you briefly, and to take before you the oath prescribed by the Constitution of the United States to be taken by the President "before he enters on the execution of his office." **I** do not **consider** it necessary at present for me to **discuss** . . .

Or he could have written this:

> Fellow-countrymen: As **we** meet together for this second taking of the oath of the presidential office, **we** have less need for an extended address than **we** had at the first. Then **we** felt a statement, describing in detail, the course **we** would pursue, fitting and proper . . .

And that is close to the style of the Gettysburg Address:

> Now **we** are engaged in a great Civil War, testing whether that nation, or any nation so conceived and so dedicated, can long endure. **We** are met on a great battlefield of that war. **We** have come to dedicate a portion of that field, as a final resting place for those who here gave their lives that that nation might live. It is altogether fitting and proper that **we** should do this.

In fact, Lincoln seems so intent on being impersonal in this first paragraph that he opened its last sentence with a DANGLING MODIFIER (see pp. 185–86):

> **With high hope for the future,** no prediction in regard to it is ventured.

Either Lincoln dozed, or he had something else in mind.

What he did in this first paragraph, intentionally or not, is tell a story not about himself or his audience, but about the occasion. Here are the topics of his opening paragraph. They deflect our attention from the participants and focus it on the event and message:

> this second appearing to take the oath of presidential office, there is less occasion . . .
>
> a statement . . . seemed fitting
>
> public declarations . . . have been constantly called forth
>
> little that is new . . . could be presented
>
> The progress of our arms . . . is well known
>
> it [progress of arms] . . . is encouraging to all.
>
> no prediction is ventured.

The question, of course, is why he did that. If we work through the rest of the Second Inaugural in the same way, we might understand not only why Lincoln wrote this first paragraph as he did, but why the speech itself is part of our national heritage. As you read, notice his subjects (underlined). We will come back to them.

> On the occasion corresponding to this four years ago, all thoughts were anxiously directed to an impending civil war. All dreaded it—all

sought to avert it. While the inaugural address was being delivered from this place, devoted altogether to saving the Union without war, insurgent agents were in the city seeking to destroy it without war— seeking to dissolve the Union, and divide effects, by negotiation. Both parties deprecated war, but one of them would make war rather than let the nation survive; and the other would accept war rather than let it perish. And the war came.

One eighth of the whole population were colored slaves, not distributed generally over the Union, but localized in the southern part of it. These slaves constituted a peculiar and powerful interest. All knew that this interest was, somehow, the cause of the war. To strengthen, perpetuate, and extend this interest was the object for which the insurgents would rend the Union, even by war; while the government claimed no right to do more than to restrict the territorial enlargement of it. Neither party expected for the war the magnitude or the duration which it has already attained. Neither anticipated that the cause of the conflict might cease with, or even before, the conflict itself should cease. Each looked for an easier triumph and a result less fundamental and astounding. Both read the same Bible, and pray to the same God; and each invokes His aid against the other. It may seem strange that any men should dare to ask a just God's assistance in wringing their bread from the sweat of other men's faces; but let us judge not, that we be not judged. The prayers of both could not be answered; that of neither has been answered fully. The Almighty has His own purposes. "Woe unto the world because of offences! for it must needs be that offences come; but woe to that man by whom the offence cometh. "If we shall suppose that American slavery is one of those offences which in the providence of God, must needs come, but which, having continued through His appointed time, He now wills to remove, and that He gives to both North and South, this terrible war as the woe due to those by whom the offence came, shall we discern therein any departure from those divine attributes which the believers in a Living God always ascribe to Him? Fondly do we hope—fervently do we pray—that this mighty scourge of war may speedily pass away. Yet, if God wills that it continue until all the wealth piled by the bondman's two hundred and fifty years of unrequited toil shall be sunk, and until every drop of blood drawn with the lash shall be paid by another drawn with the sword, as was said three thousand years ago, so still it must be said, "the judgments of the Lord, are true and righteous altogether."

With malice toward none; with charity for all; with firmness in the right, as God gives us to see the right, let us strive on to finish the work we are in; to bind up the nation's wounds; to care for him who shall have borne the battle, and for his widow, and his orphan—to do all which may achieve and cherish a just, and a lasting peace, among ourselves, and with all nations.

Now we can look at the speech in some detail.

In the first sentence of the second paragraph, Lincoln continues the same impersonal style of the introduction, both nominalized and passive:

> On the occasion corresponding to this four years ago, <u>all thoughts</u> were anxiously directed to an impending civil war.

He could have written, *everyone was anxiously thinking.* Then for two short clauses, he switches to the simplicity we expect of him:

> <u>All</u> dreaded it—<u>all</u> sought to avert it.

But in the next sentence, he returns to the impersonal passive:

> While <u>the inaugural address</u> was being delivered from this place . . .

And then he returns to the direct, subject / agent-verb / action style, this time for several consecutive sentences:

> <u>insurgent agents</u> were in the city seeking to destroy it
> <u>Both parties</u> deprecated war
> <u>one of them</u> would make war
> <u>the other</u> would accept war
> And <u>the war</u> came.

(Think, for a moment: How can a war just "come?")

He then writes an oddly awkward and passive sentence about the demographics of slavery:

> <u>One eighth of the whole population</u> were colored slaves, not distributed generally over the Union, but localized in the southern part of it.

This would have been more direct:

> One eighth of the population were slaves, most of them in the South.

In fact, in the indirectness of that sentence and in some that follow, Lincoln seems to hold slavery at a distance.

The next two sentences begin clearly enough but toward their ends, they both slip into impersonality, especially the second:

<u>These slaves</u> constituted a peculiar and powerful interest.

<u>All</u> knew that <u>this interest</u> was, somehow, the cause of the war.

Most of the subjects and verbs in the rest of the sentences represent the kind of direct prose style that we associate with Lincoln, but notice how indirectly he goes on referring to slavery (I boldface his references to it):

<u>To strengthen, perpetuate, and extend this **interest**</u> was the object

<u>the insurgents</u> would rend the Union

<u>the government</u> claimed no right to do more than to restrict the territorial enlargement of **it**

<u>Neither party</u> expected for the war the magnitude or the duration

<u>it</u> has already attained

<u>Neither</u> anticipated

the **cause** of the conflict might cease

the conflict itself should cease

(Think for a moment how a cause and an effect like slavery and the war can just "cease.")

At this point, Lincoln's style quickens through a series of short clauses as he introduces God as a character, not yet as an agent, but as a seeming passive OBJECT of prayers and requests.

<u>Each</u> looked for an easier triumph

<u>Both</u> read the same Bible, and pray to the same **God.**

<u>each</u> invokes **His** aid against the other.

<u>It</u> may seem strange that

~~any men should dare to ask a just~~ **God's** assistance in wringing their bread from the sweat of other men's faces

but let <u>us</u> judge not

Notice too how after dealing with slavery indirectly, in those last three clauses, he suddenly invokes its concreteness.

Then in three short passive clauses, Lincoln implies that God can act, but has not as either side wished:

that <u>we</u> **be** not judged [by God?]

<u>The prayers of both</u> could not be answered;

<u>that of neither</u> has been answered fully.

Lincoln then returns to the direct active style, now naming God in the subject of four of the next nine clauses as an acting, purposeful agent :

> **The Almighty** has His own purposes.
> If <u>we</u> shall suppose that
> <u>American slavery</u> . . . must needs come
> **He** now wills to remove
> **He** gives to both North and South this terrible war
> shall <u>we</u> discern therein any departure from those attributes
> <u>the believers in a living God</u> always ascribe to Him?
> Fondly do <u>we</u> hope—fervently do <u>we</u> pray
> <u>this mighty scourge of war</u> may speedily pass away
> Yet, if **God** wills that
> <u>it</u> continue until
> <u>all the wealth piled . . . toil</u> shall be sunk,
> <u>every drop of blood</u> . . . shall be paid by another
> <u>the judgments of the lord</u>, are true

Then he concludes with the majestic climax that we all remember:

> With malice toward none . . . let <u>us</u> strive on to finish the work we are in

In other words, once Lincoln gets past that first abstract and indirect paragraph and a half, he generally demonstrates what we take to be his classic American style: clear, simple, direct, and honest.

With one big and curious exception.

I think that of all the great sentences crafted by American writers, none is craftier than this one, the longest and by far the most complex in the speech, in some ways more complex than it has to be.

> If we shall suppose that American slavery is one of those offences which in the providence of God, must needs come, but which, having continued through His appointed time, He now wills to remove, and that He gives to both North and South this terrible war as the woe due to those by whom the offence came, shall we discern therein any departure from those divine attributes which the believers in a living God always ascribe to Him?

In this sentence. Lincoln expresses the heart of his argument, that the North has no right to exact retribution from the South, for it was not the South that caused the terrible war, but God:

> <u>He</u> gives to both North and South this terrible war . . .

Nor was it the North that ended slavery. God did that too . . .

> <u>He</u> now wills to remove [this offence of American slavery] . . .

And (as we see later) it will not be a triumphant North that ends the war, but God, and at a time of His own choosing:

> If <u>God</u> wills that [the war] continue . . .

In other words, the North has no right to visit its wrath on the South for starting the war or to take take credit for ending either it or slavery; it was God.

But before he wrote those clear and direct clauses assigning to God the historical responsibility for the war, he wrote this oddly indirect passage about the history of slavery:

> American slavery is one of those offences which in the providence of God, must needs come

American slavery seems to have a different origin: Just as he wrote at the end of the second paragraph that "the war came," apparently on its own, so did the offense of slavery.

This clause about American slavery is also ambiguous in two curious ways: How, for example, do we understand the phrase "American slavery": Do we take "American" to be the agent of slavery as in "American slavers," or its object, as in "Americans enslaved?" Or both?

And how are we to construe the verb *continued?*

> one of those offences . . . **which, having continued** through His appointed time, He now wills to remove

That *which having continued* at first seems to imply that the offenses continued on their own through a time that God has appointed. But as we read on, we see it could also mean that God continued the offense of slavery. Which is it? Or is it somehow both?

But it is the nominalizations that distinguish this passage. There are only five of them in these seventy-eight words, an unusually low proportion, but three of them occur in the first sixteen words. We could revise them into verbs and assign them agents:

American **slavery**	→	Americans ENSLAVE Africans
is one of those **offences**	→	Americans OFFENDED God
which in the **providence** of God	→	God PROVIDES [something]

If we reassemble these three clauses into a complete sentence, we get a claim that perhaps startles us:

> <u>God</u> PROVIDED that <u>Americans</u> ENSLAVE Africans, and <u>that</u> OFFENDED God.

Is it reasonable to suppose that Lincoln thought such a statement might raise a theological issue so thorny that, at least on this occasion, he would just as soon deflect it?

To be sure, Lincoln believed that God determined every terrible thing that had happened to both North and South, and in any event the providence of God is mysterious. But he had no problem saying clearly that God *gave* the war to both sides, that God *willed* to remove slavery (as opposed to its just "ceasing," as he wrote earlier in the speech), and though he prays the war will "pass away," he also knows that God might *will* it to continue.

But Lincoln seems less willing to be candid about his belief in God's responsibility for slavery. At least he stylistically finesses the problem: In contrast to using direct verbs to express God's agency in bringing the war and ending both it and slavery, he nominalizes verbs that would make God responsible for slavery, then buries that agency (*in the providence of God*) in the middle of the sentence.

That seventy-eight word sentence is, I think, the stylistic tour de force of American literature. And I have not touched on the doubly conditional nature of the whole sentence, a negative supposition framed as a rhetorical question:

> If we shall suppose [all this], shall we discern therein any departure from [God's attributes]?

The answer is, presumably, "No," but as a question, it allows a "Yes, we do."

But what does all this have to do with that impersonal, indirect opening paragraph? Perhaps this: Lincoln believed that the enormity of the war was God's doing, that the North and South were the guilty objects of God's just punishment. The only time he referred to North or South by name, he made them the guilty recipients of a war willed by God:

> He gives to both North and South this terrible war . . .

He made all the other subject / topic / agents general, nonspecific, even vague: *agents, parties, one, the other, both, all, each, neither, any man.* In fact, Lincoln appears deliberately to avoid naming any specific agent of any action, until he reaches the last third of his speech, where he introduces the only agent whom he names: God.

And perhaps that helps us better understand the impersonality of the opening paragraph. Knowing that he would later introduce God as the only specific agent, he wanted to create an indefinite, impersonal blue / gray–gray / blue background to subordinate everyone else's role in American history, especially his own, to the direct agency of God.

It is a great speech, especially that last sentence whose words are engraved in our national conscience. But even the parts that feel uninspired may now seem at least explicable. And when we look at the way Lincoln managed his explanation of how God directly willed (almost) everything, we see why we include this document among our sacred secular texts.

But now recall the question that motivated this discussion: What are we to make of these stylistic sleights-of-hand, of the inordinate complexity of that key sentence? How do we judge the way Lincoln (what word do we use—manipulated? handled? managed?) shaped the responses of his audience then and of us today? In so doing, was he unethical? The easy answer is no, and I think that's the right answer, at least if we judge by his intentions. But the question forces us to think hard about the ethic of clarity as an unqualified, foundational value. Lincoln was not clear, and, I think, deliberately so.

Exercise 10.5

There are 702 words in the Second Inaugural. In most prose, the proportion of nominalizations to other words is roughly 1:10, with

1:6 being high and 1:20 being unusually low. Count the nominal-izations in this speech. What do you make of the proportion of nominalizations to all words? Do you think that it affects how we respond to this speech? We saw that nine nominalizations ap-peared in the first 134 words, or about 1:15. What is the propor-tion in the rest of the speech? Are the other nominalizations con-centrated anywhere? If so, why?

Exercise 10.6

Pick out every mention of the word *war* in this speech. Look in particular as its function in each sentence: Is it an object or a sub-ject? Does there seem to be any systematic way that Lincoln used the word? (There are sixteen references.) Compare it to how we use the word *slavery* and other words for it, such as *interest* and *cause.*

Exercise 10.7

Lincoln was as deliberate in distancing God from slavery as the writer of the automobile recall letter was in distancing the manu-facturer from its defective product, or the writer of the gas com-pany letter was in distancing the company from its increase in rates. What kinds of ethical distinctions, if any, would you make among these three?

In the Second Inaugural, break up that long sentence begin-ning "If we shall suppose" into shorter, simpler clauses. What is the effect? You could begin

Suppose that American slavery . . .

Exercise 10.8

Read the Declaration of Independence. It is divided into three parts:

- A philosophical explanation of when one form of government may be thrown off and another instituted;
- Beginning at "To prove this, let facts be submitted to a candid world," a list of charges imputed to King George;

- Beginning at "In every stage of these Oppressions We have Petitioned," an account of attempts to avoid separation followed by the long last sentence declaring independence.

Identify the subject of every sentence (of every verb, if you can). If you look at the topic / subjects of each sentence in each part, you can see that Jefferson seemed deliberately and systematically to focus on a different character in the last two sections, and to focus on a different *kind* of topic in the first section. Here is the first sentence of the first section:

> When in the Course of human events, **it becomes necessary** for one people to dissolve the political bands which have connected them with another

He could have written it like this:

> In the course of human events, **we** decided that **we** had to dissolve

He wrote the first charge against King George like this:

> **He** has refused his Assent to Laws.

He could have written it like either of these two:

> There have been **repeated refusals** of Assent to Laws.
> **We** have been refused his Assent to Laws.

And he wrote the first sentence of the last part like this:

> Nor have **We** been wanting in attentions to our British brethren.

He could have written it like either of these two:

> Nor have **our British brethren** been wanting for our attention.
> **Attention** has been directed to our British brethern as well.

First determine how Jefferson systematically varied the topics in the three parts of the Declaration. Then revise some sentences in first part so that they are more like the last part, some sentences in the last part so that they are more like the first part, then some of the sentences in the middle part so that they are more like either the first or last parts. What effect do those changes have? Can you explain why Jefferson varied the style of the parts as he did? What effect was he seeking? In particular, what do you make of these constructions (review pp. 212–15)? Subjects are underlined, verbs capitalized:

> a decent respect to the opinions of mankind REQUIRES
>
> Prudence, indeed, will DICTATE
>
> all experience hath SHEWN
>
> the necessity ... CONSTRAINS them to alter their ... Government
>
> the necessity ... DENOUNCES [proclaims] our Separation

Exercise 10.9

Revise Lincoln's Gettysburg Address so that the topics are not human characters, but abstractions or the place. The first sentence might be,

> Fourscore and seven years ago, **this continent** witnessed a new nation being brought forth by our fathers. **It** was conceived in Liberty and dedicated to the proposition that **equality** is the birthright of all.

How do the new topics change the impact of the speech?

Exercise 10.10

There are 262 words in the Gettysburg Address. Count the abstract nominalizations (ignore the words *living* and the *dead,* but include *battle* in *battleground*). What do you think is the effect of the relative frequency of nominalizations on the way this speech strikes you? Where do most of the nominalizations occur? Why there?

SUMMING UP

Now, at the end of this book, how do we judge what to count as "good" writing? Is it clear, graceful, and candid, even if it fails to achieve its end? Or is it writing that gets the job done, regardless of its intention and means? The best writing is both, of course. But so long as *good* can mean either ethically sound or instrumentally effective, we'll have a problem distinguishing the two. We can resolve that dilemma by our First Principle of Writing: We write well when we would willingly experience what our readers do when they read what we've written. That puts the burden on us as writers to imagine ourselves as our readers.

If you are even moderately advanced in your academic or professional career, most of the issues we've examined here are familiar. You've already keenly experienced the consequences of unclear writing, especially when it is your own. But now that you have some control over your own writing, you may feel reluctant about applying it to the writing of others. When I work with younger writers in the professions, I tell them this: "In the first five or six years of your career, your success will likely depend on how well you write. Thereafter, it is likely to depend increasingly on the writing of those who work for you." So if you expect to achieve some level of success in your profession, you can expect to find yourself managing the writing of others. The more you practice that now, the better you'll do it then.

If you are in your first or second year of college, though, you may wonder whether all this talk about clarity, ethics, and *ethos* is just so much pedagogical finger wagging. At the moment, you may be happy just to find enough words to fill up three pages, never mind how clear they are. And it may be that you are reading textbooks that have been laboriously written and rewritten and revised and edited specifically to make them clear to first-year students. So you may not yet have experienced carelessly dense writing. But it's only a matter of time before you will.

When that happens, your teachers should still be urging you, even coercing you into writing clearly and concisely. But at the same time, you may be reading academic prose that seems anything but clear and concise. So why struggle toward clarity when obscurity seems to pay off? And on top of that, why not follow your entirely predictable and virtually irresistible desire to sound like someone who belongs in the academic world you're struggling to join? This is a dilemma that only experience resolves. What experienced readers know, and you eventually will, is that those writers we judge to be not just clear but graceful are so relatively few that we are desperately grateful when we find them.

The satisfactions of style include, of course, the pleasure we take in the admiration and compliments of our readers. But I also know that for many writers the pleasure of crafting a good paragraph is often just in the sheer achievement of it. That pleasure finally comes down, I think, to the responsibility we feel for our language and the satisfaction we take in meeting it. It is a satisfaction, though, that we find not just in writing, but in all parts of our lives: We take pleasure in doing good work, no matter the job, a view expressed by the philosopher Alfred North Whitehead, with both clarity and grace.

> Finally, there should grow the most austere of all mental qualities; I mean the sense for style. It is an aesthetic sense, based on admiration for the direct attainment of a foreseen end, simply and without waste. Style in art, style in literature, style in science, style in logic, style in practical execution have fundamentally the same aesthetic qualities, namely, attainment and restraint. The love of a subject in itself and for itself, where it is not the sleepy pleasure of pacing a mental quarter-deck, is the love of style as manifested in that study. Here we are brought back to the position from which we started, the utility of education. Style, in its finest sense, is the last acquirement of the educated mind; it is also the most useful. It pervades the whole being. The administrator with a sense for style hates waste; the engineer with a sense for style economizes his material; the artisan with a sense for style prefers good work. Style is the ultimate morality of mind.

> —Alfred North Whitehead, *The Aims of Education and Other Essays*

APPENDIX

Punctuation

I know there are some Persons who affect to despise it, and treat this whole Subject with the utmost Contempt, as a Trifle far below their Notice, and a Formality unworthy of their Regard: They do not hold it difficult, but despicable; and neglect it, as being above it. Yet many learned Men have been highly sensible to its Use; and some ingenious and elegant Writers have condescended to point their Works with Care; and very eminent Scholars have not disdained to teach the Method of doing it with Propriety.

JAMES BURROW

In music, the punctuation is absolutely strict; the bars and rests are absolutely defined. But our prose cannot be quite strict, because we have to relate it to the audience. In other words we are continually changing the score.

SIR RALPH RICHARDSON

One who uses many periods is a philosopher; many interrogations, a student; many exclamations, a fanatic.

J. L. BASFORD

There are some punctuations that are interesting and there are some that are not.

GERTRUDE STEIN

Anyone who can improve a sentence of mine by the omission or placing of a comma is looked upon as my dearest friend.

GEORGE MOORE

Most of us view commas and semicolons about as aesthetically interesting as sorting socks. In fact, many think punctuation is just a matter of following rules. It is not, of course. Used thoughtfully, punctuation can help readers not only see the structure of a complex sentence but respond to its intended nuances, even note modest moments of elegance. It takes more than a few commas to turn a monotone into the Hallelujah Chorus, but a little care can produce gratifying results.

SOME BASIC CONCEPTS

I begin with the least anyone has to know about punctuation, then explore its finer points. I'll address the matter not by describing how to use periods, commas, and so on, but as a functional problem: How do you punctuate the end of a sentence, its beginning, and its middle? I address them in that order because how you end a sentence determines how most of your readers judge your basic literacy. But before I do that, I have to distinguish two kinds of sentences.

Punctuated and Grammatical Sentences

I'll call anything that begins with a capital letter and ends with a period or question / exclamation mark a "punctuated sentence."

But we have to distinguish two kinds of punctuated sentences, because readers do; the one you are reading, for example, is one long punctuated sentence, but it does not feel as long as another long sentence you will read in a moment; I have chosen to punctuate as one sentence what I might have punctuated as a series of shorter ones; those semicolons and the comma before *but* could have been periods, for example—and that dash could have been a period too.

Here is the sentence you just read repunctuated with virtually no change in its grammar:

> We have to distinguish two kinds of punctuated sentences because readers do. The one you are reading, for example, is one short punctuated sentence. But it does not feel as long as another sentence you will read in a moment. I have chosen to punctuate as separate sentences what I earlier punctuated as one long one. The period before *but*, for example, could have been a comma, and last two periods could have been semicolons. And that period could have been a dash.

On the other hand, I can write a different kind of long punctuated sentence, one like this one that I can not break into shorter sentences merely by replacing commas and semicolons with periods, because it is a sentence consisting of several SUBORDINATE CLAUSES, all depending on one MAIN or INDEPENDENT CLAUSE—a sentence like this one that you have almost finished but that probably feels longer than that first long sentence, even though it is actually shorter.

The difference between those two long punctuated sentences is this: Both let us pause often enough, but the first one doesn't force us to hold in mind one grammatical relation after another. At the comma, semicolons, and dash, our minds treat what follows as a new sentence.

On the other hand, the second long sentence forces us to keep sorting out its grammar, right to the end. Just as that first long sentence does, the second one starts with an independent clause:

I can write a different kind of sentence . . . .

But instead of continuing with a series of independent grammatical sentences that we can process individually, it continues with a series of subordinate clauses that we have to keep integrating into a whole:

. . . a sentence

[1][that I can not break into shorter punctuated sentences merely by replacing a comma and semicolons with periods],

[2][because it is a sentence consisting of several subordinate clauses, all of them depending on one main or independent clause]—a sentence like this one

[3][that you have almost finished] but

[4][that probably feels longer than that sentence in the previous paragraph]

[5][even though it is actually shorter]

In this second sentence, we have to keep figuring out to the end how all the subordinate parts fit together, and that requires a lot more mental work.

You have to distinguish those two kinds of punctuated sentences, because your readers will: They may complain about the length of both, but it is easier for them to read a long sentence consisting of a series of short independent clauses than a long sentence consisting of a series of subordinate clauses.

Exercise A.1

Revise that second long sentence beginning with "I can write a different kind of sentence" making at least some of the subordinate clauses independent clauses. Then set those independent clauses off first with commas, semicolons, and colons. Then punctuate that revised sentence a second time, this time with periods. How have you changed the style of the sentence? Which revision changes the style of the original sentence more radically: periods, or commas and semicolons?

THE STYLE OF SIMPLE, COMPOUND, AND COMPLEX SENTENCES

At this point, you may be thinking about the standard definitions of "simple," "compound," and "complex" sentences: Most of us learned that if a sentence consists of a single independent clause, it is *simple*.

> SIMPLE: English dictionaries date back more than 400 years.

If it consists of two or more independent clauses, it is *compound:*

> COMPOUND: [English dictionaries date back more than 400 years][1], [but the greatest of them all is the *Oxford English Dictionary*][2].

If it has an independent clause and at least one subordinate clause, it is *complex*.

> COMPLEX: [While there are many good dictionaries]subordinate clause, [the greatest of them all is the Oxford English Dictionary]independent clause.

But that terminology is misleading, because it encourages us to think that a grammatically simple sentence should *feel* stylistically simpler than one that is grammatically complex. But most readers think that of the next two, the grammatically simple sentence *feels* more complex than the grammatically complex one:

> GRAMMATICALLY SIMPLE: Our review of the test resulted in a decision as to its suspension as a result of complaints from teachers.

GRAMMATICALLY COMPLEX: When we reviewed the test, we decided to suspend it because teachers complained about it.

Like the words *active* and *passive,* the terms *simple* and *complex* confusingly refer both to our impressions and to grammatical structure.

THOUGHTFUL PUNCTUATION

In what follows, then, I use terms a bit different from those you might recall.

- The term *grammatical sentence* refers to a single independent clause plus all of its attached subordinate clauses, if any. The term therefore covers both simple and complex sentences:

    I left.

    I left because I was tired.

- What we learned to call a *compound* sentence comprises at least two grammatical sentences.

    I left,_{grammatical sentence 1} but I returned_{grammatical sentence 2.}
- A *punctuated* sentence may therefore consist of a single grammatical sentence or several.

Those are the basics; now we can discuss how to apply them.

Punctuating the Ends of Grammatical Sentences

Beyond all other considerations, you have to let readers know where one grammatical sentence stops and the next begins. This one does not:

In 1957 and again in 1960, Congress passed civil rights laws that remedied problems of registration and voting this had significant political consequences throughout the South.

You have ten ways to punctuate a pair of grammatical sentences. Three are most common:

Three Common Forms of End-punctuation

1. Period (or Question/Exclamation Mark) Alone   The simplest way to signal the end of a grammatical sentence is with a period, thereby turning the one punctuated sentence into two:

✓   In 1957 and 1960, Congress passed laws that remedied problems of registration and <u>voting. This</u> had significant political consequences throughout the South.

But if you end up with too many short punctuated sentences, your readers may feel your prose is choppy, even simplistic. Experienced writers often revise a series of short grammatical sentences into subordinate clauses or phrases, turning two or more grammatical sentences into one:

✓   **After Congress passed laws in 1957 and 1960 to remedy problems of registration and voting,** those laws had significant political consequences throughout the South.

✓   The laws **that Congress passed in 1957 and 1960 remedying problems of registration and voting** had significant political consequences throughout the South.

Be cautious, though: Combine too many short grammatical sentences into one, and you create one sentence that is long and shapeless. To avoid that kind of baggy complexity but still avoid the choppiness of one short grammatical sentence after another, you can connect grammatical sentences in other ways.

2. Semicolon Alone   A semicolon is like a permeable period; whatever is on either side of it should be a grammatical sentence. When readers see a semicolon end a grammatical sentence, they assume that the grammatical sentence that follows is closely linked to the one they just finished:

✓   ~~In 1957 and again in 1960, Congress passed laws that remedied prob-~~ lems of registration and <u>voting; those</u> laws had significant political consequences throughout the South.

But if readers can't see any clear conceptual link between the two, they experience a small twinge of confusion as they try to figure it out:

In 1957 and again in 1960, Congress passed laws in order to remedy problems of registration and <u>voting; by 1995</u> Southern states had thousands of sheriffs, mayors, and other officials from their Afro-American communities.

A few shared concepts would make the connections clearer:

✓ In 1957 and again in 1960, Congress passed civil rights laws in order to remedy racial problems of registration and voting, particularly in the South; by 1995 Southern states had elected thousands of sheriffs, mayors, and other officials from their African-American communities.

A SPECIAL PROBLEM WITH *HOWEVER:* There is a common occasion on which even well-educated writers confuse readers by using a comma where they should use a semicolon or period: when they end one grammatical sentence and begin another with *however.* The punctuation in this next example is wrong because we don't know whether the *however* goes with the first grammatical sentence or with the second:

> [Taxpayers have supported public education through <u>taxes,]</u> **however, [they** are beginning to resist because taxes have been rising so steeply].

That first grammatical sentence must end with a period or a semicolon to signal readers that they have finished one grammatical sentence and are beginning a new one. If the *however* goes with the second sentence, then the semicolon should precede it:

✓ [Taxpayers have supported public education through <u>taxes]</u> [1] ; [<u>how-ever,</u> they are beginning to resist because taxes have been rising so steeply][2].

Writers mistakenly use a comma there probably because they often see *however* inside a grammatical sentence, where it should be set off by commas on either side:

✓ [Taxpayers have been willing to support public education through taxes]. [They are beginning to <u>resist, **however,** because</u> taxes have been rising so steeply].

A fairly reliable rule: If you have more than ten or so words before a *however* and as many after, you may well need to change the comma *before* the *however* to a semicolon or period, because that *however* probably begins a new grammatical sentence. But double-check to be sure.

3. *Comma + COORDINATING CONJUNCTION*   Readers recognize the end of a grammatical sentence when they see a comma followed by

- a coordinating conjunction: *and, but, yet, for, so, or, nor,* and
- followed by another grammatical sentence.

✓ In the 1950's religion came to be viewed as a bulwark against <u>communism, **so**</u> it was not long after that that atheism was felt to threaten national security.

✓ American intellectuals have often followed <u>Europeans, **but**</u> our culture has proven inhospitable to their brand of socialism.

But prefer the period if the two grammatical sentences are long and have their own internal punctuation.

When readers begin a coordinated series of three or more grammatical sentences, they accept just a comma between the first two, but only if they are short and have no internal punctuation:

✓ Baseball satisfies our love of leisurely <u>skill, basketball</u> speaks to our admiration for speed and <u>grace, and football</u> appeals to our lust for violence.

If either of the first two clauses has internal punctuation, separate them with semicolons:

✓ Baseball, the oldest indigenous American sport and essentially a rural one, satisfies our admiration for precise <u>skill; basketball</u>, our newest sport and now more urban than rural, speaks to our love of speed and <u>grace; and football</u>, a sport both rural and urban, appeals to our lust for violence.

AN EXCEPTION: You introduce a coordinated pair of short grammatical sentences with a modifier that applies to both of them. In that case, omit the comma between them:

✓ By 1995, the economies of the Soviet Union's former satellites had begun to <u>rebound but Russia's</u> had yet to hit bottom.

Four Less Common Forms of End Punctuation

4. *Period + Coordinating Conjunction*   Some readers think it an error to begin a punctuated sentence with a coordinating conjunction such as *and* or *but*. But they are wrong; this is entirely correct:

✓ Education cannot guarantee a <u>democracy. But</u> without it, democracy cannot survive.

A *however* there would be too heavy.

Like any rhetorical device, of course, this way of linking sentences can become pointless when used to excess. No more than once or twice every page or so is about right, especially for *and*.

5. Semicolon + Coordinating Conjunction   Writers rarely end one grammatical sentence with a semicolon and begin the next with a coordinating conjunction, so generally avoid this:

> In the 1950s religion came to be viewed as a bulwark against <u>communism; so it</u> was not long after that atheism was felt to threaten national security.

Use a comma there. Of course, readers are grateful for a semicolon if the two grammatical sentences are long with their own internal commas:

✓ Problem solving, one of the most active areas of cognitive psychology, has made great strides in the last decade, particularly in regard to understanding the problem-solving strategies of <u>experts; so it</u> is no surprise that educators have followed that research with interest.

But they would probably appreciate a period even more.

6. Comma Alone   Though readers ordinarily do not expect to see just a comma separate two grammatical sentences, they are not confused if the two sentences are short, balanced in length, and closely linked in meaning, such as cause-effect, first-second, if-then, this-but-not-that, etc. Be sure, though, that neither has internal commas. This would be confusing:

> Women, who have always been underpaid, no longer accept that discriminatory <u>treatment, they</u> are now doing something about it.

This is clearer:

✓ Women have always been <u>underpaid, they</u> are now doing something about it.

But a warning: Though writers of the best prose do this, many teachers consider it an error, so be sure of your readers before you experiment.

7. Conjunction Alone   Nor is it uncommon to signal the close linkage of two short grammatical sentences with a coordinating conjunction alone, omitting the comma:

✓ Oscar Wilde brazenly violated one of the fundamental laws of British <u>society **and** we</u> all know what happened to him.

But the same warning: Writers of the best prose do this, but many teachers consider it an error.

Three Special Cases: Colon, Dash, Parentheses

8. Colon   Discerning readers think you are a more than common writer if you end a sentence with an appropriate colon: They take it as shorthand for to *illustrate, for example, that is, let me expand on what I just said, therefore:*

✓   Only one question <u>remains: What</u> if we lose money?

✓   Dance is not widely <u>supported: No</u> company operates at a profit, and there are few outside major cities.

A colon also lets you signal more obviously than with a comma or semi-colon that you are self-consciously balancing the structure, sound, and meaning of one clause against that of another:

✓   Civil disobedience is the public conscience of a <u>democracy: mass</u> enthusiasm is the public consensus of a tyranny.

A rule of thumb, however: Avoid inserting a colon if it breaks a clause into two pieces, neither of which would be a grammatically complete sentence, like this:

> Genetic counseling <u>requires: a thorough</u> knowledge of statistical genetics, an awareness of choices open to parents, and the psychological competence to deal with emotional trauma.

Neither chunk before or after that colon could be a grammatical sentence. Instead, put the colon after a whole SUBJECT-VERB OBJECT structure:

✓   Genetic counseling <u>requires the following: a thorough</u> knowledge of statistical genetics, an awareness of choices open to parents, and the psychological competence to deal with emotional trauma.

In that sentence, the reader completes a chunk of a clause that could stand as a punctuated sentence, even though what follows is part of it.

If what follows the colon is a grammatical sentence, capitalize the first word or not, depending on how much you want to emphasize what follows. I tend to do so regularly, because it helps a reader anticipate that what follows is a grammatical sentence

9. *Dash* You can signal the same balance more informally with a dash—it suggests the casual immediacy of an afterthought:

✓ Stonehenge is a <u>wonder—only</u> a genius could have conceived it.

Try that with a colon: it makes a difference.

10. *Parentheses* You can attach a short grammatical sentence to another grammatical sentence with parentheses, if what is in the parentheses is like a short afterthought. Put the period outside the last parenthesis:

Stonehenge is a wonder <u>(only a genius could have conceived it)</u>.

Summary: Ten Ways to End a Grammatical Sentence

1. Parenthesis	I win (you lose**)**.
2. Comma alone	I win, you lose.
3. Conjunction alone	I win **and** you lose.
4. Dash	I win—you lose.
5. Comma + coordinating conjunction	I win**, and** you lose.
6. Semicolon	I win**;** you lose.
7. Colon	I win: you lose.
8. Semicolon + coordinating conjunction	I win**; and** you lose.
9. Period + coordinating conjunction	I win. **And** you lose.
10. Period	I win. You lose.

Readers take these ways of ending grammatical sentences as increasingly emphatic (personal taste, however, varies). If you choose punctuation that separates grammatical sentences only slightly—just a comma or conjunction—be certain your readers can recognize that those clauses are closely linked, because they look for that linkage.

PUNCTUATING BEGINNINGS

Punctuation at the beginning of a sentence is not an issue when the sentence begins directly with its SUBJECT, as this one does. However, as with this one, when it forces a reader to plow through several introductory modifying phrases and clauses, especially when they have their own internal punctuation, and that readers might be confused by it all (as you probably are right now), forget trying to punctuate it right: Rewrite it:

✓ If you open a sentence with complicated phrases and clauses, you are likely to confuse your readers, so rewrite it.

There are a few other rules that your readers expect you always to follow, but more often you have to rely on your judgment to decide how best to help them.

Five Reliable Rules

1. Always separate an introductory element from the subject that follows it if a reader might misunderstand the structure of the sentence. Do **not** do this:

   When a lawyer <u>concludes her argument</u> has to be easily remembered by a jury.

   Do this:

   ✓ When a lawyer <u>concludes, her argument</u> has to be easily remembered by a jury.

2. Never put a semicolon at the end of an introductory element, no matter how long and complicated. Readers take semicolons to mean they have come to the end of a grammatical sentence (but see p. 270). Do not do this:

   Although the Administration knew that Iraq's invasion of Kuwait threatened American interests in Saudi <u>Arabia; it</u> did not immediately prepare a military response.

   Always use a comma there. But if that element is long and complicated, consider breaking it out as a grammatical sentence:

   ✓ The Administration knew that Iraq's invasion of Kuwait threatened American interests in Saudi <u>Arabia, but it</u> did not immediately prepare a military response.

3. Never put a comma right after a subordinating conjunction. Not this:

   <u>Although, the</u> practice of punctuation is not complicated, it is rarely mastered.

4. Do not put a comma after the coordinating conjunctions *and, but, yet, for, so, or,* and *nor,* if the next element is the subject. Do not do this:

   <u>But, we</u> cannot know whether life on other planets realizes that we're here and simply prefers to ignore us.

Some writers who punctuate heavily put a comma after a coordinating conjunction if an introductory word or phrase follows:

✓   Yet, *during this period,* prices continued to rise.

Such heavy punctuation retards a reader a bit, but it's your choice. These are also correct and for the reader, perhaps a bit swifter:

✓   Yet during this period, prices continued to rise.

✓   Yet during this period prices continued to rise.

5. Put a comma after an introductory word or phrase that comments on the whole of the following sentence or a conjunction that connects one sentence to another.

These include elements like *fortunately, possibly, perhaps,* etc., and conjunctions like *however, nevertheless, regardless, instead,* etc. Since readers hear sentences in their mind's ear, they expect a pause after such words.

✓   <u>Fortunately, we</u> found that these groups are as healthy as others.

Consider revising, however, if you find yourself starting many sentences with an introductory element and a comma. A series of such sentences make a whole passage feel hesitant.

Three common exceptions: We typically omit a comma after *now, thus,* and *hence:*

✓   <u>Now it is</u> clear that many will not support this position.

✓   <u>Thus the only</u> alternative is to choose some other action.

Three Reliable Principles

1. Readers need no punctuation after a short introductory phrase directly before a subject:

✓   <u>Once again we</u> find similar responses to such stimuli.

✓   <u>In 1945 few</u> realized how the war had transformed us.

It is not wrong to put a comma there, but again, it slows readers just as you may want them to be picking up speed.

2. Readers often need a comma after a *long* introductory phrase or clause:

✓   When a lawyer begins her opening statement with a dry recital of the law and how it must be applied to the case before the <u>court, the jury</u> is likely to nod off.

But there are other considerations: How long does a reader feel is too long and how closely do you want to connect the meanings of the two clauses? Readers don't need a comma when the clause is shorter than, say, 10 or so words, its subject is the same as the subject of the main clause, and its meaning closely depends on the meaning of the main clause:

✓ When **Hitler** realized that he had lost the war **he** ordered his army to raze every city through which it retreated.

But if the subjects of the clauses differ and the ideas contrast, a comma helps the reader sense the opposition. Compare:

✓ Since **we** accepted the IRS' data **we** dropped further appeals.

✓ Although the **IRS** overruled us, **we** will still follow our original procedures.

3. Readers do not expect a comma to separate a subject from its verb. Do not do this:

> A sentence that consists of many complex subordinate clauses and long phrases that all precede a verb, **may** seem to some students to demand a comma somewhere.

As we've said before, readers generally dislike long subjects, so the best policy is to keep subjects short, making a comma unnecessary. Readers need a comma between a subject and a verb only when a phrase or clause clearly *interrupts* that expected connection. (See the next section on interruptions.)

Occasionally, you cannot avoid a long subject, especially if it consists of a list of items with internal punctuation:

> The President, the Vice-President, the Secretaries of the Departments, Senators, members of the House of Representatives, and Supreme Court Justices, take an oath that pledges them to uphold the Constitution.

In these circumstances, help your readers sort out the subject from the rest of the sentence by creating a SUMMATIVE SUBJECT, a second one or two word subject that sums up the longer one.

✓ The President, the Vice-President, the Secretaries of the Departments, Senators, members of the House of Representatives, and Supreme Court Justices: **all** take an oath that pledges them to uphold the Constitution.

To create such a subject:

- Insert a colon or a dash at the end of that long subject:
  > The President, the Vice-President, the Secretaries of the Departments, Senators, members of the House of Representatives, and Supreme Court Justices:

- Then insert a word that summarizes the preceding list:
  ✓ The President, the Vice-President, the Secretaries of the Departments, Senators, members of the House of Representatives, and Supreme Court Justices: **all** take an oath that pledges them to uphold the Constitution.

Choose a dash or a colon depending on how formal you want to seem.

PUNCTUATING MIDDLES

This is where explanations get messy, because to punctuate inside a grammatical sentence—more specifically, inside a clause, you have to consider not only the grammar of that clause, but the nuances of its rhythm, meaning, and the emphasis that you want your readers to hear in their mind's ear.

Interruptions

When you insert a phrase or clause between a subject and verb or a verb and object, your readers have a marginally harder time making the grammatical connections that hold those basic elements of a sentence together. So in general, avoid interruptions (see p. 170). But sometimes for reasons of emphasis or nuance, you want to interrupt those connections. In that case, you have t help your reader recognize the interruption by setting it off with *paired* commas or dashes:

> A sentence, **if it consists of many complex subordinate clauses and long phrases and that all precede a verb**, may seem to need a comma somewhere.

Readers need commas before and after shorter ADVERBIAL PHRASES, depending on what kind of emphasis you want them to feel. The general principle of emphasis is this: Readers feel that emphasis falls on whatever immediately follows a pause. Compare the different emphases in these:

✓   Modern poetry has become more relevant to the average reader in recent years.

✓   Modern poetry <u>has, in recent years,</u> **become** more relevant to the average reader.

✓   Modern poetry has <u>become, in recent years,</u> **more** relevant to the average reader.

✓   The antagonism between Congress and the president has created utter distrust among every group of voters.

✓   The antagonism between Congress and the president has <u>created,</u>
<u>among every group of voters,</u> **utter** distrust.

Loose Commentary

"Loose commentary" is different from an interruption, because
you can usually move an interruption someplace else in the sentence. But loose commentary modifies what it is next to, and so it
cannot be moved. It still needs to be set off with commas, parentheses, or dashes. It is difficult to explain exactly what counts as
loose commentary because it depends on both grammar and
meaning. One familiar distinction is between RESTRICTIVE and
NONRESTRICTIVE MODIFIERS (see pp. 24–25) and APPOSITIVES.

We use no commas with restrictive modifiers because they are not
loose commentary; they are necessary to understand the sentence:

✓   The tax deduction for child support belongs to the parent <u>with whom</u>
<u>the child resides.</u>

But we always set off nonrestrictive modifiers with *paired* commas
(unless the modifier ends the sentence), because they are loose
commentary, not necessary to understand the meaning of the
sentence:

✓   We had to reconstruct the larynx, <u>which is the source of voice,</u> with
cartilage from the shoulder.

An appositive is actually just a truncated nonrestrictive clause:

✓   We had to rebuild the larynx, <u>the source of voice,</u> with cartilage from
the shoulder.

You can achieve a more casual effect with a dash:

✓   We had to rebuild the larynx—<u>which is the source of voice</u>—with cartilage from the shoulder.

A dash is particularly useful when the loose commentary itself has internal commas. Readers find this confusing:

> The nations of Central Europe, Poland, Hungary, Romania, Bulgaria, the Czech Republic, Slovakia, Bosnia, Serbia have for centuries been in the middle of an East-West tug-of-war.

They understand this kind of structure more easily if they can see that loose modifier set off with dashes or parentheses:

✓ The nations of Central Europe—<u>Poland, Hungary, Romania, Bulgaria, the Czech Republic, Slovakia, Bosnia, Serbia</u>—have for centuries been in the middle of an East-West tug-of-war.

Use parentheses when you want your reader to hear your comment as a *sotto voce* aside:

✓ The brain <u>(at least that part that controls nonprimitive functions)</u> may comprise several little brains operating simultaneously.

or use it as an explanatory footnote inside a sentence:

✓ Lamarck <u>(1744–1829)</u> was a French naturalist and pre-Darwinian evolutionist.
✓ The poetry of the *fin de siècle* <u>(end of the century)</u> was characterized by a world-weariness and fashionable despair.

When loose commentary is at the end of a sentence, use a comma to separate it from the first part of the sentence. Be certain, however, that the meaning of the commentary is not crucial to the meaning of the sentence. Contrast these:

✓ I wandered through <u>Europe, seeking a place</u> where I could write undisturbed.
✓ I spent my <u>time seeking a place</u> where I could write undisturbed.
✓ Offices will be closed July 2<u>–6, as announced in</u> the daily bulletin.
✓ When closing offices, secure all <u>safes as prescribed</u> in the Manual.
✓ Historians have overlooked the effect of social <u>changes, at least in this country</u>.
✓ These records must be <u>maintained at least until the IRS has reviewed them</u>.

Here's the point: You can rely on four principles.

1. Inside the boundaries of a clause, you always use *paired* marks of punctuation—commas, parentheses, or dashes. Never use semicolons (but see p. 270).
2. Set off what prominently interrupts grammatical connections with commas, parentheses, or dashes. Never use semicolons.
3. Set off loose commentary with commas, parentheses, or dashes. Never use semicolons.
4. Use commas to separate items in a series. Use semicolons to set off items in a series only when they have internal commas (see p. 270).

PUNCTUATING COORDINATED ELEMENTS

Punctuating Two Coordinate Elements

Generally speaking, do not insert a comma between just two coordinated elements. Compare these:

   As computers have become <u>sophisticated, and powerful</u> they have taken over more <u>clerical, and</u> bookkeeping tasks.

✓ As computers have become <u>sophisticated and powerful</u> they have taken over more <u>clerical and bookkeeping</u> tasks.

Three Exceptions

1. To achieve a dramatic contrast, put a comma after even a short coordinate element if you want to emphasize a contradiction between the two:

✓ The ocean is nature's most glorious <u>creation, and its</u> most destructive.

   This use of a comma is especially emphatic before a *but:*

✓ Organ transplants are becoming more <u>common, but not</u> less expensive.

2. If you want your readers to feel the cumulative power of a coordinated pair (or more), drop the *and* and leave just a comma. Compare these:

✓   Lincoln never had a formal <u>education and never</u> owned a large library.

✓   Lincoln never had a formal <u>education, never owned</u> a large library.

✓   The lesson of the pioneers was to ignore conditions that seemed difficult or even <u>overwhelming and to get on</u> with the business of subduing a hostile environment.

✓   The lesson of the pioneers was to ignore conditions that seemed difficult or even <u>overwhelming, to get on</u> with the business of subduing a hostile environment.

3. Put a comma between long coordinate pairs only if you think your readers need a chance to breathe or to sort out the grammar. Compare:

It is in the graveyard that Hamlet finally realizes that the inevitable end of life is the <u>grave and clay and that</u> regardless of one's station in <u>life the end</u> of all pretentiousness and all plotting and counter-plotting must be dust.

A comma after *clay* and *life* signals a natural pause:

✓   It is in the graveyard that Hamlet finally realizes that the inevitable end of all life is the <u>grave and clay, and that</u> regardless of one's station in <u>life, the</u> end of all pretentiousness and all plotting and counter-plotting must be dust.

More important, the comma after *clay* sorts out the structure of a potentially confusing *grave and clay and that regardless*.

In this next sentence, the first half of a coordination is long, so a reader might have a problem connecting the second half of the coordination to its origin:

Conrad's *Heart of Darkness* brilliantly dramatizes those primitive impulses that lie deep in each of us and stir only in our darkest <u>dreams but asserts</u> the need for the values that control those impulses.

A comma after *dreams* would clearly mark the end of one coordinate member and the beginning of the next:

✓   Conrad's *Heart of Darkness* brilliantly dramatizes those primitive impulses that lie deep in each of us and stir only in our darkest <u>dreams, but asserts</u> the need for the values that control those impulses.

On the other hand, if you find yourself trying to make sense out of a complicated sentence with punctuation alone, you probably need to revise the whole sentence

Punctuating a Series of Three or More Coordinated Elements

Finally, there is the matter of punctuating a series of three or more coordinated elements. First decide whether in such a series you are someone who, as a matter of principle, does or does not put a comma before the *and*:

✓   His wit, his <u>charm and his loyalty</u> made him our friend.

✓   His wit, his <u>charm, and his loyalty</u> made him our friend.

Both are correct, but be consistent. If any of the items in the series has its own internal commas, then readers rely on semicolons to see how they should group the items:

✓   In mystery novels, the principal action ought to be economical, organic, and lo<u>gical; fas</u>cinating, yet not exo<u>tic; clear</u>, but complicated enough to hold the reader's interest.

SUMMING UP

Rather than summarize this detailed material, I offer just a three bits of advice:

- Always signal the end of a grammatical sentence.
- Always observe the five reliable rules.
- Always set off long interrupting elements with commas.

Beyond that, use your good judgment: Punctuate in ways that help your readers see the connections and separations that they have to see to make sense of your sentences. That means you must put yourself in the place of your reader, not easy to do, but something you must learn. On the other hand, write a clearly structured sentence in the first place, and your punctuation will take care of itself.

Exercise A.2

These passages lack their original punctuation. Slash marks indicate grammatical sentences. Punctuate them three times, once using the least punctuation possible, a second time using as much varied punctuation as you can, and then a third time as you think

improve some.

1. Scientists and philosophers of science tend to speak as if "scientific language" were intrinsically precise as if those who use it must understand one another's meaning even if they disagree / but in fact scientific language is not as different from ordinary language as is commonly believed / it too is subject to imprecision and ambiguity and hence to imperfec understanding / moreover new theories or arguments are rarely if ever constructed by way of clear-cut steps of tion deduction and verification or falsification / neither are they defended rejected or accepted in so straightforward a manner / in practice scientists combine the rules of scientific methodology with a generous admixture of intuition aesthetics and philosophical commitment / the importance of what are sometimes called extra-rational or extra-logical components of thought in the *discovery* of a new principle or law is generally acknowledged. / . . . but the role of these extralogical components in persuasion and acceptance in making an argument convincing is less frequently discussed partly because they are less visible / the ways in which the credibility or effectiveness of an argument depends on the realm of common experiences on extensive practice in communicating those experiences in a common language are hard to see precisely because such commonalities are taken for granted / only when we step out of such a "consensual domain" when we can stand out on the periphery of a community with a common language do we begin to become aware of the unarticulated premises mutual understandings and assumed practices of group even in those subjects that lend themselves most readily to quantification / discourse depends heavily on conventions and interpretation conventions that are acquired over years o practice and participation in a community.

—Evelyn Fox Keller, *A Feeling for the Organism: The Life and Work of Barbara McClintock*

2. In fact of course the notion of universal knowledge has always been an illusion / but it is an illusion fostered by the monistic view of the world in which a few great central truths determine in all its wonderful and amazing proliferation everything else that is true / we are not today tempted to search

for these keys that unlock the whole of human knowledge and

well taught it / and the more surely and deeply we know our own job the better able we are to appreciate the full measure of our pervasive ignorance / we know that these are inherent limits compounded no doubt and exaggerated by that sloth and that complacency without which we would not be men at all / but knowledge rests on knowledge / what is new is meaningful because it departs slightly from what was known before / this is a world of frontiers where even the liveliest of actors or observers will be absent most of the time from most of them / perhaps this sense was not so sharp in the village that village which we have learned a little about but probably do not understand too well the village of slow change and isolation and fixed culture which evokes our nostalgia even if not our full comprehension / perhaps in the villages men were not so lonely / perhaps they found in each other a fixed community a fixed and only slowly growing store of knowledge of a single world / even that we may doubt / for there seem to be always in the culture of such times and places vast domains of mystery if not unknowable then imperfectly known endless and open.

—J. Robert Oppenheimer, "The Sciences and Man's Community,"
from *Science and the Common Understanding*

Glossary

Grammar is the ground of all.
WILLIAM LANGLAND

Most of the grounds of the world's troubles are matters of grammar.
MONTAIGNE

There is a satisfactory boniness about grammar which the flesh of sheer vocabulary requires before it can become vertebrate and walk the earth. But to study it for its own sake, without relating it to function, is utter madness.
ANTHONY BURGESS

Thou hast most traitorously corrupted the youth of the realm in erecting a grammar school. . . . It will be proved to thy face, that thou hast men about thee that usually talk of a noun and a verb, and such abominable words as no Christian ear can endure to hear.
WILLIAM SHAKESPEARE, 2 HENRY VI, 4.7

What follows is no tight theory of grammar, just definitions useful for the terms in this book. Where the text discusses something at length, I refer you to those pages in the interest of saving space here.

Action: Action includes movement, feeling, cognition, etc. Prototypically, an action is expressed by a verb: *move, hate, think, discover*. But actions also appear in NOMINALIZATIONS: *movement, hatred, thought, discovery*. Associated with actions are conditions, typically expressed by adjectives: *able, intelligent, plausible*, etc. These may also be nominalized: *ability, intelligence, plausibility*. (pp. 48–50)

Active: Distinguish between what is by grammatical definition a VERB in the active voice and a sentence whose style *feels* active. (pp. 78–79). The first below is active but feels passive; the second is passive but feels more active than the first.

> Discovery of the deficit **required** termination of the project.

> When the deficit **was discovered,** the project **was terminated.**

A grammatically active verb has a SUBJECT that is the AGENT of its action, occurs in its PAST PARTICIPLE form only after *have* and has an OBJECT after the VERB: *I **have** bro**ken** the code.*

Adjective: A word you can put *very* in front of: *very old, very interesting*. There are some exceptions: *major, additional, resumptive*, etc. Since this is also a test for ADVERBS, you can distinguish adjectives from adverbs by trying them out between *the* and a noun: *The **occupational** hazard, the **major** reason*, etc. Unfortunately, some nouns occur in the same position—*the **chemical** hazard*.

Adjective Phrase: An ADJECTIVE and what attaches to it: *so **full** that it burst.*

Adjectival Clause: Adjectival clauses modify nouns. Also called RELATIVE clauses, they usually begin with a relative pronoun: *which, that, whom, whose, who:* There are two kinds: RESTRICTIVE and NONRESTRICTIVE.

| Restrictive | The book **that** *I read* was good. |
| Nonrestrictive | My car, **which** *you saw,* is gone. |

Adverb: Adverbs modify all parts of speech except NOUNS:

Adjectives	**extremely** large, **rather** old, **very** tired.
Verbs	**frequently** spoke, **often** slept, left **here.**
Adverbs	**very** carefully, **somewhat** often, **a bit** late.
Articles	**precisely** the man I meant, **just** the thing I need.
Sentences	**Fortunately,** we were on time.

Adverb Phrase: The adverb and what attaches to it: *as **slowly** as possible.*

Adverbial Clause: This is a kind of SUBORDINATE CLAUSE. Adverbial clauses modify a VERB or ADJECTIVE, indicating time, cause, condition, etc. They usually begin with SUBORDINATING CONJUNCTIONS like *because, when, if, since, while, unless:*

> **If you leave,** I will stop. **Because he left,** I did too.

Agent: A kind of CHARACTER. Prototypically, agents are flesh-and-blood, but for our purposes, an agent is the *seeming* source of any ACTION, the entity without which the action could not occur.

> **She** criticized the program in this report.

Often, we can make the means by which we do something into a seeming agent:

> **This report** criticizes the program.

Do not confuse agents with SUBJECTS. They prototypically are subjects, but an agent can be in a grammatical OBJECT: *I underwent an interrogation by **the police.*** (pp. 69–75)

Appositive: A word or PHRASE that modifies a NOUN but that is not necessary to identify it uniquely. An appositive is just a reduced NONRESTRICTIVE CLAUSE:

| Nonrestrictive clause | This report, **which is a devastating criticism of the program,** is true. |
| Appositive | This report, ~~**which is**~~ **a devastating criticism of the program,** is true. |

Article: They are easier to list than define: *a, an, the, this, these, that, those.*

Character: Prototypically, a flesh-and-blood person who acts or is acted on. If a character acts, it is an AGENT; if acted on, a GOAL. We also count inanimate entities as characters if a writer repeatedly refers to them, particularly in the SUBJECT/TOPIC of several consecutive sentences. By this definition, abstract NOUNS count as a kind of character. Thus *cognitive complexity* is a character if we repeatedly use it as the subject of VERBS. (pp. 73–75)

Clause: A clause has two defining characteristics:

1. It is a sequence of at least one SUBJECT + VERB.
2. The verb agrees with the subject in number and can be made past or present.

By this definition, these next are all clauses:

    She left   that they leave   if she left   why he is leaving

These next are not, because the verbal forms cannot be made past tense nor do they agree in number with the putative subject:

    for her to **go**   her **having gone**

Complement: Whatever completes a VERB:

    I am **home.**   You seem **tired.**   She helped **me.**

Compound Noun: Spelling alone does not signal when consecutive nouns constitute a compound noun. Some are separate words: *space capsule, retirement home;* some are hyphenated: *mother-in-law, eighty-two;* some are one word: *airport, bookkeeper.* A reliable test is pronunciation: If the first word is stressed, it is a compound word: *dóghòuse, skyscràper, bóok déaler.* On the other hand, some phrases that seem to be compounds are stressed on the second word: *garden páth, stone wáll, father conféssor.* (p. 91)

Conjunction: Usually defined as a word that links other words, PHRASES, or CLAUSES. (But so do VERBS and PREPOSITIONS.) They are easier to illustrate than define (the first two are also categorized as SUBORDINATING conjunctions):

ADVERBIAL conjunctions	because, although, when, since, etc.
RELATIVE conjunctions	who, whom, whose, which, that
SENTENCE conjunctions	thus, however, therefore, nevertheless
COORDINATING conjunctions	and, but, yet, for, so, or, nor
CORRELATIVE conjunctions	both X and Y, not only X but Y, either X or Y, neither X nor Y, X as well as Y

Coordination: We coordinate grammatically equal elements:

Same part of speech	*you* **and** *I, red* **and** *black, run* **or** *jump.*
PHRASES	*in the house* **but** *not in the basement.*
CLAUSES	*when I leave* **or** *when you arrive.*

(pp. 180–83)

Correlative Conjunction: Ordinarily, the second conjunction of a pair of correlative conjunctions should precede a word, PHRASE, or CLAUSE that exactly parallels the first:

| **Not** | | He **both** *had the data* **and** *the equipment* to display it. |
| But this | ✓ | He had **both** *the data* **and** *the equipment* to display it. |

Not		We will **either** *arrive on Monday* **or** *on Wednesday.*
But this	✓	We will arrive **either** *on Monday* **or** *on Wednesday.*
Or this	✓	We will arrive on **either** *Monday* **or** *Wednesday.*

Dangling Modifier: A dangling modifier is a PHRASE whose implicit SUBJECT is different from the explicit subject of the CLAUSE that the modifier attaches to. Strictly speaking, this opening phrase dangles:

> To understand this answer, the question has to be analyzed carefully.

The implicit subject of *to understand* is some unnamed person, but the explicit subject of the following clause is *the question*. To fix this, one or the other has to be changed:

> For anyone to understand this answer, the question has to be analyzed.
>
> To understand the answer, you have to analyze the question.

(pp. 185–87)

Dependent Clause: Any CLAUSE that cannot be punctuated as a MAIN CLAUSE, one beginning with a capital letter and ending with a period or question mark. It usually begins with a subordinating conjunction such as *because, if, when, which, that:*

> why he left   because he left   which he left

Direct Object: The NOUN that follows a TRANSITIVE VERB and can be made the SUBJECT of a PASSIVE verb:

> I found **the money.** → **The money** was found by me.

Distinguish this from INDIRECT objects: *I gave **my friend** the money.* Indirect objects can also be made the object of the PREPOSITION *to: I gave the money **to my friend,*** and the subject of a passive sentence: ***My friend** was given the money.*

Emphatic: A word that heightens truth or certainty: **very** old, **certainly** true, **completely** useless. (p. 153)

Finite Verb: A verb that can be made past or present. These are finite verbs because we can change their tense from past to present and vice versa:

> She **wants** to leave. ↔ She **want**ED to leave.

These are not finite verbs because we cannot change the INFINITIVE to a past tense:

> She wants to **leave**S. ↔ She wants to **leave**D.

Fragment: A PHRASE or DEPENDENT CLAUSE that begins with a capital letter and ends with a period, question mark, or exclamation mark:

> Because I left.   Though I am here!   What you did?

These are complete sentences:

> He left because I did.   Though I am here, she is not.   I know what we did.

Free Modifier: A modifier that may appear either after a MAIN CLAUSE or before. It usually begins with a VERB in its PRESENT or PAST PARTICIPIAL form, less often with an ADJECTIVE:

Hoping that everyone was happy, the dean ended the meeting.

The dean ended the meeting, **hoping that everyone was happy.**

The dean ended the meeting, **happy that the matter was settled.**

(pp. 177–78)

Gerund: A NOMINALIZATION created by adding -*ing* to a VERB:

When she **solved** the problem, she helped me.

Her **solving** the problem helped me.

Goal: That toward which the ACTION of a VERB is directed. In most cases, goals are expressed as DIRECT OBJECTS.

I see **you.**   I broke **the dish.**   I built **a house.**

But in some cases, the literal goal can be the SUBJECT of an ACTIVE VERB:

I underwent an interrogation.   **She** received a warm welcome.

Grammatical Sentence: A single independent CLAUSE plus all attached modifiers. (pp. 252–53)

Hedge: A word that softens the certainty of a claim: *possibly, probably, may, indicate, suggest, appear, seem.* (pp. 154–56)

Independent Clause: A CLAUSE that does not modify any other element in a sentence.

Infinitive: A VERB that cannot be made past or present. It often is preceded by the word *to:*

He decided to **stay.**

But sometimes not:

We helped him **repair** the door.

Intransitive Verb: A verb that does not take an OBJECT and so cannot be made PASSIVE. These are not TRANSITIVE verbs:

He **exists.**   They **left** town.   She **became** a doctor.

Linking Verb: A VERB with a COMPLEMENT that modifies its SUBJECT.

He **is** my brother.   They **became** teachers.   She **seems** reliable.

Main Clause: There are two kinds of clauses: MAIN (or INDEPEN-DENT) and SUBORDINATE (or DEPENDENT). A main or independent clause can be punctuated as an independent sentence:

I left.   Why did you leave?   We are leaving.

A subordinate or dependent clause cannot be punctuated as an independent sentence. It must be attached to a main or independent clause. These would be incorrectly punctuated:

Because she left.   That they left.   Whom you spoke to.

Main Subject: SUBJECT or the MAIN CLAUSE.

Metadiscourse: Writing about writing and reading. This includes connecting devices such as *therefore, however, for example,* and expressions of the author's attitude and intention: *I believe, in my opinion;* comment about what the writer is about to assert: *most people believe, it is widely assumed, allegedly;* remarks addressed directly to the audience: *as you can see, consider now the problem of.* (pp. 86–88, 151–157, 160–162)

Nominalization: A NOUN derived from an ADJECTIVE or VERB (pp. 48–49):

decide → **decision**   depart → **departure**   happy → **happiness**

Nominalize: To turn an ADJECTIVE or VERB into a NOUN :

decide → decision   depart → departure   happy → happiness

Nonrestrictive Clause: A clause that does not uniquely identify the NOUN PHRASE it modifies:

My birthday, **which I keep a secret,** *was last month.*

Since we have only one birthday, any clause we attach to that word must be nonrestrictive, because the word is already uniquely identified. Since it is nonrestrictive, it must begin with *which* (not *that*) and be set off with commas. (pp. 24–25)

Noun: A word that fits this frame: *The* [   ] *is good.* Some are concrete: *dog, rock, car;* others abstract: *ambition, space,* *speed.* The nouns that most concern us are NOMINALIZATIONS, nouns derived from VERBS or ADJECTIVES: *act → action, wide → width.*

Object: There are three kinds:

1. DIRECT object: the NOUN following a TRANSITIVE VERB:
   I *read* **the book.**   We *followed* **the car.**
2. PREPOSITIONAL object: the noun following a preposition:
   in **the house**   *by* **the walk**   *across* **the street**   *with* **fervor**
3. INDIRECT object: the noun between a VERB and its direct object:
   I *gave* **him** a tip.

Parallelism: PHRASES or CLAUSES are parallel when they have similar grammatical elements, similar sound patterns, and/or similar or deliberately contrasting semantic elements:

(pp. 192–97)

Passive: A passive verb has three and sometimes four characteristics: (1) the SUBJECT is the GOAL of the ACTION of the verb. (2) The main verb appears after a form of *be*. (3) The verb is in its PAST PARTICIPLE form. (4) The AGENT of the action may be in a PREPOSITIONAL PHRASE after the verb:

The cryptologists broke the code.

→ The code[1] **was**[2] broken[3] [by **cryptologists**[4]].

(pp. 78–79)

Past Participle: Usually the same form as the past tense *-ed: jumped, worked, investigated.* Irregular VERBS have irregular forms: *seen, broken, swum, stolen,* etc. Past participle forms of TRANSITIVE verbs also function as modifiers:

a **broken** arm   a **twisted** leg   a **scratched** face

Phrase: A group of words constituting a unit but not including a SUBJECT and a FINITE VERB: *the dog, too old, was leaving, in the house, ready to work.*

Possessive: *my, your, his, her, its, their* or a NOUN ending with *-'s* or *-s':*

the **dog's** tail

Predicate: Whatever follows the whole SUBJECT, beginning with the VERB PHRASE, including the COMPLEMENT and whatever attaches to it.

He **[went downtown yesterday to buy a hat]**_{predicate}.

Preposition: Easier to list than to define: *in, on, up, over, of, at, by,* etc.

Prepositional Phrase: The preposition plus OBJECT: *in the house, by the door.*

Present Participle: The *-ing* form of a VERB. It has three functions:

1. The PROGRESSIVE form of a verb following a form of *be:* He *was* **running.**
2. A MODIFIER: ***Running*** streams are beautiful.
3. A GERUND: ***Running*** can kill you. (though the participle *-ing* and the gerund *-ing* descend into Modern English from different ancestors.)

Progressive: The PRESENT PARTICIPLE form of the VERB:

Running streams are beautiful.

Punctuated Sentence: Whatever begins with a capital letter and ends with a period, question mark, or exclamation point. (pp. 252–53)

Relative Clause: A CLAUSE that modifies a NOUN:

I read the book **that you reviewed.**   I know **whose book this is.**

Relative Pronoun: *who, whom, which, whose, that.*

Restrictive Clause: A restrictive clause is also called a "defining" clause. A restrictive clause uniquely identifies a thing. Most of us own more than one book, so when I refer to a book that I have not yet mentioned, I'd have to "restrict" my reference to a particular book: *Let me tell you about a book **that I just bought.*** In this case, we introduce the clause with *that* or *which* (but check p. 24 for this debatable question), and we do not set it off with commas. (pp. 24–25)

Resumptive Modifier: A modifier that repeats a word toward the end of a CLAUSE and adds to it a RELATIVE CLAUSE (pp. 176–77):

> We need to create new opportunities,
> > **opportunities** *that will be open to everyone.*

Running Modifier: Includes three kinds of modifiers:

FREE MODIFIER	Police protect us, **sacrificing their lives if necessary.**
RESUMPTIVE MODIFIER	They have a tough job, **a job that few others are willing to do.**
SUMMATIVE MODIFIER	We should honor them, **an act that few remember to do.**

(pp. 176–78)

Run-on Sentence: A PUNCTUATED SENTENCE consisting of two or more GRAMMATICAL SENTENCES not separated by either a COORDINATING CONJUNCTION or any mark of punctuation this entry illustrates a run-on sentence.

Simple Subject: The simple subject is the smallest unit inside the WHOLE SUBJECT that determines whether a verb will be singular or plural:

> The **books** that each person must read **are** listed.

Stress: The last part of a CLAUSE that receives the strongest emphasis (pp. 122–24):

> The program succeeded not because of luck but because of **hárd wórk.**

Subject: The subject is what the VERB agrees with in number:

> **Two men** *are* at the door.   **One man** *is* at the door.

We can see in these sentences that *there* is the subject of neither verb.

> **There** *was a man* at the door.   **There** *were two men* at the door.

Distinguish the WHOLE SUBJECT from its SIMPLE SUBJECT.

Subjunctive: A form of the VERB that we use when we talk about events that are contrary to fact: *If he* **were** *President.* . . .

Subordinate Clause: A clause that usually begins with a SUBORDI-NATING CONJUNCTION such as *if, when, unless,* or *which, that, who:* There are three kinds of subordinate clauses: nominal, ADVERBIAL, and ADJECTIVAL.

> I know **that I left.**   I left **because he did.**   I am the man **who left.**

Subordinating Conjunction: *Because, if, when, since, unless, which, who, that, whose,* etc.

Summative Modifier: A modifier that modifies a whole CLAUSE. It begins with a NOUN that sums up what has gone before and contin-ues with a RELATIVE CLAUSE (p. 177):

> Japan is downsizing its industrial base,
> > *a process* **that will affect world trade.**

Summative Subject: A SUBJECT that sums up in a word or two a series of preceding words (pp. 264–65):

> Poland, Hungary, Bulgaria, Romania—**they all** know the meaning of government oppression.

Theme: The key concepts that run through a series of sentences (pp. 130–32).

Topic: The unit of information that the rest of the sentence com-ments on. It is the psychological SUBJECT of a sentence. The topic of a sentence is usually also its grammatical subject:

> **China** will eventually become a major industrial nation.

We cannot define topic in grammatical terms, however, because topics can appear in a variety of grammatical constructions, in-cluding in an introductory PREPOSITIONAL PHRASE:

> *In regard to* **China,** it will eventually become democratic.

Topics can appear in other constructions, especially after METADISCOURSE.

I believe that **China** will eventually become democratic.

There is wide agreement as to **China's** becoming a world power.

(pp. 104–07)

Topic String: A topic string is the sequence of TOPICS through a single passage. (pp. 130–32)

Transitive Verb: A VERB with a DIRECT OBJECT. The direct object prototypically "receives" an ACTION. The prototypical direct object can be made the SUBJECT of a PASSIVE verb:

We **read** the book. → The book **was read** by us.

By this definition, *resemble, become,* and *stand* (as in *He stands six feet tall*) are not transitive.

Verb: The word that must agree with the SUBJECT in number and that can be inflected for past or present:

The book **is** ready.   The books **were** returned.

Whole Subject. You can identify a whole subject once you have identified the VERB: Put a *who* or a *what* in front of the verb and turn the sentence into a question. The fullest answer to the question is the whole subject:

The ability of the city to manage education is an accepted fact.

Question: **What** is an accepted fact?

Answer (and whole subject): The ability of the city to manage education.

This doesn't work with sentences beginning with *there.*

Suggested Answers

There is no perfect revision to any of these exercises, so do not feel that your revision has to match my suggested one word-for-word. I have no doubt that many of you will come up with revisions better than those here.

3.8

When you nominalize many verbs, you frustrate what your readers expect—that characters will appear as. . . . But when you drop characters altogether, you frustrate them even more. You no doubt felt that when you read this version of. . . . I was able to drop Little Red Riding . . . when I nominalized the verb *walk* into . . .

3.9

Nominalizations are italicized; verbs and adjectives boldfaced.

- 2a. *Smoking, pregnancy,* **may lead,** *injury;* 2b. **write, understand.**
- 4a. *Complaints, apathy,* **provide,** *suggestions, dispelling;* 4b. **have claimed, watch, tend, become, able, has demonstrated, be.**
- 6a. **need, know, are being logged, can save,** *risk;* 6b. **is,** *need, analysis, intensity, use,* **provide,** *projection.*
- 8a. **examine, influence,** *advertising, advertising,* **respond,** *influences,* **create, appeals;** 8b. **is,** *review, responses, judgments, well-formedness, knowledge, reading.*

3.10

Do not worry if your revisions are slightly different from these.

2. Writing concisely leads to easier reader understanding.
4. Claims by critics as to children becoming readers with lower ability have not been supported by demonstrations of their truth.
6. There is a need for knowledge of the extensiveness of logging in areas of our national forests for the purpose of saving virgin stands at greatest risk.
8. This article is an examination of the influence of buyers on advertising and of the responses of advertising agencies to those influences in the creation of strategies for appealing to consumers.

3.11

2. When pregnant women smoke, they may injure their fetus.
4. Although editorial writers complain that voters are apathetic, they have not suggested how to dispel it.
6. We must analyze how intensively students are using our libraries so that we can reliably project what new resources we need.
8. In this study, we review how readers respond to rhetorical patterns and judge texts to be well-formed when they know the subject matter of the text before they read it.

3.12

2. The President's aides asserted that he was immune from . . .
4. When the author analyzed our data, he did not cite sources that would support his criticism of our argument.
6. The Pope appealed to the industrialized nations of the world to assist starving Africans.
8. When the participants agreed on the program, they assumed that the federal government had promised funds.
10. The two sides agreed that they needed to revise the treaty.
12. The laboratory personnel must carefully prepare the specimen sections.

14. Though we were disappointed when the board rejected our proposal, we were not surprised because we expected that it had decided to delay new initiatives.

3.13

2. When you precisely plot the location of the fragments of a vase, you will reconstruct it more accurately.
4. When a student is not socialized into a field, she may have writing problems because she does not know enough about how professionals in the field construct arguments.
6. When we evaluated the outcome of the programs, we emphasized objective measures, even though we knew that the raters often disagreed with one another.

4.2

2. We will never solve the problem of UFOs until we understand better whether extraterrestrial life is possible.
4. In an emergency room, a doctor has to decide on the scene whether to force medication on an irrational patient who is unable to provide legal consent.
6. As we view network television less and cable and rental cassettes more, networks increasingly recognize that our tastes and viewing habits have changed and that they must program accordingly.
8. Recent critics have accurately described how the press has failed to report on the Middle East fairly. When we compare how journalists from different countries cover the same event, we see how inaccurately the news is reported by politically biased newspapers. When they omit facts and slant stories, journalists reveal that they have failed to carry out their mission objectively. As a result, because the public does not know the truth, it bases its opinion more on emotion than on reason.

4.3

2. OK
4. OK

6. Before Ann Richards was elected governor of Texas, her Republican opponent attacked her as a liberal Democrat who once used drugs, but in her campaign, she also used negative advertising.
8. Schools will improve science education sufficiently to provide American industry with skilled workers and researchers only when taxpayers/state governments/the federal government [take your pick] provide more money.

4.5

2. The model has been statistically analyzed.
4. We are considering whether we should create a database, but we have not yet evaluated how useful it would be.
6. We intend this book to help readers understand not only how the grammars of Arabic and English differ, but also how Arabic vocabulary reflects a different worldview.
8. Tissue rejection was studied by methods developed when we discovered that dermal sloughing increases when cells regenerate.

4.6

2. We now make almost all home mortgage loans for thirty years. With inflated prices of housing, you cannot repay a loan more quickly. (eye-ball to eye-ball with the borrower)
4. Many Victorian scientists and theologians argued against Darwinian evolution because it contradicted what they assumed about their place in the world. It defined humans not as divinely privileged but as a product of nature.
6. We can most clearly explicate why smoking is socially significant if we analyze how adolescents interact. In particular, we should study how their social class determines how they relate.
8. We have undervalued how the brain solves problems because we have not studied it in scientifically reliable ways.

4.7

As you probably have heard, over the last several weeks, some of our students have been racially and sexually harassing other students. Even though on other campuses some students also harass other students, we are just as offended when some of our students harass others here. In most of the ten to twelve incidents here, students have written graffiti or verbally insulted someone. In only two cases did one of our students physically contact another, and in neither case did that student injure the other one. A commitment exists to providing an environment where life, work, and study can take place without fear of racial, sexual, religious, or ethnic taunting or harassment. It has been made clear that bigotry and intolerance will not be permitted and that a commitment to diversity is unequivocal. Steps are being taken to improve security in campus housing. There is pride here in a tradition of diversity. . . .

4.8

2. We can reduce the blood pressure of diabetic patients if we apply renal depressors.
4. On the basis of these principles, we can formulate rules that allow readers to extract information from narratives.
6. The Federal Trade Commission should enforce guidelines for the durability of tires on new automobiles.
8. When we visited offices and reviewed assessments of what the agency needed for training, we identified issues that we can use to create an initial questionnaire for the staff.

5.1

In order to demonstrate Abco's advantages versus competitors, our report will highlight various components of Abco's current profitability, particularly growth in Asian markets. We will base this analysis on revenue returns along several dimensions: product type, end-use, distribution channels, distributor type, etc. We project that Abco's newest product lines will grow if it can develop distribution channels in China. To support the introduction of these new products, Abco will need a range of innovative strategies.

5.2

2. In their natural states, most animals lack the power to create and communicate a new message to fit a new experience. Their genetic code enables them to communicate only a lim-

ited number and kind of messages. Bees, for example, can communicate information only about distance, direction, source, and richness of pollen in flowers. In all significant respects, animals of the same species are able to communicate a limited repertoire of messages delivered in the same way, for generation after generation.

5.6

2. After Peter the Great, seven out of eight reigns of the Romanov line had to deal with some sort of palace revolt or popular revolution. In 1722, Peter the Great terminated the principle of succession by heredity and based succession on achievement by merit. As a result many tsars, including Peter, died before they named successors. Czarina Anna appointed Ivan VI when he was only two months old, but she was defeated by Elizabeth, daughter of Peter the Great, who ascended the throne in 1741. Because succession did not depend on authority, the boyars regularly disputed who was to become sovereign. In 1797, Paul I codified a new law basing succession on male primogeniture. But he was strangled by conspirators, one of whom was probably his son, Alexander I.

5.7

This is only one of many possible versions. Yours could be quite different.

We create a "moral climate" when we accept an objectivized moral ~~standard for approving of people if they conform, shunning them if~~ they don't, thereby discouraging nonconformity.

5.8

The people of this village, I have said, hear something from the cathedral at Chartres that I cannot, but it is important to understand that I hear something that they cannot. Perhaps it is the power of the spires, the glory of the windows that strike them; but God has made Himself known longer to them, after all, than to me, and in a different way; the slippery bottomless well to be found in the crypt, down which heretics were hurled to death, terrifies me, along with the obscene, inescapable gargoyles jutting out of the stone and seeming to say that the devil and God can never be divorced. I doubt that the devil enters the villagers' minds when they look at the cathedral because the devil has never been identified with them. But the status which myth imposes on me in the West must be accepted before I can hope to change it.

6.1

Your revisions may well differ from these, depending on what you think is most important in each sentence.

2. These studies may produce a new political philosophy that could affect our society well into the twenty-first century.
4. According to everyone in the industry, "turnkey" means responsibility not only for the manufacture and installation of a new piece of equipment, but for its satisfactory performance as well.
6. Clearly, those who have overbuilt suburban housing developments in floodplains have in recent years caused widespread flooding and economic disaster.
8. Economically speaking, however, it is feasible to rent rather than buy textbooks for basic courses such as mathematics, foreign languages, and English, that do not change from year to year.
10. Speakers and writers should adhere to the guidelines set forth in the MLA style sheet and the NCTE guidelines for nonsexist language to the best of their ability.

6.2

2. The apparent issue here is whether during contract bargaining, management has the duty to disclose the date it intends to close down its operation. The rationale for management's duty to bargain in good faith is to minimize conflict. Though the case law on this matter is scanty, companies are obligated during bargaining to disclose major changes in an operation in order to allow the union to put forth proposals on behalf of its members.
4. One current hypothesis to explain this kind of severe condition is that a toxin elaborated by the vibrio alters mucosal and vascular permeability. In favor of this hypothesis are changes

in small capillaries located near the basal surface of the epithelial cells and the appearance of numerous microvesicles in the cytoplasm of the mucosal cells. It is believed that when capillaries become more permeable, fluid is hydrodynamically transported into the interstitial tissue and then through the mucosa into the lumen of the gut.

6.5

Words that provide conceptual connective tissue are highlighted.

2. The next century the situation changed, because after Peter the Great seven out of eight reigns of the Romanov line were plagued by **turmoil** over **disputed** *succession* to the THRONE.

The **problems** began in 1722, when Tsar Peter the Great passed a law of *succession* that terminated the principle of heredity and required the SOVEREIGN to appoint a *successor* when he died. But because many TSARS, including Peter, died before they named *successors,* those who aspired to RULE had no authority by appointment, and so their *succession* was often **disputed** by the boyars, lower-level aristocrats. There was **turmoil** even when *successors* were appointed. In 1740, Ivan VI was adopted by Czarina Anna Ivanovna and named as her *successor* at age two months, but his *succession* was **challenged** by Elizabeth, daughter of Peter the Great. In 1741, she defeated Anna and *ascended* to the THRONE herself. In 1797 Paul tried to eliminate these **disputes** by codifying a new law: *primogeniture in the male line.* But **turmoil** continued. Paul was **strangled** by conspirators, one of whom was probably his son, Alexander I.

7.1

If you cancel within the first thirty days, you will not be charged the first monthly fee.

7.2

2. Science needs accurate data if its theories are to advance the world safely.

4. Agencies that assist our participants have reversed their recently announced policy.
6. Most patients in a public clinic do not expect special attention because their problems usually are minor and can be treated with minimal expertise and attention.
8. When investors think that prices will rise, they usually put most of their discretionary resources into art objects.
10. Educators have long wanted to help readers remember information better, but they have not been able to identify the features that make passages differ in difficulty. The first problem is to identify common and different features among comparable passages. The second is that they have not been able to evaluate the quality and quantity of information that a reader remembers.

7.3

2. A second set of rules includes those whose observance we ignore, and whose violation we ignore as well.
4. While it is unclear what counts as "too many" prepositions, it is clear that when you avoid abstract nouns, you need fewer of them.

7.4

2. Stop taking the medicine only if you are not dizzy and nauseous for six hours.
4. Cosmologists disagree on an open or closed universe, a dispute that will likely continue until they compute its mass.
6. If we wish to be independent of imported oil, we must develop oil shale and coal as sources of fuel.
8. The Insured must provide the Insurer with all relevant receipts, checks, or other evidence of costs that exceed $250.
10. Though we are not certain whether life exists elsewhere in the universe, statistical evidence makes it likely that somewhere among the immense number of planetary systems, it does.

7.5

2. At the end of his career, Frost used imagery of seasons in his longer poems.

4. The traditional values that once showed us how to be good mothers and wive were self-contradictory.
6. When Freud interpreted dreams, he was mistaken in his assumptions about their role in the subconscious.
8. Order of birth may or may not relate to academic success.

7.6

2. In this section, I argue that we must dispense with plea bargaining because it lets hardened criminals avoid punishment and encourages contempt for the judicial system.
4. We cannot assume that ground snakes in unmapped areas are larger than those in mapped areas.
6. Most investigators of life stages think that midlife is most critical for our mental health because most of us decide then whether we are winning or losing the game of life.

8.1

2. Even if the film industry and television producers agreed to limit how often they would show characters using cigarettes, it would do little to discourage young people from smoking.
4. Copyright laws regulate software downloaded into users' computers, whether they use it for commercial or entertainment purposes. If they copy it for any purpose without authorization, they violate the law.

8.2

2. Teachers, administrators, and even newspapers have debated grade inflation because they think it can undermine student achievement, but employers have not had difficulty identifying job candidates with high levels of technical and analytical skills.
4. School officials responsible for setting policy about security have said that local principals may require students to pass through metal detectors before entering a school building. Therefore, it is necessary for them to educate parents and students about the seriousness of bringing on to school property (or better: that they must not bring to school) anything that looks like a weapon.

8.3

2. For whatever reason, such conduct is prejudicial to good discipline.
4. Given the low quality of elected officials, the merit selection of judges is an idea whose time came long ago.
6. Unless we reduce the emission of carbon dioxide by the end of the century, we will change the climate of the world.

8.4

Again, your revisions will be completely different from these.

2. For the last few years, automobile manufacturers have been trying to meet more stringent mileage requirements, **a challenge** that has tested American ingenuity / **requirements** that Detroit has strenuously tried to change / hoping that new technologies will provide them with a breakthrough in engine design.
4. Most young people cannot grasp the insecurity that many people felt during the Great Depression, **a failure** that makes it impossible for them to share their grandparents' experiences / **an insecurity** that shaped them for the rest of their lives / believing that the stories they hear from their grandparents are exaggerations.
6. Many Victorians were appalled when Darwin suggested that their ancestors might have included creatures such as apes, **a concept** that offended not only their personal self-respect, but their fundamental religious beliefs, as well / **creatures** that they had seen as utterly different from themselves / choosing to believe instead that they were created by God 6000 years before.
8. Scientific inquiry began when primitive people began to think about the regularities of nature, **an intellectual breakthrough** that forever changed our relationship to nature/**regularities** that were invisible to only those whose intellectual development made the ordinary interesting.
10. Recently, journalism has focused on news once considered only salacious gossip, **gossip** that only the supermarket tabloids stooped to/**a trend** that will continue until the public becomes intelligent enough to demand substantive news.

8.7

2. Though we expect to succeed, we need to resolve immediately the differences that have interfered with communication.
4. After we audited internal operations in the summer of 1996, we audited foreign affiliates that had not been audited by their local headquarters.

9.2

2. While the strong are often afraid to admit weakness, the weak often fail to assert the strength they possess.
4. When parents raise children who do not value the importance of hard work, the adults those children become will not know how to work hard for what they claim to value.

9.3

2. The blueprint for the political campaign plan was concocted by those with the least sensitivity to our most critical needs.
4. Nothing has changed America more than the power of federal government.
6. Boards of education can no longer expect that taxpayers will support the extravagancies of incompetent bureaucrats.

10.2

As the Illinois Commerce Commission has authorized, **we** are charging you . . . .

We-version:
We have not raised rates . . . but **we** are restructuring the rates now . . . so that **we** can we charge you for what **we** pay to provide you with service. **We** are charging you a sum that **we** have prorated over the period during which **we** changed our rates. When **we** prorate, **we** base part of the bill on former Service Charges, which **we** identify on your bill as . . . service charges, which **we** identify as "New Rate"

***You*-version:**

As the Illinois Commerce Commission has authorized, **you** will have to pay. . . . **You** have not had to pay . . . but **you** will now pay rates that have been restructured consistent with the policy of The Public Utilities Act that lets us base what **you** pay on what it costs to provide you with service. **You** will pay a sum that is pro-rated over the period during which the rates changed. When **you** pay prorated rates, **you** pay part of the bill based on former service charges, which **you** can identify on your bill as "Old Rate," and part of the bill that **you** can identify identify as "New Rate."

10.3

Your car may have a defective part that connects the suspension to the frame. If you brake hard and the plate fails, you won't be able to steer. We may also have to adjust the secondary latch on your hood because we may have misaligned it. If you don't latch the primary latch, the secondary latch might not hold the hood down. If the hood flies up while you are driving, you won't be able to see. If either of these things occurs, you could crash.

10.9

Four score and seven years ago, **this continent** witnessed the birth of a new nation. . . . Now **a great Civil War** engages us. . . . **That war** has given us this great battlefield for a meeting place. **A portion of that field** is ready to receive its dedication. . . . **This** is an altogether fitting . . . But in a larger sense, **this ground** will not let us dedicate, . . . **It** has already received that consecration . . . **The words we say here** [You finish the rest.]

A.2

1. Scientists and philosophers of science tend to speak as if "scientific language" were intrinsically precise, as if those who use it must understand one another's meaning, even if they disagree. But, in fact, scientific language is not as different from ordinary language as is commonly believed; it, too, is subject to imprecision and ambiguity and hence to imperfect understanding. Moreover, new theories (or arguments) are rarely, if

ever, constructed by way of clear-cut steps of induction, deduction, and verification (or falsification). Neither are they defended, rejected, or accepted in so straightforward a manner. In practice, scientists combine the rules of scientific methodology with a generous admixture of intuition, aesthetics, and philosophical commitment. The importance of what are sometimes called extra-rational or extralogical components of thought in the *discovery* of a new principle or law is generally acknowledged. . . . But the role of these extralogical components in persuasion and acceptance (in making an argument convincing) is less frequently discussed, partly because they are less visible. The ways in which the credibility of effectiveness of an argument depends on the realm of common experiences, on extensive practice in communicating those experiences in a common language, are hard to see precisely because such commonalities are taken for granted. Only when we step out of such a "consensual domain"—when we can stand out on the periphery of a community with a common language—do we begin to become aware of the unarticulated premises, mutual understandings, and assumed practices of the group. Even in those subjects that lend themselves most readily to quantification, discourse depends heavily on conventions and interpretation—conventions that are acquired over years of practice and participation in a community.

2. In fact, of course, the notion of universal knowledge has always been an illusion; but it is an illusion fostered by the monistic view of the world in which a few great central truths determine in all its wonderful and amazing proliferation everything else that is true. We are not today tempted to search for these keys that unlock the whole of human knowledge and of man's experience. We know that we are ignorant; we are well taught it, and the more surely and deeply we know our own job the better able we are to appreciate the full measure of our pervasive ignorance. We know that these are inherent limits, compounded, no doubt, and exaggerated by that sloth and that complacency without which we would not be men at all. But knowledge rests on knowledge; what is new is meaningful because it departs slightly from what was known before; this is a world of frontiers, where even the liveliest of actors or observers will be absent most of the time from most of them. Perhaps this sense was not so sharp in the village—

that village which we have learned a little about but probably do not understand too well-the village of slow change and isolation and fixed culture which evokes our nostalgia even if not our full comprehension. Perhaps in the villages men were not so lonely; perhaps they found in each other a fixed community, a fixed and only slowly growing store of knowledge-a single world. Even that we may doubt, for there seem to be always in the culture of such times and places vast domains of mystery, if not unknowable, then imperfectly known, endless and open.

ACKNOWLEDGMENTS

D. H. Lawrence, *Studies in Classic American Literature*. New York: The Viking Press, 1961.

Norman Mailer, *Armies of the Night*. New York: The New American Library, Inc., 1971.

From *Science and the Common Understanding* by J. Robert Oppenheimer. Copyright © 1954 by J. Robert Oppenheimer, renewed © 1981 by Robert B. Meyner. Reprinted by permission.

From "The Aims of Education" in *The Aims of Education and Other Essays* by Alfred North Whitehead. Copyright © 1929 by Macmillan Publishing Co., Inc., renewed 1957 by Evelyn Whitehead. Reprinted by permission.

From Strunk, William Jr. & White, E. B. *The Elements of Style* 3/e. Copyright © 1979 by Allyn & Bacon. Reprinted by permission.

INDEX

Aphasia, temporary, 10–11
Absolute words, 33
Abstraction: analysis of, 53; as causative agents, 214–15; as characters, 233–34; diagnosis of, 53; revision of, 53; passive combined with nominalization and, 79
Abstractions: as characters, 62–63, 73–75, 212–15, 214–15, 233–34; as characters in Second Inaugural, 240–44
Academic prose, and first person, 85
Academic writing, 5, 8, 10–11, 85–91, 93–94; metadiscourse, 86–91; telling stories in, 45–47
Accept vs. *Except*, 31
Actions: as verbs, 41–67, 44–49, 58; as verbs or nouns, 42–46; in adjectives, 49–50
Active voice: and coherence, 82; and cohesion, 80–82, 99; and focus, 81; and stress, 125; defined, 78
Active, choosing between passive, 79–85
Active, impressions vs. grammar, 78
Adjectives, as actions, 49
Affect vs. *effect*, 31
After vs. *than* after *different*, 20
Agents: abstractions, 214–15; metaphorical, 214–15
Aggravate vs. *annoy*, 30
Ain't, logic of, 18
Among vs. *between*, 20
Analysis, lack of emphasis, 123; of abstraction, 53; of impersonality, 70–73; of incoherence, 108; of old-new problems, 107
And, 262; begin sentence with, 21, 23, 258–59
Annan, Noel Gilroy (Lord Annan), 26
Annoy vs. *aggravate*, 30
Anticipate vs. *expect*, 30

Anxious vs. *eager*, 30
Any, with singular, 29
Appositive, 267
Aristotle, 211, 219
Arnold, Matthew, 1
Aronowitz, Stanley, 9, 229, 231
As vs. *like*, 32
As vs. *since*, 26
As vs. *while*, 26

Balance, 192–97; coordinated, 193–95; non-coordinated, 195–97; topics and stress, 193–95
Baldwin, James, 114
Barzun, Jacques, 23, 24
Basford, J.L., 251
Because, begin sentence with, 23
Bernstein, Theodore M., 62
Between vs. *among*, 20
Between you and I, 27–28
Blackmail vs. *coercion*, 30
Blackmail vs. *extort*, 30
Blair, Hugh, 14
Blake, William, 165
Brand, Myles, 75
Bureaucratese, 4, 79
Burgess, Anthony, 273
Burns, Robert, 17
Burrow, James, 251
But, 262; begin sentence with, 21, 23, 258
Campbell, George, 14
Capote, Truman, 139
Carr, E.H., 210, 211
Carroll, Lewis, 97
Categories, redundant, 142
Causative agents, 214–15
Chadwick, Douglas, 8
Character, 42–50; and metadiscourse, 86–87; and passive verbs, 78; as abstractions, 233–34; as abstractions in *Second Inaugural*, 240–44; as nominalizations, 62–63, 73–75; as point of view, 81; as reified abstractions, 214–15; as subjects, 42–46, 69; finding and

relocating, 70; importance of, 69; missing, 72; finding and relocating, 70–72; importance of, 69–70; with passive verbs, 78–79; reconstructing missing, 72–73;
Chiasmus, 199–200
Churchill, Winston, 197
Clarity, 93, 119; subversive, 231–32; in complexity, 166, 167; diagnosis of, 69; and emphasis 119–122; local versus global, 98–99; making judgments about, 42; measures of, 42; simpleminded-ness vs., 64–65
Coercion vs. *blackmail*, 30
Coherence, 98, 103–112; and active vs. passive, 82; and stress, 130–31; as focus, 104–05; beginning sentence well, 110–15; diagnosis, analysis, and revision for, 107–108; sense of focus and, 103–104; system for, 108–109; topics for, 104–107, 130–31
Cohesion, 98–102; and active vs. passive voice, 80–82; and active vs. passive voice, 99; and flow, 99, 101; and focus, 80, 103; and nominalizations, 62; and old-to-new, 101–02; illusory, 115–16
Cohort vs. *consort*, 30
Coleridge, Samuel Taylor, 41
Colon, use of, 260, 64–65, 267
Comma, use of, 257–58, 259, 262–69
Complete, 33
Complexity, 42; balance and symmetry in, 192–97; of style, appropriate, 64, 166, 175–78, 180–83, 200–04; appropriate, 64–65; at end of sentence, 81, 120, 121; clarity in, 166, 167; necessary, 75, 224, 230–32; salutary, 230–32; *See also* Obscurity

Complex sentence, 254–55
Compose vs. *consist*, 31
Compound noun, 91
Compound sentence, 254–55
Comprise vs. *constitute*, 31
Concepts as characters, 73–75
Concision, 140–57; and grace, 140; metadiscourse, 151–62; productive redundancy, 159–62
Concrete writing, 59
Confusion, period of stylistic, 10–11
Conjunctions: coordinating, 257–60; illusory cohesion with, 115–16; subordinating, 32, 262
Connections, unclear, 185
Consist vs. *Compose*, 31
Consort vs. *cohort*, 30
Constitute vs. *comprise*, 30–31
Continual vs. *continuous*, 30
Cooper, James Fenimore, 6
Coordination, shorter to longer, 182
Coordinating conjunction, punctuating with, 258
Coordinating elements, punctuating, 268–70
Coordination, 180–84; balanced, 192–95; faulty, 183–84, 195–97; unclear connections, 185
Correctness, 14–37; logic, 18; as choice, 15, 20–21; as historical accident, 17–18; history of, 19; kinds, 19; as unpredictability, 36–37; folklore, 16, 22–26; options signaling deliberate care, 26–29; reasons for rules, 16–19; rules observed thoughtfully, 20–22; words attracting special attention, 29–31
Crichton, Michael, 8, 10
Crick, F.H.C., 155
Criterion vs. *criteria*, 31

Dangling modifiers, 87, 185–86; and passives, 186
Dash, use of, 261, 64–65, 267; paired, 266
Datum vs. *data*, 31
Democracy: and clarity, 93; and correctness, 19; and style, 19
Dennett, Daniel C., 211
De Quincey, Thomas, 97
Diagnosis, for lack of emphasis, 124–27; of abstraction, 53;

of impersonality, 70–73; of incoherence, 107–08; of old-new problems, 107; of sprawl, 167
Discreet and *discrete*, 31
Disinterested vs. *uninterested*, 30

Eager vs. *anxious*, 30
Educationese, 79
Effect vs. *affect*, 31
Einstein, Albert, 219
Elegance, 191–216; balance and symmetry and, 192–197; and climactic emphasis, 197–200; and metaphor, 209–15; extravagant, 200–206; nuances of length and rhythm, 206–209
Eliot, T.S., 118
Elision, 32
Emerson, Ralph Waldo, 41
Emphasis: and clarity, 119–22; and metadiscourse, 153–54; and pronoun substitution, 126; at end of sentence, 122; climactic, 197; managing, 124–27, 135, 198–200; punctuation, 265, 266; and stress, 122–24; 130–32, 135; and themes, 132; and topics, 130–32
Endings, of sentence, 124–27
Enormity vs. *enormous*, 30
Enormous vs. *enormity*, 30
Erasmus, 14
Ethics, 5, 219–49; and style, 220–235; of metaphor, 212–15; artful misdirection, 232–35; defining, 222; and intended obscurity, 225–28; mutual obligations of writers and readers, 94, 220–23; and rationalized obscurity, 228–30; and salutary complexity/subversive clarity, 230–32; and style, 222–23; and unintended obscurity, 223–25
Ethos, 221
Except vs. *accept*, 31
Exclamation mark, 255–56
Expect vs. *anticipate*, 30
Extort vs. *blackmail*, 30
Explanation, unnecessary, 143

Famous vs. *notorious*, 31
Fewer vs. *less*, 25–26
Finalize vs. *finish*, 33
First person, in academic prose, 85; in metadiscourse, 85–87
Fitzgerald, F. Scott, 139

Flaunt vs. *flout*, 30
Flow, 256; and logic, 116; and passive voice, 80; as cohesion, 99, 101; and grammatical connections, 170; and unclear connections, 185
Focus, 130–31; and active vs. passive voice, 81; and cohesion, 80, 103–104; and passive vs, active, 81; as coherence, 104–05
Folklore, 16, 22–26
Follett, Wilson, 23
Fortuitous vs. *fortunate*, 30
Fowler, Francis, 21, 24–25
Fowler, H.W., 21, 24–25, 29
Fragments, urgency conveyed by breaking sentences into, 207
Franklin, Benjamin, 97, 139
Free modifier, 177–78
Fulsome vs. *full*, 30

Gass, William, 41
Gay, Peter, 199
Gender, and style, 34–35; sexism and pronouns, 33–34
Gerunds, 48
Gibbon, Edward, 198
Gilbert, John P., 86
Godard, Jean-luc, 3
Golden Rule of Writing, 50–51, 94
Goldstein, Tom, 8
Gowers, Sir Ernest, 21, 28
Grace, 140
Grammatical connections, 170; interrupting, 170; unclear, 185
Grammatical sentences, 252–54; defined, 255; punctuating, 255–61

Hedging, 153–56
Hiding behind language, 10
Hisself, logic of, 18
Hobgoblins, 32–33
Hoffman, Eva, 180–81
Hofmann, Hans, 139
Hopefully, impersonal, 20, 32
However, 257, 263; punctuation of, 257–58
Huxley, Julian, 210–11

I, in academic writing, 85–86, 87
Illogical grammar, 18
Illusory cohesion, 115–16
Impact, as a verb, 33
Impersonal style, 70–73, 85

Impersonality: analysis of, 70–73; diagnosis of, 70–73; revision of, 70–73

Implications, general, 142–43

Impressions: language of, 42, 99; unreliability of, 60

Imply vs. *Infer* 31

Incoherence, analysis of, 108; diagnosis of, 107–108; revision of, 108

Infer vs. *imply*, 31

Infinitives, split, 20, 26–27

Information, new vs. old, 80–81, 99–102, 171

Intensifiers, 156–57

Interrupting subject and verb, 171

Interruptions, 170–71; punctuating, 264–68

Intrinsic sense, 187–88

Introductory phrases and clauses, 110–11, 152–53, 168–69; punctuating, 261–65

Irregardless, 15; vs. *regardless*, 33

It-shift 1, 126

It-shift 2, 126

Johnson, Samuel, 191

Keller, Evelyn Fox, 271

Kennedy, John F., 12

La Rochefoucauld, 68, 219

Lack of emphasis: analysis of, 123; diagnosis of, 124–27; revision of, 124–27

Langland, William, 273

Language: of impressions, 78; technical, 120

Law, language of 4, 8, 79

Lawrence, D.H., 207

Lederman, Leon M., 211

Legalese, 4, 8, 79

Length: nuances, 206–209; sentence, 167, 175–87, 206–209

Less, 25–26; vs. *fewer*, 25

Like, vs. *as*, 32

Lincoln, Abraham, 235–248; analysis of Second Inaugural, 235–44

Lippmann, Walter, 193–95

Logic, 17–19; and correctness, 18; and flow, 116; and style, 59

Long sentences: writing 175–87; trouble shooting, 183–87

Long subjects: punctuating, 264–65; revising, 169–70

Loose commentary, punctuating, 266–68

Lucas, F.L., 191, 27

MacDonald, Dwight, 27

Mailer, Norman, 208

Marquez, Gabriel Garcia, 118

Maugham, Somerset, 191

McPeek, Bucknam, 86

Medium vs. *media*, 31

Mencken, H.L., 12

Metadiscourse, 86,–91, 151–62, 186; and characters, 86–87; and emphasis, 153–54; and hedging, 154–56; and intensifying, 156–57; and stress, 124; attribution to source, 152; autobiographical, 160–52; redundant, 151–57; topic focus, 152–53; unnecessary, 110

Metaphor, 209–215; deceptive, 213–14; ethics of, 212–15; silly, 212

Mill, John Stuart, 165

Mills, C. Wright, 8

Misdirection, artful, 232–34

Modifiers, dangling, 87, 185–86; dangling and nominalizations, 186; free, 177–78, 185, 188; misplaced, 186–87; redundant, 141–42; resumptive, 176–77, 201, 202; running, 176–78; squinting, 186; summative, 177; nonrestrictive, 266–67

Monotony, and topics, 112, 176; and nuances of length and rhythm, 206

Montaigne, 273

Moore, George, 251

Moore, Marianne, 139, 140

Morton, Donald, 221, 231

Mosteller, Richard, 5

Mulcaster, Richard, 5

Narrative style, 42–50; in academic writing, 45–47; telling stories about characters and actions, 42–44

Negative words, 147

Negatives, to affirmatives, 146–48

New information, 81; at end of sentence, 102

Newton, Sir Isaac, 87–88

Nietzsche, Friedrich Wilhelm, 41

Nominalization, 48–49, 53–58, 59, 69; and cohesion, 61–62; concision, 62; and dangling

modifier, 186; and elegance, 197–98; as character, 62–63, 73–75; common patterns of, 54–55; with of, 198–99; with passive voice, 79; coordinate, 201, 202; doubled, 201, 202; useful, 61–64, 67

None, with singular, 29

Nonrestrictive modifiers, 24–25, 266–67

Nonstandard English, 18–19

Not only X, but Y, 126

Notorious vs. *Famous*, 31

Oates, Joyce Carol, 200–201

Object, getting to quickly, 171

Objective style, and active vs. passive voice, 85

Objective style, and passive, 85–86

Obscurity, 223–230; defended, 228–32; intended, 225–28; unintended, 223–25

Ochs, E., 223

Old-to-new, 101–103, 120–122; analysis of, 107; and cohesion, 101–02; diagnosis of, 107

One, as character, 72–73

Ong, Walter S.J., 23, 25, 28

Oppenheimer, J. Robert 272

Organic Cohesion, 115

Orwell, George, 3, 7, 28–29

Paine, Thomas, 5

Parallelism, 183–84, 199–200

Parentheses, use of, 261, 267

Parsons, Talcott, 93–94

Passages, introduction of, 132

Passive voice. 78–91; and focus, 81; and coherence, 82; and cohesion, 80–82, 99; and flow, 80, 99–101; and metadiscourse, 86–91; and objective style, 85; and stress, 125; as syntactic device, 125; defined, 78; with nominalization, 79; characters, and 78–79; combining negatives and negative words with, 147; dangling modifiers and, 87, 186; impression of, 78–79; nominalizations to create, 79; objective point of view, 85–86; sense of flow and, 99–101

Perfect, as absolute word, 33

Period, use of, 255–56, 258

Phenomenon vs. *phenomena*, 31

Phrase, replaced with a word, 143–46

Poe, Edgar Allan, 68
Point of view, 81–83, 130–31; and active, passive, 82–83; and passive vs. active, 81
Pound, Ezra, 207
Precede vs. *proceed*, 31
Precision, real vs. false, 36
Prentice, George D., 219
Preposition: begin sentence with, 23–24; end sentence with, 24, 28
Prepositional phrases, too many, 59
Principal vs. *principle*, 31
Proceed vs. *precede*, 31
Productive redundancy, 159–62
Professional voice, 8, 10–11, 92–94
Pronoun substitution, and emphasis, 125–27; and sexist language, 33 –35; substitution for stress, 125–27
Proust, Marcel, 219
Punctuated sentences, 208, 252–54, 255
Punctuation, 251–72; beginning of sentences, 261–65; coordinated elements, 268–70; end-punctuation, 255–61; loose commentary, 266–68; middle of sentences, 265–68

Quiller-Couch, Sir Arthur, 139, 219

Rationalized obscurity, 228–30
Read, Sir Herbert, 165
Reader's obligations to writers, 222
Redundancy: categories, 142; productive, 159–62; redundant modifiers, 141–42; replacing phrase with word, 143–46; *See also* Metadiscourse
Redundancy, productive, 159
Regardless, 15, 263; vs. *irregardless*, 33
Reification, 214–15, 232–34
Relative clauses, reducing, 169–175
Relative pronoun, for restrictive clauses, 24
Repeated words, 126–27
Restrictive clauses, 24, 25
Resumptive modifiers, 176–77, 201, 202
Revision, for lack of emphasis, 124–27; of abstraction, 53;

of impersonality, 70–73; of incoherence, 108; of old-new problems, 107; of sprawl, 167–171, 174–75; starting sentence briskly, 167–74; common patterns of nominalizations for, 54–55; of compound nouns, 91–92; coordination, 181–182; diagnosing need for, 60–61; finding and relocating characters, 70–72
Rhythm, 167, 169 – 170, 192, 198–99, 206–209, 256, 263, 265
Richardson, Sir Ralph, 251
Rules: as folklore, 22–26; history of, 16; kinds, 16, 19–20, 22–29; reasons for, 16–19; thoughtful observation of, 20–22
Running modifiers, 176–80
Russell, Bertrand, 217

Sales, St. Francis de, 68, 219
Salience, echoing, 199
Salutary complexity, 230
Schieffelin, B., 223
Schopenhauer, Arthur, 3
Scholarship, language of, 8
Scientific prose, 87
Scientific writing, 85–91; *See also* Academic writing
Second Inaugural Address, 235–248
Semi-colons, use of, 256–57, 259, 262, 270; plus coordinating conjunction, 259
Sentence, beginning, 104, 110–115; 120, 121; ending, 119–30, 197–200, 124–27; length, 175–83, 206–08; opening, 110; psychological geography of, 106, 122; punctuated vs. grammatical, 167, 208; punctuating beginning of, 261–65; shape, 166–83, 208; starting, 167; grammatical, 252–61; length, 175–187, 206–209; maintaining internal connections, 185; punctuating endings, 255–61; punctuating middles, 265–68
Sentences: elegant, 192–97; flow, 256; punctuated vs. grammatical, 252–254; punctuating ends of, 255; simple vs. complex, 254–55; sprawl, 256
Series, punctuating, 269–70

Sexist language, 33–34
Shakespeare, William, 41, 118, 273
Shall vs. *will*, 27
Shape, sentences, 165–83, 192–204; clarity in complexity, 166, 167; controlling sprawl, 174–75; intrinsic sense and 187–88; long sentences, writing, 175–87; urgency conveyed by short sentences, 206
Shaping stories, 232–34
Shaw, George Bernard, 191, 210, 211
Shenstone, William, 165
Short subjects, 169–70,
Short to long, coordination, 182
Similes, 210
Simplicity, 166; excessive, 64–65, 94, 192; inappropriate, 64–65, 112
Since vs. *as*, 26; vs. *because*, 26
Social sciences, language of, 8
Sociologicalese, 79, 93
Sotto voce aside, 266
Split infinitives, 26–27
Sprat, Thomas, 5
Sprawl, 256; controlling, 174–83; diagnosis of, 167, 175; revision of, 167–171, 174–75
Squinting modifiers, 186–87
Standard English: and Logic, 17–19; and social control, 16–19, 36–37, 231–232; history of, 16–18
Stein, Gertrude, 165, 251
Sterne, Laurence, 137
Stratum vs. *strata*, 31
Stress, 130, 132; and balance, 193–95; and coherence, 130–31; and elegance, 197–200; and metadiscourse, 124, 153–154; and passive vs. active voice, 125; and pronoun substitution, 126; defined, 122–23; in coordination, 182; managing, 124–17
Strunk, William, 161
Style: and ethics, 220–235; and gender, 34–35; and logic, 59; and point of view, 81–83; appropriate complexity, 64, 166, 175–178, 180–183, 200–204; as choice, 4, 10, 15, 29, 35, 37, 50;, 83, 233–34; ethics, 5; history of, 5–9, 231; impersonal, 70–73, 85;

objective, 85; of Lincoln's Second Inaugural, extended analysis of, 235–44

Subject: as characters, 42–46, 69; as topics, 106–107; long, 264–65; grammatical, 104–106; psychological, 104–107; short vs. long, 169–170; summative, 202, 264–65

Subjunctive, 28–29

Subordinate clauses: breaking out, 175; replacing nominalizations, 54–55, 59

Subordinating conjunction, 32, 262

Subversive clarity, 230–32

Summative modifier, 177

Summative subjects, 202, 264–65

Symmetry, 192–197

Syntactic complexity, 120, 121

Syntactic devices for emphasis, 125–127

Than, vs. *after* after *different*, 20

That vs. *which*, 20, 24–25

Their, as singular, 35

Theirselves, logic of, 18

Themes, 130–31

There, 54, 125, 153; for emphasis, 62, 125

Thoreau, Henry David, 14

Three or more coordinating elements, punctuating, 269–70

Throat–clearing, 110–12

Topic, 104–107, 130, 122; and balance, 193–95; and coherence, 104–107, 130–31; and emphasis, 130–132; and grammar, 105–106; and metadiscourse, 152–53; and monotony, 112; sequence of, 108–109

Topic String, 103–04, 106–08, 132

Topics, 104; as subjects, 106–07; in coordination, 182

Trotsky, Leon, 206

Troubleshooting long sentences, 183–87

Turner, Frederick Jackson, 202–204

Twain, Mark, 7

Unclarity: private causes, 9–11; short history of, 5–9

Uninterested vs. *disinterested*, 30

Unique, as absolute word, 33

Verbs, as actions, 42–46, 44–49

Voice: personal, 134; professional, 92; actions and, 48–49; actions as, 44, 46

Watson, J.D., 155

Watts, Alan W., 209

We, 72–73; in academic writing, 85, 87

Wesley, John, 139

What–shift, 126

Which vs. *That*, 20, 24–25

While vs. *As*, 26

White, E.B., 14, 161

Whitehead, Alfred North, 249

Who vs. *Whom*, 27

Whom vs. *Who*, 27

Wilde, Oscar, 3

Will vs. *Shall*, 27

Wittgenstein, Ludwig, 39, 165, 230

Words, doubled, 141

Words, light and heavy, 126–27, 197–99; meaningless, 141–42; doubled, 141; redundant, 141–42; repeated, 126–27; replacing phrase with word, 143–46

Writers: experienced and inexperienced, 20–21, 112, 115–16, 159–61, 212; inexperienced, 181

Zinsser, William, 27